THE GOLDEN THREAD

For my wife
Fiona Cadwallader

THE GOLDEN THREAD

The Life and Gifts of Miss Frances Ellis

Patrick Heren

GRACEWING

First published in England in 2024
by
Gracewing
2 Southern Avenue
Leominster
Herefordshire HR6 0QF
United Kingdom
www.gracewing.co.uk

No part of this publication may be reproduced, stored in a retrieval system, or transmitted in any form or by any means, electronic, mechanical, photocopying, recording or otherwise, without the written permission of the publisher.

The right of Patrick Heren to be identified as the author of this work has been asserted in accordance with the Copyright, Designs and Patents Act 1988.

© 2024 Patrick Heren

ISBN 978 085244 976 9

Typeset by Gracewing

Cover design by Bernardita Peña Hurtado

Contents

Acknowledgements viii

Foreword ix

Introduction: Our Most Generous Benefactress ... xiii

1 The Catholic Church Returns to England............1

2 Called from Comfort to Build True Wealth........17

3 To Advance the Kingdom of Heaven 23

4 A Scandalous Episcopal Dispute........................49

5 A Missionary in Cornwall 87

6 Letters From Hayle...107

7 Churches Financed by Frances Ellis 155

Glossary 291

Bibliography..293

Index of churches 295

Index of names...299

Acknowledgements

My thanks are due first to Jenny Delves, the archivist of the Archdiocese of Southwark, who cheerfully provided me with endless boxes of parish records and other material, not to mention welcome cups of tea. I was helped immeasurably by Anselm Nye, who had just catalogued the archives of the Daughters of the Cross, including the letters of Miss Ellis. He also helped me to understand this remarkable order of nuns, and their chief characters.

Among the clergy, Fr Christopher Basden (Ramsgate), Fr Jack Dillon (Peckham Rye), Mgr Timothy Galligan (Altenburg Gardens), Fr Marcus Holden (Clapham Park), Fr Antony Megalan (Catford) and Canon Martin Edwards (Wandsworth East Hill) were generous with their time and wisdom.

I owe a great debt of gratitude to the three people who read my manuscript in earlier drafts and made a number of recommendations which improved it immeasurably: my wife Fiona Cadwallader, Rachel Edwards and Anselm Nye. Any remaining errors of fact or interpretation are my responsibility.

Photographs of the churches were mostly taken by Richard Stonor, with a few contributions by Fiona Cadwallader. Other pictures are from the archives of the Daughters of the Cross and from the online photographic archive of David Knights-Whittome, an early 20th century photographer based in Sutton.

Foreword

Since my appointment, in July 2019, as the Archbishop of Southwark I have become familiar with certain parishes being described as having 'an Ellis church'. Apart from appreciating this referred to a past benefactor, I knew little else. It is, therefore, a great joy to introduce this delightful account of Miss Frances Ellis' remarkable life and gifts, what might rightly and properly be called her vocation and mission.

As Patrick Heren reveals, Frances' motivation was evangelisation, although it would not have been identified as such in her day. With the passionate zeal of a convert to Catholicism, she understood the profound significance of place. It mattered that Catholics had places, churches, in which to worship. It mattered that children had places, schools, in which to learn. It mattered that the sick had places, hospitals, in which to receive treatment and care. Such places and, in particular, such Catholic places were vitally important given the historical and political setting in which Catholicism struggled to emerge again on the streetscape and skyline of England.

Venturing out from the shadows of the English Reformation, the Catholic Church began a mid-nineteenth century programme of formal re-establishment and expansion. This necessitated the practical means for Catholicism to, quite literally, put itself on the map. Step forward Miss Ellis. She grasped better than many the need to build, and so set to work funding construction projects which have stood the test of time. Anyone who attends Mass today in an 'Ellis church' owes Frances a debt of gratitude and the occasional lighted candle and prayer.

Miss Ellis was an achiever, but never, it seems, at the expense of kindness or good manners. Her shrewd management of inheritance and investment amassed a portfolio which would be the envy of any property magnate today. She put this at the service of the Gospel, first as an Anglican and then as a Catholic. In the pages that follow you will encounter both her simplicity and directness. She was not afraid to keep to her principles, nor to stand by her friends. I suspect she suffered fools charitably.

Frances' great generosity towards the Daughters of the Cross is brought out beautifully in the letters recorded here. They provided a spiritual anchor for her apostolic endeavours. The author records Frances' devotion to St Gertrude of Nivelle, a saint whom he recalls was a 'courageous woman who lived at a time of evangelisation'. In her own way, imitating her adopted patroness, the same can be said of Frances.

Thanks to Patrick Heren the life and spirit of Miss Frances Ellis, and her prestigious catalogue of buildings, is now made more widely available. In changing times, may we learn from her the importance of place and, especially, the importance of sacred Eucharistic space, where heaven touches earth and calls us to new life.

Most Rev. John Wilson
Archbishop of Southwark

Introduction

Our Most Generous Benefactress

This is the story of how a retiring middle-aged woman spent her considerable fortune to extend the benefits of the Catholic faith to the mostly poor people of the Diocese of Southwark and beyond. Her benefactions ranged from churches to schools, hospitals, orphanages and convents. She worked by personal contact. The money for new churches in Southwark was made available to the diocesan treasurer Canon Edward St John, as and when he asked for it. And the support for the projects of the Daughters of the Cross of Liège was channelled through their Provincial, Mother Iphigènie Butner. Most of this charity was dispensed during the reign of King Edward VII, between 1901 and 1910.

Frances Elizabeth Ellis, usually remembered as Miss Ellis, if she is remembered at all, never sought public thanks or recognition for her generosity. More than ninety years after her death, there remains remarkably little documentary evidence of her benefactions. The Daughters of the Cross, who remember her with love and admiration, have preserved several hundred letters she wrote to Mother Iphigènie and other nuns. But the archives of the Archdiocese (as it now is) of Southwark have little to say about her. Partly this is fallout from the dispute between the leaders of Westminster and Southwark, partly because Canon St John was ostracised, after a financial scandal for which he was not responsible.

But it also speaks of a certain clerical complacency, of taking for granted a woman few in authority knew.

Frances Ellis would not have minded her anonymity, indeed she probably welcomed it. She may have regretted what happened to Canon St John, but as will become clear, she remained in touch with him until the end of her long life.

The typical church she founded—modest, square and built in London stock brick—is sometimes referred to as an 'Ellis Box'. None could be compared to St Paul's Cathedral. But of Frances Ellis one could say, as it was said of Sir Christopher Wren: *Si monumentum requiris, circumspice.*

'If you seek her monument, look around you.'

I first encountered Miss Frances Ellis in 2001 while researching the centenary history of our former parish of St Francis de Sales & St Gertrude, Larkhall Lane, Stockwell. I had been asked to write a history by the parish priest, the late and much-missed Fr Tom Heneghan. As with most churches, little documentation was held by the parish itself, and I spent many hours in the archives at Archbishop's House. I also spoke to the then-archivist, Fr Michael Clifton, who was parish priest at St Thomas Aquinas, Ham. Fr Michael had just written a history of the Archdiocese and was shortly to publish his biography of Archbishop Amigo. He told me what he knew about Miss Ellis and sketched in some of the background, including her collaboration with the diocesan treasurer Canon Edward St John, who he regarded as a rogue or a fool, or both. Fr Michael was a humorous man, and he told me that Miss Ellis' churches were all so plain because she employed an architect whose day job was designing railway engine sheds. I took him at his word, and that particular error appeared in the parish history, *A Spoonful of Honey*. Unfortunately, since then it has been picked up and repeated on several Ellis parish websites.

Many years later, after I had retired from active journalism, I began thinking about Miss Ellis again, and saw that there was a story to be told. My idea was to piece together what I could about her life and combine this with a survey of the Ellis churches. At that point I thought there were probably fifteen or twenty.

I began, in early 2019, in the Archdiocesan archives. These now had a professional archivist, the excellent Mrs Jenny Delves, but there was a problem: there was no information about Miss Ellis, apart from brief mentions in some parish archive boxes. Then Jenny Delves told me that a large cache of her letters was held by the Daughters of the Cross of Liège at Tite St, Chelsea, and that they had recently been archived by her freelance colleague, Mr Anselm Nye. I got in touch with him, and, with the permission of the Superior, I began to work through the two large boxes of her correspondence.

As I began reading the letters, an extraordinary and unexpected character began to emerge. Frances Ellis, a wealthy and devout convert, had devoted herself and her wealth not only to building churches but, perhaps more importantly for her, to the charitable works of these admirable nuns. She was an intelligent, imaginative and strong-minded woman who created a religious community and care home in her house at Hayle in the far west of Cornwall. She understood money and was determined to give hers away in as effective a manner as possible. She liked people, and she had a gently ironic sense of humour.

The letters are handwritten, and not always easy to read. I suspect she wrote many of them on her lap while sitting in the garden. They are dated just with the date and the month, and only a few can be ascribed to a particular year. Most are addressed to senior nuns at Carshalton, including the Provincial, Mother Iphigènie.

The discovery of the letters changed the book I was trying to write. Frances Ellis was already living at Hayle when her first churches were being built, and she did not mention them in her letters to nuns. No letters to Canon St John, or to anyone else concerned with the church-building programme, have survived. I saw that I would have to rely largely on the Southwark archives to build a picture of the Ellis churches, while her letters would provide the material for her biography. In that I was aided by biographical information given to the Daughters of the Cross by some of her descendants in the 1980's.

Three works published privately by the Daughters of the Cross provided context and much additional information. These were the history of the order and the biography of their founder, both listed in the bibliography; there is also a useful pamphlet on the order's history in Cornwall available only in a partial photocopy.

The range and quality of the information about parishes held by the Archdiocese is variable. There was little or nothing about the building of the churches, but there was usually enough from visitation forms and correspondence to build up a picture of the early years of each mission. There was nothing to shed light on the relationship between Miss Ellis and Canon St John, or on the process by which her money was paid over to build the churches. But there was a fair amount of documentation of Canon St John's fall from favour, and his eventual transfer to Liverpool as a prison chaplain. His professional demise was also bound up with the bizarre rift that opened up between Bishop Amigo and Archbishop Bourne within a few months of the latter's translation from Southwark to Westminster. This strange dispute is well known among Catholic historians, and it is particularly well told by Fr Mark Vickers in his biography of Bourne, *By The Thames Divided*.

The more I read and tried to make sense of the St John saga—bound up as it is with Southwark's chronic poverty—I saw that this made a third strand to the story, which I have told in Chapter 4. It is relevant to the life and work of Frances Ellis because she stopped funding churches for Southwark after St John resigned as treasurer, although she still had funds at her disposal. It also fills in the real-world background to the struggle to meet the needs of Southwark Catholics.

At a late stage, after I had completed the first draft of the book, I discovered that there was information relevant to the St John story in the Westminster archives, and I was able to include this.

The information available on parish websites varies from zero to reasonably extensive. Some parishes, like St Bede's Clapham Park or St Vincent de Paul's, Altenburg Gardens, have benefited from excellent published histories.

For the buildings themselves, Evinson's *Catholic Churches of London* is an indispensable guide. Online, the website taking-stock.org.uk catalogues all Catholic churches in England and Wales, often in great detail. Both sources are primarily architectural, but they include some historical information.

I was unable to consult the records of the Benedictine community of St Augustine's Ramsgate which might have thrown more light on Miss Ellis' early activities. In 2011, the monks left Ramsgate for a new monastery in Surrey, but they have not yet unpacked their archives. In particular I had hoped to consult the Chronicle of Abbot Thomas Bergh, which is referenced in Dom David Parry's centenary history of the monastery.

There is a handwritten list of Ellis churches in the Southwark archives, which proved vital in establishing the extent of her charity. Mrs Delves thinks it was written by a priest-archivist in the late 20th century, but not Fr Clifton. It shows that someone at St George's was thinking about the subject. But otherwise, very little information about Miss Ellis and her church-building programme is held by the Archdiocese. It may be that papers were lost in the wartime bombing of the Cathedral, but this is unlikely as Archbishop's House, where the archives were then situated, escaped serious damage. She and her benefactions are not even a topic in the Southwark archive, and no one seems to know why. Bourne and Amigo both knew Frances Ellis, and gratefully acknowledged her contribution throughout their terms at St George's.

This oversight may be due to the dispute with St John, which caused such scandal at the time, and led to him becoming a non-person at Southwark. Might it be that St John's official correspondence was destroyed as part of the effort to restore the diocese's reputation for financial competence after the Bishop affair?

One document that has been preserved is the Minute Book of the Council of Temporal Administration (finance committee), but this throws up more questions than answers. The enormous gaps—1894–1900 and 1900–

1907—suggest that Canon St John, the Council's secretary, kept his real records elsewhere, and that they no longer exist.

In the end, the true record of Frances Ellis' benefactions is found in the bricks and mortar of the churches she supported, not in paper files.

When we recall the state to which the long years of persecution had reduced the Catholic body at the dawn of the nineteenth century, we may well wonder at what has been accomplished since then. Who shall say how it has come about? Where out of our poverty, for example, have been found the sums of money for all our innumerable needs? Churches and colleges and schools, monastic buildings and convents, have all had to be built and supported; how, the Providence of God can alone explain ... From the first years of the nineteenth century, there have been signs of the dawn of the brighter, happier days for the old religion. Slight indeed were the signs at first, slight but significant, and precious memories to us now, of the workings of the Spirit, of the rising of the sap again in the old trunk, and of the bursting of bud and bloom in manifestation of that life which, during the long winter of persecution, had been but dormant. Cut down almost to the ground, the tree planted by Augustine has manifested again the divine life within it; it has put forth once more new branches and leaves, and gives promise of abundant fruit.

Francis Gasquet, *Short History of the Catholic Church in England*, p. 128.

1

THE CATHOLIC CHURCH RETURNS TO ENGLAND

Frances Elizabeth Ellis (1846–1930) was one of English Catholicism's great benefactors, but her piety and modesty have ensured that her name remains unknown to the world at large. At best, she is remembered as 'Miss Ellis', or occasionally 'our generous benefactress'. In fact, her support and encouragement resulted in the building of dozens of much-needed new churches, and, perhaps closest to her heart, the rapid development of the Daughters of the Cross of Liège, one of the most active orders of nuns in the early 20th century.

She began her great programme of charitable works in 1900, fifty years after the restoration of the Catholic hierarchy in Britain. The Church had struggled throughout that time to build cathedrals, churches, schools and other institutions. The pre-Reformation churches belonged to the Church of England, and there was no chance of getting them back.[1] Everything had to be bought and paid for.

The restoration of the Catholic Church took place during a time of unprecedented population growth. Between 1851 and 1901 the population of the United Kingdom increased by more than half, from 27 million to 41 million. In the same period, the population of London more than doubled, from 2.65 million to 6.5 million. Irish immigration was significant from the great famine in the late 1840's onward, with at least half a million arriving in

Britain, many settling in London. Most struggled against desperate poverty and cruel discrimination. Yet they stayed and worked and raised families, giving rise to that distinctive strain of the city's population, the London Irish. As the 19th century progressed, they were joined by other Catholic migrants, notably from Italy and Germany.

This rapid demographic change was accompanied by enormous growth in London, north and south. The railways, and from 1863 the Tube, enabled the city to sprawl in all directions, providing jobs and requiring new homes. The Catholic church tried constantly to build churches and schools for its children but was hamstrung by lack of money. It depended largely on the gifts of the faithful, rich or poor.

Frances Ellis was not alone in her generosity, but she was unique in carefully targeting her largesse so as to ensure the greatest and most lasting impact, especially in the Diocese of Southwark. Though a recent convert, she completely understood the Church authorities' desperate concern for Catholic families in danger of losing their faith because they had no access to Mass or to Catholic schools. Her work was both fruitful and enduring, as nearly every one of her churches has grown and flowered into the 21st century. It was as if, in the Parable of the Sower, all the seeds 'fell upon good ground; and brought forth fruit that grew up, and increased and yielded, one thirty, another sixty, and another a hundred.'[2]

The 19th century Catholic revival in Britain

Since the 16th century Reformation, and more particularly after the English Civil War (1641–1649), Britain had become profoundly hostile to Catholics and Catholicism. Protestants were raised on ferociously anti-'Papist' accounts such as Foxe's *Book of Martyrs*. Although the last Catholic martyr, Blessed Oliver Plunkett, had been executed in 1681, strict penal laws remained in force through most of the 18th century. Catholics kept quiet and worshipped in secret, supported by brave priests trained abroad who lived in disguise and were in constant danger of betrayal.

Popular feeling was strongly anti-Catholic, especially in London. The number of English practising Catholics in the late 18th century was probably less than 50,000, their ranks depleted by punitive taxation and the many legal disabilities visited on them.[3]

In the 1770's, Parliament relaxed some of the penal laws, and Catholics were allowed to swear oaths of loyalty to the monarch and to inherit property. Yet even these relatively minor reliefs provoked violent reaction among the more extreme Protestants, notably the Gordon Riots of 1780. Ironically, these violent disturbances began at St George's Fields, site of today's St George's Cathedral, Southwark. After several days of rioting, including attacks on Parliament, Newgate prison and the Bank of England, the army was deployed, shooting dead 285 rioters. 30 more were tried and hanged. Lord Gordon, who had whipped up the mob, was tried for treason but acquitted. The riots proved a diplomatic disaster for Britain, which had been seeking support in Catholic Europe for its war against the American colonists.

Despite this setback, after 1789 Catholic refugees from the French revolution were welcomed in Britain, including houses of exiled English monks and nuns who were able to resume their communal lives in the English countryside. These included the communities familiar today as Stanbrook, Downside, Ampleforth, Douai and Stonyhurst.

Under the penal laws, Mass had typically been celebrated secretly in private homes or other secular venues until the Catholic Relief Act of 1791 legalised the construction of new Catholic churches. Despite this new freedom, the habit of concealment remained, and for the next few decades new Catholic churches were designed to look from the outside like ordinary houses. A good example is St Benet's, Netherton, Liverpool (1793), where the church is tucked away behind the priest's house.

The culmination of these gradual relaxations came in 1829 with the Roman Catholic Relief Act. This removed most of the remaining legal impediments, and allowed Catholics to vote, practise law, join the judiciary, serve as officers in the armed forces of the Crown and generally take a full part in British society. Some restrictions remained, but primarily to maintain the role of the Church of England and the Protestant nature of the Crown itself.

Paradoxically, a key influence on the political establishment was the flood of continental Catholic refugees after the French Revolution; as Britain entered a long war with France, the country began to see itself as a beacon of liberty and a refuge for the oppressed—even Catholics. At least 6,400 French Catholic priests were exiled in Britain and the Channel Islands, including six hundred who were housed by the British government in the King's House, Winchester. The activities of the French priests raised the profile of Catholicism and emboldened English Catholics. Most of the French clergy returned to France in 1801, when Napoleon reached a Concordat with Pope Pius VII, but some stayed on. The Abbé Morel, for instance, built St Mary's Holly Mount in Hampstead (1816), one of London's most charming churches.

Despite his personal antipathy to Catholicism, the Duke of Wellington, prime minister in 1829, felt a debt of honour to the many Catholic Irish soldiers who had fought for him in the Peninsular War and at Waterloo. But the main reason he rammed through the Relief Act was the dangerous state of Ireland, where Daniel O'Connell had been elected MP for Clare, but as a Catholic was prevented from taking his seat at Westminster.

The Catholic church gradually emerged from underground. For 250 years English priests had been trained on the continent before returning to Britain in disguise, risking torture and death in order to minister to the faithful. At least 237 were martyred between 1537 and 1681, often at Tyburn, usually by the terrible method of hanging, drawing and quartering.[4] Now new seminaries were established at St Edmund's Ware in Hertfordshire and St Cuthbert's Ushaw in Co. Durham, where English men could train openly for the priesthood.

Forward in faith: Evangelism, the Oxford Movement and Newman

In addition to Catholic emancipation, the 19th century saw a resurgence in the Christian religion generally. Most significant for English Catholics were two very different Anglican movements:

- Evangelism, with its serious moral concerns such as anti-slavery, came first, championed by William Wilberforce and other luminaries. Many evangelicals, though on the low church, anti-ritualist wing of the Church of England, were in favour of freedom of worship, for Catholics as much as other denominations.
- The Oxford Movement, so named because it arose among a group of young Anglican dons at Oriel College, Oxford,

championed a return to the historic roots of the Christian church: John Keble, Edward Pusey, John Henry Newman and others argued that the Church of England should acknowledge Catholic traditions, especially the sacraments and 'proper' liturgy.

The Oxford Movement developed its thinking in a series of 'Tracts'—what might today be called white papers—hence its members were called Tractarians. John Henry Newman, who was vicar of St Mary's the University church, and a star of the Oxford Movement, argued in Tract 90 that because the Church of England regarded itself as descended from the early Church, it must by definition share the beliefs of the Apostles and the Fathers of the Church. Newman then took the 39 Articles of the Church of England—universally understood as a thoroughly Protestant set of anti-Catholic principles—and showed that, apart from a number of philosophical errors and omissions, they were consistent with Catholic belief. Therefore, he argued, the Church of England could not deny the validity of the sacraments, or the doctrine of the Real Presence, or the authority of the Bishop of Rome. This challenge was rejected by the Church of England, and Newman was received into the Catholic church shortly afterwards.

Newman—Saint John Henry Newman as he became in 2019—was the greatest Catholic thinker, and, according to James Joyce, literary stylist of the 19th century, but he was also a dedicated priest and a tireless worker for Catholic education. His life and work were immensely influential throughout Britain during the second half of the 19th century. In the 20th century his writings underpinned the reforms enacted by the Second Vatican Council. As Pope Benedict XVI said at his beatification in 2010:

It is right and fitting that we should recognise today the holiness of a confessor, a son of this nation who, while not called to shed his blood for the Lord, nevertheless bore eloquent witness to him in the course of a long life devoted to the priestly ministry, and especially to preaching, teaching, and writing.[5]

Newman and other high-profile educated converts helped make Catholicism respectable, even fashionable. But the growth in Catholic numbers was due principally to migrants from Ireland in the wake of the potato famine. And their impact was greatest in the big cities, especially London.

The Catholic hierarchy returns to a chorus of outrage

Around the time that Frances Ellis was born into a respectable Anglican family, a series of significant events accelerated the restoration of Catholic life in Britain. Newman became a Catholic in 1845, the Irish potato famine ran from 1845 to 1849, and in 1850 Pope Pius IX restored the English Catholic hierarchy in the bull *Universalis Ecclesiae*. Bishops replaced the Vicars Apostolic who had represented—often secretly—the authority of the Pope in England and Wales.

The Pope divided England and Wales into thirteen dioceses. London would have two: Westminster and Southwark, separated by the Thames. These were the first Catholic bishops in England since the end of Queen Mary's reign in 1558—292 years earlier. This decision was to have unforeseen consequences in the early 20th century, forming an odd backdrop to Frances Ellis' philanthropy.

Westminster covered all of 'official' London north of the river—Parliament, Whitehall, Downing St, the law courts, Buckingham Palace and the City of London—while Southwark initially took in Kent, Surrey, Sussex, Hampshire, Berkshire, the Isle of Wight and the Channel Islands as well as the vast and rapidly growing suburbs of South London.

On 29 September 1850, the Pope appointed Nicholas Wiseman as first Archbishop of Westminster along with twelve bishops for the other dioceses. Wiseman was also made a cardinal. It was unusual in that era for a cardinal not to live in Rome, close to the Pope. But Pius IX, who knew Wiseman well, wanted to bolster his position in hierarchical British society.

Having travelled to Rome to receive his red hat, Wiseman sent home a pastoral letter entitled 'From Out the Flaminian Gate'.[6] Couched in Wiseman's characteristically exuberant style, the letter exulted in the restoration of the English church to the company of Catholic Europe. Yet it was greeted with fury by many English Protestants, who called it 'papal aggression'. The text hardly seemed to justify such reaction, except for one passage which could, if one was so minded, be read as Wiseman and Pius IX claiming dominion over Britain:

> His Holiness was further pleased to appoint us, though most unworthy, to the archiepiscopal see of Westminster, giving us at the same time the administration of the episcopal see of Southwark. So that at present, and till such time as the Holy See shall think fit otherwise to provide, we govern, and shall continue to govern, the counties of Middlesex, Hertford, and Essex as ordinary thereof, and those of Surrey, Sussex, Kent, Berkshire, and Hampshire, with the islands annexed, as administrator with ordinary jurisdiction.

Perhaps Wiseman should have made it clearer that his mission to 'govern' Westminster and the home counties was a matter purely internal to the Catholic church, but those large parts of British society, including the Church of England, which feared the return of Catholic—and Papal—influence, exploited the ambiguity. Many seemed to believe that the Catholic Church was claiming title to the historic dioceses of the Church of England, or even setting up a sort of shadow Papal government of the country itself. There was also a widespread conviction that bishops could only be (a) Anglican and (b) appointed by the monarch. All the anger of 300 years of separation from the Catholic Church bubbled to the surface, along with the view that Rome was a haunt of superstition under a tyrannical Pope.

The Prime Minister Lord John Russell, supported by *The Times*, stoked the outrage. As a result, Parliament passed the Ecclesiastical Titles Act, which imposed a £100 fine on anyone assuming a title to a 'pretended see'—although the Act was regarded almost immediately as a dead letter.

Russell's violent reaction was surprising, as he had for many years been a leading advocate of greater liberty for Catholics. In part this was because he hoped that by pleasing the Irish church, he would make Ireland a more enthusiastic member of the United Kingdom. But the prospect of a second hierarchy threatening the bishops of the established church was too much for him, and for many other Protestant Englishmen. The hatred and fear of Catholicism was deep-rooted in British society, and it would not be dispelled by legalisation or reluctant tolerance.

Public meetings gave vent to these feelings all across the country. For instance, a packed and heated meeting at the York Guildhall heard from a Mr Barstow, whose sentiments chimed with many others, whether bishops, politicians or laymen:

> He was not actuated by any ill-will towards any of the Catholic persuasion. Far from it. He was in the habit of holding familiar intercourse with many of them, and he entertained towards the whole of them the highest respect. Still it did not follow that we were to surrender the rights and privileges of this country on account of our individual regard for those who entertained different religious sentiments to ourselves (cheers). But he did not think that in the present instance the Catholic inhabitants of this country were so to blame as the Bishop of Rome... Hitherto the Roman Catholics had had their own regulations—their own Ecclesiastical superiors, by whatever name they chose to call them, and none had attempted to interfere with them in that respect... It was very well to say that the Romish church had enjoyed this power before, and that the mere giving of these titles would not increase her influence; but it must be remembered that the Queen, according to the law of England, was the fountain of all rank and honour. Therefore for the Pope (uproar, cries of 'He wants to plant his cloven hoof on our soil'), without any consultation with her Majesty or her Ministers, to appoint persons to bear ecclesiastical titles such as had recently been put forward, was undoubtedly an act of aggression.[7]

Cardinal Wiseman learned of the furore while still on the continent and reacted with typical force and clarity in an 'Appeal to the English People'. It sold 30,000 copies and was published in five London daily papers, including *The Times*—an indication that the storm was already abating.

Although it did publish Wiseman's appeal in full, *The Times* introduced it in a feverishly hostile manner:

> We received last night a copy of the following address by Dr Wiseman in explanation of his appointment by the Pope as bishop of Westminster, and hasten to lay before our readers what must be considered as the authorized defence of this monstrous act of presumption.

Wiseman appealed to English common sense and fairness, and ridiculed the exaggerated fears of the established church. He pointed out that Westminster, his intended see, was nothing to do with Westminster Abbey, which in any case was not the seat of an Anglican bishop, rather a 'royal peculiar'.[8] Here Wiseman showed his steel:

> (Westminster Abbey), its treasures of art and its fitting endowments, form not the part of Westminster which will concern me. For there is another part which stands in frightful contrast, though in immediate contact, with this magnificence. In ancient times, the existence of an abbey on any spot, with a large staff of clergy, and ample revenues, would have sufficed to create around it a little paradise of comfort, cheerfulness, and ease. This, however, is not now the case. Close under the Abbey of Westminster there lie concealed labyrinths of lanes, and courts, and alleys, and slums, nests of ignorance, vice, depravity, and crime, as well as of squalor, wretchedness, and disease; whose atmosphere is typhus, whose ventilation is cholera; in which swarms a huge and almost countless population, in great measure, nominally at least, Catholic; haunts of filth, which no sewage committee can reach—dark corners which no lighting board can brighten. This is the part of Westminster which alone I covet, and

> which I shall be glad to claim and to visit as a blessed pasture in which sheep of holy Church are to be tended, in which a Bishop's godly work has to be done, of consoling, converting, and preserving.[9]

In other words, the Dean and Chapter of Westminster Abbey were welcome to continue unmolested with their grand state occasions and ignore the grinding poverty outside their gates. The Catholic church, led by the Archbishop of Westminster, would concern itself with the care of the bodies and souls of the poor.

This episode helped define the development of the English Catholic church for the next few decades. Although it welcomed converts from other confessions, as an institution Holy Mother Church would turn its gaze to the spiritual and temporal needs of the poor. It relied on Providence to find the means to build churches, schools and orphanages, whatever was required to succour its urban flock in their often-desperate need. And while the Protestant fear of 'Rome' receded—though it has never entirely disappeared—so also the Catholic ambition for the wholesale conversion of England retreated.

The impoverished Diocese of Southwark

From the outset, Southwark was Westminster's poor relation, politically and literally: it had little money, and was heavily dependent on donations from wealthy Catholics such as the Duke of Norfolk, Lord Petre and the Earl of Shaftesbury. St George's Cathedral, designed by A. W. N. Pugin and opened in 1848, was unable to be completed to the architect's satisfaction. The necessary money was found in the nick of time by a certain Michael Forristal. Rewarded with the job of diocesan treasurer, he repaid this trust by losing £18,000 of Southwark's money, a dereliction which caused many years of enforced austerity.[10]

In one sense only, Southwark had an advantage over its neighbour across the Thames: it possessed a ready-made Cathedral in St George's. The archbishops of Westminster, by contrast, had to content themselves with Our Lady of Victories in Kensington until Westminster Cathedral was opened in 1903.

In fact, Cardinal Wiseman lived at St George's Cathedral for a year, until Thomas Grant was appointed Southwark's first bishop. Grant, only 36 in 1851, was immediately plunged into the gruelling business of developing a diocese and negotiating with government. A brilliant theologian and canon lawyer, Grant had spent his entire career as a priest in Rome. He had been Rector of the English College and helped the Pope plan the restoration of the English hierarchy. The huge Diocese of Southwark, where he knew almost no one, was therefore a tremendous challenge.

Grant was also called upon to represent his friend Cardinal Wiseman in negotiations with the government over the provision of chaplains for the armed services—in those days disproportionately Catholic—and in prisons. Himself the son of a soldier, born in 1816 near the battlefield of Waterloo, Grant was well suited to the task. Discussions were made more urgent by the outbreak of the Crimean War in 1854, to which Grant sent two chaplains. He also despatched several Sisters of Mercy from Bermondsey and a group of Sisters of the Faithful Virgin from Norwood to work with Florence Nightingale at the Scutari hospital. He is credited with achieving the Chaplains Act that regularised the status of armed services chaplains of all denominations.

Grant, like his successors, worked tirelessly for the diocese. He wrote constantly to his clergy, to whom he was greatly devoted. The challenge of expansion was enormous, especially once 'quasi-parishes' came into being in 1855, followed by the deaneries and the college of canons at St George's Cathedral. Unhappily the latter development foreshadowed the tension with Westminster that would mark the English church during Frances Ellis' period of generosity to Southwark after 1900. The first canons included a number of eminent and learned men, who were nevertheless regarded with suspicion by Cardinal Wiseman. He suspected them of 'Gallicanism'—a disposition to think independently of Rome in an era when the Popes were becoming more conservative and controlling.

When Wiseman died in 1865, Grant was considered as his successor at Westminster. But he was exhausted and already ill with the cancer that was to kill him in 1870, and the top job went instead to Henry Edward Manning, a former Anglican. Bishop Grant himself was succeeded by James Danell, the Vicar General of the Diocese, who like many of Southwark's senior clergy had trained at St Sulpice in Paris and was ordained by the Archbishop of Paris. This French—or Gallican—influence would have consequences in the period that Frances Ellis was supporting Southwark.

During Bishop Danell's reign it became clear that Portsmouth and the surrounding area would need a new diocese, which was to be taken from Southwark. As Danell was dying in 1882 the Pope, at the urging of Cardinal Manning at Westminster, constituted the new Diocese of Portsmouth. This covered Hampshire, Berkshire, the Isle of Wight and the Channel Islands. Southwark was left with South London, Kent, Surrey and Sussex.

Although the population of the reduced Southwark Diocese was about five times the population of the new diocese, Portsmouth nevertheless received 40% of the funds available to Southwark. This imbalance further exacerbated Southwark's chronic financial difficulties just at the point of enormous expansion. And this created the need which Providence, in the shape of Miss Frances Ellis, was to meet.

Notes

1. A notable exception is the 13th century St Etheldreda's, Ely Place, Holborn, London EC1. This had been the chapel of the medieval palace of the Bishops of Ely. After falling into disuse, in 1873 it was purchased by the Rosminian priest Fr Lockhart and restored to Catholic use.
2. Mark 4:8.
3. 50,000 was less than half of one percent of the overall population at the time.
4. Near Marble Arch, London. Today the nuns of the Tyburn convent pray constantly before the Eucharist for the glory of God, the souls of the Martyrs, and the needs of the human family.
5. Pope Benedict XVI, *Homily at Beatification of John Henry Newman* (19 September 2010).
6. An ancient city gate of Rome (now known as the Porta del Popolo) through which ran the Via Flaminia, the road from Rome to the north, and by implication Cardinal Wiseman's return voyage home.
7. *The Tablet* (23 November 1850), p. 739.
8. In the Church of England, a Royal Peculiar is a church that belongs directly to the monarch and thus does not come under the jurisdiction of a bishop. Others include the Chapel Royal, St James's Palace; the Queen's Chapel, St James's Palace; the Chapel Royal, Hampton Court; the Chapel of St John the Evangelist in

the Tower of London; the Chapel of St Peter ad Vincula in the Tower of London; the Queen's Chapel of the Savoy.

9. *The Times* (20 November 1850), pp. 5–6. Through the rest of November and December 1850, the correspondence columns of The Times and other periodicals seethed with angry and violent denunciations of Wiseman, the Pope and Catholic doctrine. But it is clear that Wiseman's Appeal had drawn the sting from the initial reaction.

10. Equivalent to tens of millions of pounds in 21st century terms. This was the first of several severe blows that weakened Southwark's finances.

2

CALLED FROM COMFORT TO BUILD TRUE WEALTH

Fanny, as she was known to her family, was born at Brighton, the younger daughter of Charles and Catherine Ellis. Charles, who gave his profession as 'Gentleman', was a man of independent means, derived from the family stockbroking firm of Ellis & Co, which flourished between 1770 and 1920. Catherine, née Conant, was descended from a family of lawyers and Anglican clergymen. Charles and Catherine lived first at Ulcombe in Kent, then from 1868 at Waltham Place, a large and comfortable house near Maidenhead with extensive grounds. There they enjoyed a life of wealthy Victorian respectability, with a butler, cook and numerous other domestic servants. The family were devout Anglicans and did much for their parish church at White Waltham.

Charles and Catherine's first daughter, Rose (1841–1925), was born in Italy, five years before Frances.[1] She was born with an unspecified mental disability, although the evidence shows she was able to write. No photograph of her survives. Fanny cared for Rose throughout her life, a sign of her gentle and devoted nature.

In a note compiled by the nuns with whom Frances later lived, it is recorded that Catherine Ellis became blind, and relied on her younger daughter as a help and guide. In one of Frances' letters from around 1910, advising a change of scene for an ill nun, she refers to her mother's afflictions:

> I write from bitter experience. My own dear mother, in a time of extreme pressure of worry and work, did not have the change she needed, and for 23 years lived in broken down health and blindness after a paralytic stroke.

As Catherine died in 1890, and the 23 years of blindness takes us back to 1867, it seems no coincidence that the Ellis family moved from Kent to Berkshire in 1868. What came before this can only be conjecture. Perhaps the 'extreme pressure of worry and work' was caused by taking care of her mentally disabled elder daughter. In any case the pressure would not have been financial.

Other than this one memory of her mother, there is little recorded evidence of the life the Ellis family lived together. Frances did not marry, and it seems the family was a close and happy one. Her surviving scrapbooks evince an interest in landscape and historic places, such as the Lake District, Cheddar Gorge and the ruins of Glastonbury Abbey, perhaps mementos of family holidays. She took a close interest in the weather (as her later letters confirm), and in religious matters.

As a young woman, one newspaper story especially caught her attention: the Rev. C. H. Craufurd, rector of Old Swinford, Worcs, defended from the pulpit his decision to marry his cook-housekeeper, thereby provoking a great deal of public comment, some critical, some supportive and some merely ribald. Frances kept a number of cuttings relating to this episode, though without annotation. From her later correspondence, and her evident generosity of spirit, it seems likely that she took the rector's side.

Frances was a sophisticated woman. Later, largely retired from the world, she showed signs of her cultivation when writing to her Godmother, Mother Iphigènie of the Daughters of the Cross. One example is in 1904 when she sends her a parcel of fine German wine—a Bernkasteler—which she has snapped up at a good price (£2 a case—the equivalent of £25 a bottle today) after a talk given by a man from the Wine Society. Though it is probable that she drank little of it herself, and kept it for visiting bishops, Mother Iphigènie, being German, must have particularly appreciated the gift.

Frances also demonstrated business acumen and shrewd practicality when dealing with builders and tradesmen. In this she showed the influence of her father. As he had no sons, and Rose was an invalid, it is likely that Charles Ellis taught his intelligent and industrious daughter how to manage the family affairs.

In addition to the large household at Waltham Place and their involvement with improvements to the church at White Waltham, the Ellis family invested in property in different parts of England. The second half of the nineteenth century was a period of rapid population growth and rising prosperity—circumstances propitious to investment in bricks and mortar.

The Ellis family's placid comfortable life came to an end with the deaths of Charles in 1885, and of Catherine in 1890. At the age of 44, Frances inherited £113,537, the equivalent of at least £20 million today. Interestingly, this money did not come to her entirely from her father Charles, who had left Catherine £57,000 at his death. This implies that Catherine was either wealthy in her own right (possible, given her own family background) or that Charles had divided his fortune with her during his lifetime. In either case, Frances was well equipped to be head of her little household of two. Indeed, over the next forty years she gave away at least twice the sum she had inherited, which suggests shrewd investment skills and money management.[2]

Frances never married, and no evidence survives of any admirers, or indeed of any male friends outside the clergy. She was a handsome woman, and an heiress, and would no doubt have been seen as a 'catch'. Her wealth and position must have reinforced her natural independence. If she had chosen to marry, all her money and property would by law have belonged to her husband. Her philanthropic activities in the second half of her life testify to a strong character with decided views and a determination to put her wealth to good use. This might have been difficult, or impossible, if she had married.

One picture survives of Frances as a young woman, posing for the photographer in the garden at Waltham Place. The hat and dress she is wearing suggests it was taken in the late 1860's, when she would have been in her early twenties.[3] Her lively expression, good looks and fashionable clothes do not suggest a retiring disposition.

Frances' health may have been delicate. In later life she suffered from asthma and bronchial trouble, and her letters hint at a life-long affliction. That too might have deterred her from contemplating marriage in her youth. And it emphasised for her the attractions of clean air, especially at the seaside.

Frances' first care was for her sister Rose and would always remain so. The house and establishment at Waltham Place, however comfortable and familiar, began to feel too large for two middle aged spinsters. At the 1891 census, a year after the death of their mother, they still employed 17 servants. The Misses Ellis continued to reside at Waltham Place for several years, during which

Frances took her first steps in philanthropy. In 1897, as her ideas crystallised, Frances opted for a radical change.

The young Frances Ellis at Waltham Place

Notes

1. Frances usually referred to Rose as 'Kate', from her middle name Catherine.
2. Frances sold Waltham Place before or around 1900, though no record survives of the sale. It is likely that the price on the open market would have been in the range of £20–30,000, adding considerably to her wealth. It was purchased by her cousin Frances Anne Conant and her husband Byam Martin Davies, possibly at a sub-market rate. They moved there in 1901, the year that Frances moved to Cornwall.
3. Thanks to the Victoria and Albert Museum's textiles and fashion department for dating the clothes.

3

To Advance the Kingdom of Heaven

As new head of the household and custodian of a large fortune, Frances Ellis began to consider a life programme that responded lovingly to the teachings of Jesus. She had read the Bible since a child, and she knew there was no ambiguity in His injunctions. Jesus said to the rich young man who wanted to know what he needed to gain eternal life:

> If thou wilt be perfect, go and sell that thou hast, and give to the poor, and thou shalt have treasure in heaven: and come and follow me.' But when the young man heard that saying, he went away sorrowful: for he had great possessions.[1]

She saw that she must be braver than the young man who clung to his wealth, though he knew it was wrong. And she also heeded Jesus' command not to use one's charity for self-aggrandisement:

> Take heed that ye do not your alms before men, to be seen of them: otherwise ye have no reward of your Father which is in heaven. Therefore when thou doest thine alms, do not sound a trumpet before thee, as the hypocrites do in the synagogues and in the streets, that they may have glory of men. Verily I say unto you, they have their reward. But when thou doest alms, let not thy left hand know what thy right hand doeth: That thine

alms may be in secret: and thy Father which seeth in secret himself shall reward thee openly.[2]

While still living in the old family home, Frances resolved that she would use her money to advance the Kingdom of Heaven, quietly but with maximum effect, only maintaining the basics of life for her sister and herself.

Frances' first major religious benefaction came in 1893 at the hamlet of Littlewick Green, a couple of miles from Waltham Place. She gave £15,000—a huge sum at the time—for the construction and endowment of St John the Evangelist as a new Anglican parish church.[3] This charming neo-Gothic church in blue Pennant stone replaced an early 19th century wooden chapel which had been used by a variety of congregations. A plaque records that St John's was donated by Frances 'to the glory of God, and in memory of Catherine Ellis of Waltham Place, Berks, widow of Charles Ellis Esq.'

Four years later, to commemorate Queen Victoria's diamond jubilee, Frances installed a fine stone water fountain at Waltham Place, between the house and the farm. A brass plaque recorded: 'This fountain of pure water was erected on Monday 22 June to commemorate 60 years of the reign of her most gracious majesty Queen Victoria by Frances Elizabeth Ellis'. Many years later an old gardener recalled that villagers treated it as a sort of shrine, and left jars full of flowers there.

These were both generous gifts and much appreciated by the people of Littlewick Green and White Waltham. However, everyone was aware of the source of this charity, and that Frances lived in the 'big house' next to St Mary's. She herself wondered what more she could do in the local area, and to what effect. Here she was effectively the lady of the manor, socially as well as financially secure. Whatever she did locally would be visible to everyone. She concluded that the scope for really making a difference lay elsewhere.

Frances had turned fifty in 1896—a good age for an Englishwoman in the late 19th century—and was always conscious of the needs of her disabled sister. She began planning for their old age, which in her view would have to involve fresh air: her bronchial problems were getting worse, and she was determined to remain well enough to care for Rose.

The Isle of Thanet, at the eastern extremity of Kent, and swept by winds from the Channel and the North Sea, was her first resort. In 1897, she bought a large Georgian house and garden in Ramsgate High Street, and was immediately plunged into a society radically different from the one she had grown up in. She also discovered a very different type of Christianity to the established church she had known in Berkshire. Catholic clergy, religious and lay people were much in evidence on Thanet, and especially in Ramsgate.

Although its heyday had been in the early 19th century, Thanet in 1897 remained more fashionable than it has since become. The railway brought it within two hours of London. A building boom had produced a good number of agreeable houses for the well-to-do.

Thanet, as everywhere in Britain, had a large number of poor and very poor people, and many social problems. There was no NHS, no social security, no welfare state as we understand it today. Relief of the poor and sick was left largely to private charity, which often meant the church. Here again, Thanet was blessed with Anglican, Catholic and other denominations, all active in works of charity and corporal works of mercy.

In particular, many orders of Catholic nuns, mostly French, German and Belgian refugees from anticlerical governments, had settled along the coast.[4] Their encounter with one of these orders would lead to a new life for the Ellis sisters.

The ancient town of Ramsgate had played a significant role in the mid-19th century Catholic revival. In 1843 the designer of the Palace of Westminster, Augustus Welby Pugin, came in search of the historic roots of English Catholicism: St Augustine, the Apostle of the English, despatched by Pope Gregory the Great in 597, had landed with forty Roman monks at nearby Ebbsfleet. Pugin, a fervent Catholic convert, accordingly chose Ramsgate for the site of his ideal community, designing a Gothic church, house and school.

Bede's account of St Augustine's arrival in Kent

In his *History of the English Church and People*, St Bede (672–735) gave a dramatic account of Augustine's mission to the English, beginning with his approach to King Ethelbert of Kent. It is worth quoting at length.

> In this island (Thanet) landed the servant of our Lord, Augustine, and his companions, being, as is reported, nearly forty men. They had, by order of the blessed Pope Gregory, taken interpreters of the nation of the Franks, and sending to Ethelbert, signified that they were come from Rome, and brought a joyful message, which most undoubtedly assured to all that took advantage of it everlasting joys in heaven and a kingdom that would never end with the living and true God. The king having heard this, ordered them to stay in that island where they had landed, and that they should be

furnished with all necessaries, till he should consider what to do with them. For he had before heard of the Christian religion, having a Christian wife of the royal family of the Franks, called Bertha; whom he had received from her parents, upon condition that she should be permitted to practise her religion with the Bishop Luidhard, who was sent with her to preserve her faith. Some days after, the king came into the island, and sitting in the open air, ordered Augustine and his companions to be brought into his presence. For he had taken precaution that they should not come to him in any house, lest, according to an ancient superstition, if they practised any magical arts, they might impose upon him, and so get the better of him. But they came furnished with Divine, not with magic virtue, bearing a silver cross for their banner, and the image of our Lord and Saviour painted on a board; and singing the litany, they offered up their prayers to the Lord for the eternal salvation both of themselves and of those to whom they were come. When he had sat down, pursuant to the king's commands, and preached to him and his attendants there present, the word of life, the king answered thus: 'Your words and promises are very fair, but as they are new to us, and of uncertain import, I cannot approve of them so far as to forsake that which I have so long followed with the whole English nation. But because you are come from far into my kingdom, and, as I conceive, are desirous to impart to us those things which you believe to be true, and most beneficial, we will not molest you, but give you favourable entertainment, and take care to supply you with your necessary sustenance; nor do we forbid you to preach and gain as many as you can to your religion.' Accordingly he permitted them to reside in the city of Canterbury, which was the metropolis of all his dominions, and, pursuant to his promise, besides allowing them sustenance, did not refuse them liberty to preach.[5]

From this auspicious beginning, St Augustine's mission grew rapidly. Ethelbert, and with him all the people of Kent, soon agreed to be baptised. A Cathedral was raised in the middle of Canterbury, as well as a new monastery just outside the Roman walls. Drawn from the ranks of Augustine's monks, bishops were established at Rochester, York and London. The word of God spread among the pagan Anglo-Saxons throughout the land that would one day be known as England. And the representatives of Papal authority began to meet with the Celtic monks and missionaries who themselves were reintroducing an older Christianity from the remote fringes of Britain and Ireland whither it had been driven after the collapse of the Roman empire. This fusion was the true birth of the English church.

The great commemoration of 1897 and a new evangelisation of England

By 1897, the 1300th anniversary of St Augustine's mission, a number of religious communities were living and working on the Isle of Thanet. At Pugin's Abbey of St Augustine, a community of Benedictine monks had come initially from Subiaco in Italy, the site of St Benedict's original monastery. The community flourished and attracted many British monastic vocations. They built their abbey, designed by Pugin's son Edward, across the road from the church. Although A. W. N. Pugin had paid for the church himself, he had given it to the Vicar Apostolic of the English church in 1846. Since the restoration of the English hierarchy in 1850, it had been vested in the new Diocese of Southwark. Although architecturally impressive, it was too small to serve happily as parish church for Ramsgate. By the 1890's, a new church was needed for the town itself.

Events began to move swiftly for Frances Ellis. Once in Ramsgate she met a certain James Leahy, who became her financial advisor and property agent.[6] Mr Leahy was a Catholic, and in later years Frances ascribed her own first interest in Catholicism to his steadfast faith, citing his example of walking daily to Mass in all weathers.

St Augustine's anniversary in 1897 was marked by fervent celebrations, in London as well as Ramsgate. The Catholic church put on a huge demonstration that emphasised the profound and enduring links between the early church and modern Catholicism, and between Britain and the rest of Christendom. Cardinal Perraud, Archbishop of Autun, in Burgundy, and the Archpriest of Arles, whose 6th-century predecessors had encouraged Augustine when he was wavering in his mission, joined Cardinal Vaughan, Archbishop of Westminster, first at the Brompton Oratory, then at Ramsgate.

On Monday 13 September, an open-air Mass was celebrated in fields at Ebbsfleet, two miles from Ramsgate, where tradition placed Augustine's landing in 597. The Mass was led by Cardinals Vaughan and Perraud, assisted by the entire English hierarchy, representatives of their Chapters, the Abbot of Ramsgate and his monks, the Abbots of all the other English Benedictine houses, the heads of the Jesuits, Dominicans, Franciscans, Redemptorists and other communities, as well as hundreds of nuns and priests.

The Ramsgate monks chanted the very invocation sung by their Roman predecessors 1300 years before:

> *Deprecamur te Domine in omni misericordia tua*
> *ut auferatur furor tuus et ira tua a civitate ista et*
> *de domo sancta tua quoniam peccavimus alleluia.*[7]

The Duke of Norfolk and thousands of other lay Catholics from all over the country were also present, as were the mayors and dignitaries of Ramsgate and the other Thanet towns. This extraordinary gathering marked the confident resurgence of Catholicism in the country which three centuries earlier had rejected St Augustine's gift.

Later that day, at the Granville Hall in Ramsgate (also designed and built by Edward Pugin), Cardinal Vaughan spoke powerfully about the golden thread linking Augustine's 6th century mission to the 19th century Catholic revival. Gregory the Great's papal authority, he said, was the same authority wielded by Pope Leo in 1897. The Benedictine monks who accompanied Augustine followed the same rule and 'sing the same litanies to the same chant' as the Benedictine monks who now occupied Pugin's abbey.

The Catholic revival had a deliberate, almost pugnacious air about it. Since 1850, Catholics had put up with a great deal of prejudice and abuse from the Protestant establishment, but they were sure of the faith and the justice of their cause. About Anglicanism, Cardinal Vaughan did not mince his words:

> All England knows that the fair line of continuity in faith and doctrine falls among those who no longer hold the ancient cathedrals or dispose of the ancient revenues. We hold the ancient faith, others hold the ancient foundations.

Vaughan also spoke of the efficacy of prayer, to which he attributed the return of so many modern-day English men and women to Roman Catholicism.

And as the prayers of her children rise and fall, so
does the work of salvation advance or recede.

Cardinal Vaughan's words deeply moved Frances Ellis that September evening in the Granville Hall, to which she had been escorted by Mr Leahy. Her heart responded to her Saviour's call, though she was four years away from her reception into the Catholic church.

That she was still an Anglican makes it all the more extraordinary that her next benefactions were to the Catholic church.

Mother Iphigènie and the Daughters of the Cross

In these last years of the 19th century, Frances Ellis formed four important friendships with leading Catholics: Francis Bourne the Bishop of Southwark; his diocesan treasurer Canon Edward St John; Thomas Bergh OSB Abbot of Ramsgate; and Mother Iphigènie Butner, Provincial of the Daughters of the Cross of Liège.

Bourne (later to succeed Vaughan as Cardinal Archbishop of Westminster) and St John would have told her of the desperate shortage of churches across their diocese. The work of finding the resources to build new churches fell to the treasurer.

Edward St John was a convert, the son of the head of the Customs service and the nephew of Fr Ambrose St John, close friend of St John Henry Newman. Before becoming a Catholic, Edward had worked in a bank in Brighton, apparently his principal qualification as treasurer.

A great networker, Abbot Bergh maintained contacts with the others and advised Frances on matters spiritual and practical.

Mother Iphigènie pointed her towards the works of mercy being carried out by the Daughters of the Cross. Of the four, Iphigènie was closest to Frances Ellis' heart.

Mother Iphigènie, Provincial of the Daughters of the Cross

The Daughters of the Cross had arrived in Britain in 1863, originally intending to recruit English-speaking women for their recently founded missions on the Indian sub-continent. However, they swiftly put down roots in

England. Members of the German province arrived as exiles from the *Kulturkampf*, moving from Düsseldorf to Bury in Lancashire in 1878. Iphigènie was the superior of this group.

Sister Honorine Kersten was the Superior at the Margate convent, where they had run a Catholic Poor Law school for sick children since 1879. She and the Provincial explained to Frances their ambition to build a tuberculosis (TB) hospital at Ramsgate. Before the development of penicillin in the mid-twentieth century, TB was a major health scourge, and there were TB hospitals all across the country.

The nuns were well placed to answer Frances' questions about the Catholicism to which she was increasingly attracted. They also explained the special charism of their order, which combined active works of charity with time for contemplation and prayer. In light of subsequent events, we must assume that Frances began to receive instruction in the Catholic faith from these devout sisters.

The Daughters of the Cross had been founded at Liège, Belgium, in 1833 by Mère Marie Thérèse (born Jeanne) Haze (1782–1876). Mlle Haze came from an impeccable Catholic background, her father having been secretary to the last Prince-Bishop of Liège. The order's first work was caring for orphans and ensuring their education. They also ministered in women's prisons and tried to keep the inmates from going astray after release. They ran hospitals for people with TB and sexually transmitted diseases, gruelling work that few others were prepared to contemplate.

The Daughters never had much money, and their efforts were marked by trust in the Lord's mercy, and in the Holy Spirit to provide them with the bare necessities of their work: buildings, books, food, cash. They also had to contend with the hostility of the Belgian authorities, who regularly tried to undermine or close down their schools for poor girls. Despite these obstacles, their work increased rapidly across Belgium, as did the numbers of women joining the order. As the 19th century progressed, the Daughters of the Cross began working in Germany, Holland, India and England—where they established a house at Cheltenham in 1863 and Chelsea in 1869.

The English province became central to the Daughters' missionary work over the succeeding century. Mother Iphigènie, born Julie Butner in Prussia in 1841, joined the Daughters of the Cross in 1860. As a young nun she experienced the *Kulturkampf* loosed on the German church by Chancellor Bismarck, who wanted to eradicate the church's participation in education. A strong character with a gift for organisation, she was appointed to run the new English province in 1885. At that date there were four houses in England—Chelsea, Bury, Kensington and Margate—but by the time she died in 1912 there were fifteen. Importantly, she established the order's novitiate at Carshalton, Surrey, where she also started a girls' boarding school, St Philomena's.

From Frances' later letters, it is clear that she and Iphigènie became firm friends. On Frances' side, at least, the friendship was a passionate one. She deeply admired Iphigènie, from whom she learned not only about the Daughters' work and ambitions, but also what it meant to be a nun: the unrelenting work, the devotion and the readiness to sacrifice oneself for the sake of others and the love of Jesus.

Frances Ellis had arrived at middle age wealthy and self-contained, but with few close friends. Her admiration for Iphigènie perhaps filled a gap in her life, and focused her growing determination to use her money for the relief of distress and the good of the church.

Iphigènie reciprocated the friendship but inevitably in a manner defined by her vocation as a nun, and by her duties as the order's British Provincial. The life of a Daughter of the Cross—the life of any nun—is extremely disciplined, more disciplined in truth than the lives of many monks. In addition to the cycle of prayer, there was work, sometimes hard, unpleasant and even dangerous, willingly undertaken in obedience to one's superiors and for the love of God. There were to be no cliques within a house, and nuns were warned against the danger of having a 'particular friend'. Friendship between two nuns within a convent is permissible but should be centred on the shared desire to know, serve and love Our Lord better, without competition and without excluding other members of the community.

The philanthropy begins, and the Ellis sisters join the Catholic church

In 1900, Frances Ellis' first recorded Catholic benefaction was the gift to St Augustine's Abbey of Chartham Terrace, a substantial property immediately next to the Abbey church. Ironically Chartham Terrace had been built some years before by an anti-Catholic architect, Charles Habershon, deliberately to try to block the light entering the east window of the Abbey church. Frances intended it as a rental asset that would boost the community's income. Shortly afterwards she gave money to Abbot Bergh to build St Mildred's church five miles away at Minster-in-Thanet. This modest building was the first of 36 churches she would fund in the Southwark Diocese.

Also in 1900, Frances gave the diocese a substantial house in Ramsgate known as Victory Villa, together with £3,100 for the construction of a new parish church, badly needed because the Catholic population had outgrown the use of St Augustine's Abbey church. The architect was Peter Paul Pugin, younger son of A. W. N. Pugin, and the church, in Hereson Road, was dedicated to St Ethelbert and St Gertrude.

Frances had been receiving instruction not only from the nuns but also from Abbot Bergh, who remained her friend and confidant for the rest of his life. On the 8th of January 1901, Frances and her sister Rose were received into the Catholic Church, and the following day made their first Holy Communions. Mother Iphigènie was her Godmother. Frances took St Gertrude as her patronal saint, while Rose chose St Winefride.

Fifteen years later, on the occasion of her seventieth birthday, one of the Daughters of the Cross wrote a poem in tribute to Frances which reads in part:

> *For we can see how, down the changing years,*
> *The guiding star of His dear love appears*
> *Lighting your life with its pure silver ray*
> *That star, unseen by the dim eyes of men*
> *That led you in sweet ways past human ken,*
> *Into the noon-tide of the Church's day.*
> *It shone above you on that thrice-blessed morn*
> *When in the sacred fount your soul was born*
> *To a new life of faith, and joy and praise:*
> *It shone with a yet deeper, tenderer light*
> *When first your Saviour would in love unite*
> *His Heart to yours for endless length of days.*

Also in 1900, according to the DoC's history, Bishop Bourne approached Sr Honorine and Mother Iphigènie with a request that they open a hospital in Ramsgate for tuberculosis patients. The Bishop, in this account, had been given a house for the purpose by Miss Ellis. This may be the wrong way round. It is more likely that the nuns had told their new friend of the need for such a hospital and that she had agreed to support the plan.

In fact, Frances Ellis gave the DoC three houses for the hospital, separated by a strip of land which she had been unable to buy from yet another anti-Catholic Ramsgate resident. This separation later caused difficulties with the local authority, which did not welcome TB patients (or Catholics) in the middle of the town.

The houses were numbers 142, 144 and 146 High Street, Ramsgate. According to the Daughters of the Cross, when she actually handed them over to the nuns, she had been living in one of the houses. The Georgian house at 144 High St, the largest and most attractive of the three, was probably her Ramsgate base before she moved to Cornwall.[8]

In early 1901, around the time of her reception, Frances had already moved to a rented house at Penzance, Cornwall, even as these developments were taking shape on Thanet. But it's clear that she regularly travelled the 300 miles from one end of England to the other. She was certainly in Ramsgate in January 1901, and then again in April.

The English province of the DoC could not spare enough sisters for the new hospital, so reinforcements were sent from Belgium. On 16 April 1901, three German nuns—Srs Mary Emmanuel Ditges, Mary Aloysie Marix and Georgia Gietmann—left Liège and travelled to Margate via Carshalton. One of the Daughters wrote an account of their arrival and the start of the hospital.

On the following day, Chère Sr Honorine took them to Ramsgate. They first drove to the monastery of the Benedictines to ask the Blessing of the Right Revd the Abbot T.S. Bergh, then went to the future hospital then called Cunningham House where they were introduced to Miss F.E. Ellis, the lady foundress of the establishment who kindly gave them tea & then showed the premises. They consisted of three houses—one, the largest, was still partly inhabited by Miss Ellis and a small staff, the other two were empty but for some furniture heaped up in one of them ... There were also about twenty bedsteads in the to be hospital. There was also the installation of the Ellis treatment of chest and throat by inhalation which included pneumatic chambers, a pump and a gas motor.

The first work done was to fit up the little Chapel. On the 27th March, H. Mass was first said by Fr Abbot Bergh and on the Feast of the Ascension, 16th May, the first Benediction was given by Fr Prior Swithburt (Palmer). Miss Ellis soon gave a sewing machine on condition the Sisters would make the mattresses. It was fixed by Sr Provincial that the first house called 'The Limes' should be for the Sisters, the second for the male patients & the third & largest was the inhaling for the female patients.

St Catherine's Hospital owed its very existence to Frances Ellis. Her involvement was more than simply financial. As soon as possible, it opened to provide urgently needed care to 70 patients, both men and women. It was formally opened by Bishop Bourne on Wednesday 26 June 1901 during a visitation dedicated to three Ellis foundations. On the Tuesday he had laid St Ethelbert's foundation stone, and on Wednesday morning he consecrated St

Mildred's in Minster. Frances Ellis was there for all three ceremonies, before returning to Cornwall.

Devotion to St Gertrude of Nivelles

Perhaps the seeds of Frances Ellis' devotion to St Gertrude, to whom the first four of her churches were dedicated, were sown during her initial conversations with Mother Iphigènie and Sister Honorine: she took Gertrude as her confirmation name.

This St Gertrude was a seventh century Frankish nun, founder of an important double monastery of men and women at Nivelles.[9] The daughter of the steward of King Dagobert, she was born in 626, and raised in the palace. At the age of ten she declined the offer of a political marriage, declaring:

> I have chosen for my spouse Him from whose eternal beauty all creatures derive their glory, whose riches are immense and Whom the angels adore.

The king, admiring her steadfast purpose, did not press the matter.

St Gertrude was a courageous woman who lived at a time of evangelisation on both sides of the Channel. Her monastery at Nivelles was 50 miles from Liège, where the Daughters of the Cross began their work 1200 years later. Gertrude was a great church-builder, and was devoted to the care of orphans, widows, captives, and pilgrims. She was aided at times by Irish monks who had travelled to the continent via England, and she would have been well informed about the progress of the church in Kent only a few decades after St Augustine's arrival. She was a most appropriate confirmation saint for Frances.

Miss Ellis, Bishop Bourne, Canon St John and the expansion of Southwark

During this period Frances Ellis also began working with Bishop Francis Bourne (1861–1935) of Southwark and his treasurer Canon Edward St John (1855–1934). Bourne was a driven character with a strong sense of the Church's mission to re-evangelise Great Britain, which he saw as 'Mary's dowry'. His eloquent intensity caught Frances' imagination. She already knew in a general way that she wanted to give her money to advance the faith and serve the people. Bourne's powerful sense of the 'golden thread', the work of the Holy Spirit linking early Christianity to the modern revival of the Catholic church in England, unfolded for her the work of salvation. This growing consciousness led to her greatest programme of philanthropy and her most enduring legacy.

In those days, Bourne's Diocese of Southwark covered South London, Kent, Sussex and Surrey, a vast area marked by rapid population growth. All across South London, in particular, many thousands of Catholics were living at some distance from churches where they could attend Mass. The diocese was constantly trying to find the resources to cater for the faithful, whether by building new churches or starting schools and orphanages. The hierarchy feared, with good reason, that people would fall away from the faith if they could not easily go to church and receive the sacraments, or if their children were not educated in Catholic schools.

Canon St John was at the heart of this development programme. As Bourne, by then Cardinal Archbishop of Westminster, noted in 1930, he had seen 'the necessity of erecting new missionary centres in south London, and the plan was worked out with the devoted zeal and careful accuracy of Canon St John.'

In 1913, St John himself put it like this:

> As treasurer of the Diocese, I have been engaged in a great work of church extension in the Diocese. A good convert lady who was very wealthy gave me *carte blanche* to buy land and build simple churches anywhere in South London. The work of carrying out her instructions was very great, as no less than thirty-six new parishes have been formed with her money, besides other institutions of charity. The lady preferred to transact her business through me, and both Bishop Bourne (while Bishop of Southwark) and the present Bishop encouraged her in every way to do so. She has given over £144,000 to the Diocese in ten years.[10]

An intelligent, sensitive man with a deep love for the poor, St John was the fifth of nine children of Frederick and Mary-Ann St John. The family was initially well to do, his father rising to Surveyor General (or head) of Customs.[11] His uncle, Fr Ambrose St John (1815–1875), first ordained a priest of the Church of England, later converted to Catholicism, and was a close friend of his fellow Oratorian John Henry Newman. Indeed, Newman dedicated his spiritual autobiography *Apologia pro Vita Sua* to Ambrose St John and was buried in the same grave.[12]

However, his father Frederick died when Edward St John was only eight, and the family fell on hard times. Edward converted from Anglicanism in his twenties, after five years at a bank in Brighton. This was scant training for running the finances of a cash-strapped diocese under constant pressure to build churches, schools and orphanages. Nor was his path to the priesthood an easy one. Although he was supported and encouraged by the

Provost of the Brompton Oratory Fr Philip Gordon, St John was not admitted for training at St Edmund's Ware until he had become sufficiently proficient at Latin. That suggests he had not enjoyed the standard classical education a boy of his class would have expected. He was finally ordained priest at St George's Cathedral in 1887, aged 31.

Yet only three years later, appointed by Bishop John Butt (in office 1885–1897), St John was the driving force on the Council of Temporal Administration, what would today be called the Diocesan Finance Committee. The Bishop was the chairman *ex officio*, but St John was the secretary, and all communication was directed through him. Furthermore, he coordinated the financial manoeuvres necessary to achieve Southwark's ambitions under particularly difficult conditions. In particular he seems to have been the only cleric who worked with lay advisors, two of whom later let him and the Diocese down badly.

As a senior diocesan official, St John would have been present at the 1897 celebrations at Ramsgate, attending the new bishop, Francis Bourne (in office 1897–1903). His name appears in records relating to the building of St Ethelbert & St Gertrude's, the new church at Ramsgate which Miss Ellis financed and endowed. From then on, Frances Ellis supported the diocesan expansion plans across south London. She may have been moved to support the work by her admiration for Bishop Bourne, but the direct link was with St John.

None of the early correspondence between Frances and Canon St John survives, perhaps because he became embroiled in the Southwark diocese's financial difficulties after 1905. Some papers may have been lost when the Cathedral was devastated by Luftwaffe fire-bombs in 1941, but it seems more likely that they were deliberately destroyed as part of the effort to restore Southwark's reputation. It is telling that the only records of correspondence between the two survives in the Westminster rather than the Southwark archives.

The appearance of the Ellis Boxes

Around the turn of the century, Frances Ellis told Bishop Bourne and Canon St John that her wealth was available for the diocese to use to build churches wherever they were needed. St John's later statement that she gave him '*carte blanche*' is an exaggeration: she wanted good value, not out of meanness, but so that the money would stretch as far as it could, to bring as many people as possible to church in the new Catholic communities that were spreading across south London.

The direction and planning of the church-building programme belonged to Canon St John. Even before the project started, Frances Ellis was living far away in west Cornwall. The initial intention was to place new churches between larger established ones, and thus enable Catholics to get to Mass more easily. Later St John extended the programme to the new suburbs on the fringes of Kent and Surrey.

Frances Ellis wanted the churches she financed to be architecturally simple, usually of London stock brick in a plain Romanesque style with a round window on the west front. She also preferred them to be dedicated to early English saints, to emphasise that the Catholic church was deeply rooted in Britain—that there really was a golden thread connecting the modern church to the era of St Augustine. This was especially important when resurgent Catholicism was portrayed in the hostile press as an unpatriotic foreign import. Some Anglicans sarcastically referred to the Catholic church in Britain as 'the Italian mission to the Irish'.

In practice, she did not always get her way with names: there was a period after 1903 when the newly installed Bishop Amigo decreed that new churches be dedicated to the twelve apostles. And the faithful did not always favour their places of worship being named after obscure, even comical sounding Anglo-Saxon saints.[13]

Finally, Frances stipulated that in each church, there should be an annual Mass for every parishioner who had ever worshipped there.

From 1902, the programme of church-building developed with extraordinary rapidity, especially considering the challenge of finding suitable building sites. In some years as many as seven churches were planned, built and opened in south London. For Canon St John it was a punishing addition to his already extensive workload. Frances Ellis paid over the money as and when required. By then her own day-to-day concerns were largely with the Daughters of the Cross, whom she was also supporting financially

The church-building slowed down after 1908, when St John fell out with Bishop Amigo and the Southwark Chapter. But the crucial year was 1911, when Frances Ellis became peripherally involved in the dispute between Bourne and Amigo. In particular, Bourne, with St John's help, used her dissatisfaction with Southwark's administration of her charity in his lobbying of the Pope to merge Westminster and Southwark into a single Archdiocese of London. She made it clear in writing that, if forced to choose, her loyalty was to Bourne and St John, not to Amigo.[14]

Her gifts to Southwark were certainly over by 1913, the year Canon St John left for Liverpool. If the Diocese made any attempt to maintain the arrangement with Miss

Ellis, no record of it has survived. By then she had also given away most of the money she had inherited in 1890.

In 1911, she had decided to donate £15,000, a large part of her remaining wealth, to the Pope himself. This perhaps was money she might have spent on further Southwark churches, if St John had still been in charge.

Pope Pius X replied to Frances in January 1912, imparting his apostolic blessing together with a *Pro Ecclesia et Pontifice* medal, in those days the highest papal award available to women.[15] The letter and medal were entrusted to Archbishop Bourne who had travelled to Rome in November 1911 to be appointed Cardinal.[16] With the Pope's letter, Bourne sent a note in his own hand:

> My dear Miss Ellis
>
> I am at last able to send you the Holy Father's autograph blessing and thanks. You will understand the delay in the remembrance of his constant daily cares of every kind. But I know what real and heartfelt joy and consolation your generous gift brought to his heart, for he spoke to me about it more than once. I am sending too by the same post the Medal which he entrusted to me for you.
>
> I hope you are keeping well. I am gradually getting back to my ordinary routine of work but there is much still in the way of ceremonies and receptions. Please remember me kindly to Bishop Graham, and believe me, with every blessing,
>
> Your obedient servant in J. C.
>
> Francis Cardinal Bourne

The Papal Medal has not been preserved with the Ellis papers, and it may be that it was buried with Frances at Hayle in 1930.

Notes

1. Matthew 19:21.
2. Matthew 6:1–4.
3. See Chapter 7.
4. In France religious orders were persecuted under various anti-clerical laws from 1880 onwards, particularly aimed at teaching orders. In Germany, the clergy and religious were excluded from education by a law of 1872, part of the *Kulturkampf* (culture war) waged by Bismarck and the new Prussian Empire against religious authority in general and the Catholic church in particular. There were similar struggles in Belgium in the later 19th century, though there was less persecution of religious. In fact, Belgium took in thousands of religious from Germany and France.
5. St Bede, *An Ecclesiastical History of the English People*, (London: Penguin Books, 1990) p. 74.
6. It is confusing that Frances Ellis had agents with two such similar names, James Leahy in Thanet, and James Lee in the West Country. Gertrude, the daughter of James and Frances Leahy, joined the Daughters of the Cross in 1903, taking as her religious names Frances Elizabeth in tribute to Frances Ellis. From 1900 onwards, Mr James Lee is regularly recorded as Miss Ellis' man of business in Cornwall. At the 1901 census, James and Fanny Lee were living with Frances Ellis in Penzance.
7. 'We beseech thee, O Lord, for Thy great mercy, that Thy wrath and anger be turned away from this city, and from Thy holy house, for we have sinned. Alleluia.'
8. Today 142 Ramsgate High St is the home of the Thanet Lodge of the Oddfellows' Club, 144 is divided into 3 private dwellings and 146 no longer stands.
9. There are several saints named Gertrude. The best known is St Gertrude of Helfta, sometimes called St Gertrude the Great (1256–1301), a German theologian, mystic and nun who together with St Mechtilde, developed 'nuptial mysticism', the idea of a nun being a Bride of Christ.
10. From St John's controversial pamphlet *Some Notes on the False Diocesan Balance Sheet of Jan 31 1910, Appendix No. II.*

11. The St Johns are an ancient family whose origins can be traced back to at least 1340, and possibly to a Norman knight granted land by William the Conqueror. Edward St John was from the family's senior branch which was awarded the Barony of Bletso in 1559. The current holder of the title, Anthony Tudor St John, is the 22nd Baron of Bletso.
12. Two men sharing a grave was an accepted marker of deep friendship in Victorian times, and was not, as is sometimes suggested today, an indication of homosexual love.
13. See Chapter 7 for the change of name from St Egbert's to St Matthias, Worcester Park.
14. See the detailed account in Chapter 4.
15. 'For Church and Pope'.
16. Bourne had been Archbishop of Westminster and leader of the English church for eight years when he received his red hat. His predecessor had been named cardinal only nine months into his term of office. The delay was largely due to Bourne's public falling out with Amigo.

4

A Scandalous Episcopal Dispute

Miss Ellis' church-building programme took place against a background of trouble within the Diocese of Southwark, and a bizarre rift between the Bishop of Southwark and his superior and neighbour the Archbishop of Westminster. That so many churches were built in only a few years was due to the speed and efficiency with which Canon St John deployed the cash she made available to him. The process slowed and eventually halted as Southwark was crippled by financial scandal, while Archbishop Bourne quarrelled with Bishop Amigo before launching a campaign for Westminster to take over Southwark. Ten years after the church-building programme began, Frances Ellis was persuaded to side with Bourne and St John against Amigo, and ceased supporting new churches.

To understand the dispute, it is helpful to begin with the young Fr Francis Bourne and the foundation of Southwark's diocesan seminary, St John's Wonersh.

Francis Bourne (1861–1935) was a south Londoner, born in Clapham, who was both baptised and ordained priest at St Mary's Clapham. He demonstrated a strong attachment to south London throughout his life, especially after his translation to Westminster. His father died when he was a boy, and he was close to his devout Irish mother. Highly intelligent but socially insecure, he grew up a reserved, sensitive and prickly young man. His physical health was often poor, but his faith was powerful.

Bourne had an unusual path to the priesthood, including two years' study at St Sulpice in Paris which influenced him profoundly. The English seminaries of the day, such as St Edmund's Ware and St Thomas's Hammersmith, were narrow and regimented, with an over-reliance on the study of medieval scholasticism. There was also a typically British concern with turning out clerical gentlemen.[1]

St Sulpice, while severe in its discipline, provided a sophisticated training open to a larger degree of philosophical enquiry than was usual in England. The teachers at St Sulpice aimed for holiness and simplicity in their own lives and fostered the spiritual as well as the intellectual in their students.

> A good Sulpician constitutes himself everywhere and always the companion and the model of the future priests, in their pious exercises, recreations, meals, and walks, briefly in all the details of their life.[2]

The whole seminary, teachers as well as students, constituted a spiritual community, rather different from the hierarchical English colleges. This was a model that profoundly affected the young Bourne. He was especially influenced by one professor, the Irishman Fr John Baptist Hogan, who believed in Catholic truth, and wanted the seminarians to understand and believe it themselves. So armed, they would show forth Christ's love to the faithful and to potential converts.

At St Sulpice, Bourne's teachers were unafraid to discuss modern challenges to the church, such as Darwinian evolution and the new biblical scholarship. As Fr Hogan wrote:

> It is not, nor has it ever been, the policy of the Catholic Church to close her eyes to the evidence, and cling indiscriminately to all that is old.³

Catholic doctrines, discerned over time, rested on the authority of the church, not on shifting interpretations of the Bible; these were threatening to Protestant theology, but not to Catholic doctrine founded on the teachings of the Church Fathers. On the other hand, Hogan was fiercely critical of progressivism and relativism, which would undermine 'all definite, settled beliefs.'

In 1883, Bourne met the charismatic Italian priest Don Bosco, founder of the Salesian order, who had travelled to Paris to appeal for funds for a new church of the Sacred Heart in Rome. His goodness and simplicity of heart won over the normally anti-clerical Parisians. Don Bosco's great work in Turin had been to provide for the education of poor boys, and his example had a profound effect on Bourne. As he took his leave of them, Bosco said to the St Sulpice seminarians: '*Soyez saints prêtres*'—be holy priests.

Ordained sub-deacon and deacon in Paris, Bourne moved on to study theology and philosophy at the Catholic University of Louvain in Belgium, but illness prevented him taking a doctorate. He returned to England to convalesce, and in June 1884 was ordained priest at St Mary's Clapham by Bishop Coffin, the man who had baptised him in the same church 23 years earlier. He was sent first as curate to Blackheath, where he was swiftly plunged into church-building—a new one was needed—and education—he was responsible for 90 middle class orphan boys. He ran the school, taught the boys French, supervised cricket on Blackheath and trained them in Gregorian chant to a high liturgical standard. But he did not stay long at Blackheath, having offended the parish priest, who found him opinionated and determined to have his way. He served briefly as curate at Mortlake before his appointment as curate to Mgr Denis at West Grinstead, Sussex. Denis had a high opinion of himself, and it must have been a tricky pairing—especially as the parish was too small to merit a curate. But Bourne's Bishop had bigger plans for him.

St John's Wonersh and the challenge of priestly formation

Southwark had never had its own diocesan seminary, most of its priests being trained at Westminster's college of St Edmunds in Ware, Hertfordshire. That changed under Bishop John Butt (in office 1885–1897). In 1889, Butt asked the 28-year-old Fr Bourne to launch a new seminary in temporary accommodation while a permanent home was being built. Bourne found a country house at Henfield, Sussex, near his church at West Grinstead. The future diocesan treasurer, Fr Edward St John, came down to inspect it, and thus began a close friendship that would last 45 years.

During the two years at Henfield House, Bourne also became friends with one of the young teachers, Thomas Hooley. Hooley was an ex-seminarian who had abandoned his studies; later his vocation revived, and as a priest he played an important role both at Wonersh and then for 43 years as parish priest of St Bede's Clapham Park. He also became Bourne's lifelong confessor.

Fr Bourne was the Rector of Wonersh, which meant he was responsible for the senior seminary and the students actively preparing for the priesthood. He also held the Professorship of Moral Theology and Holy Scripture. The junior seminary, which educated boys from the age of 13 or 14 who felt they might have vocations to the priesthood, was under Fr Hooley, known as the Regent.

The senior seminary was run on Sulpician lines, that is with great devotion to spiritual development and intellectual rigour, though at the same time preserving a certain informality, and a sense of community. Most of the professors were relatively young priests, because Bourne wanted his students to be intellectually and socially close to their teachers. Personal memories that have been preserved of these early days at Wonersh show a warm atmosphere under the leadership of a happy Rector.

The relative freedom of inquiry implicit in the Sulpician system encouraged some of the staff and students to adopt positions then known within the church as Modernism. This was a period of great change in the academic understanding of history and scripture. Modernism was an attempt to adapt the church and its teachings to the modern world, and Bourne was in some measure sympathetic to this approach. But the more radical Modernists decided that few of the Catholic church's fundamental doctrines had actually been given by Christ: some taught that all truth was relative, which led them into historicism and subjectivism. The Popes of the late 19th and early 20th centuries accordingly clamped down on such teachings, while also imposing ever tighter control of national churches—especially in France and Britain.

This was the period of *ultramontanism*, best described as increased centralisation of the church under Papal authority, combined with theological conservatism and strongly expressed opposition to socialism in all its forms.[4] Politically, the Papacy was at odds with the government of the newly united Italy. In 1870, Pope Pius IX retreated into the Vatican after refusing a settlement offered by the Italian government. His successors were to remain there nearly sixty years until the Lateran Treaty of 1929, which recognised the Vatican as a sovereign nation. But at the start of the 20th century, the Papacy was not inclined to compromise with the modern world.

Bishop Butt's health began to fail and in 1896, at the age of 35, Bourne was made co-adjutor (joint) Bishop of Southwark. Butt formally retired the following year and Francis Bourne was consecrated Bishop of Southwark in May 1897. Naturally this took him away from Wonersh, his first and greatest love. His elevation did not please all of the Southwark clergy, especially some of the canons at St George's Cathedral. The one priest at the Cathedral he could rely on was his friend Fr Edward St John, since 1894 busy running the perennially fragile diocesan finances.

The Society of Secular Priests: enter Fr Peter Amigo

Bishop Bourne conceived the idea that as many as possible of his diocesan clergy–spread as they were over such a large area–should feel themselves part of a wider spiritual priestly community: in essence he wanted to extend the Sulpician ideals he had fostered among his seminarians at Wonersh. Looking round for someone to help realise this vision, his eye fell on Fr Peter Amigo (1864–1949), a priest of the Archdiocese of Westminster. Amigo was a Gibraltarian who retained a slight Spanish accent throughout his life. He was a man of strong character and—perhaps because as a Gibraltarian he stood outside the class system that dominated British life—evident social self-confidence. In that he had the advantage over the nervous, lower-middle class Bourne.

Marked for advancement by Cardinal Manning (Archbishop of Westminster 1865–1892), Amigo was sent to teach at St Edmund's seminary shortly after his ordination in 1888. Cardinal Vaughan, Manning's successor, appointed him to an East End parish where he was to develop a House of Pastoral Theology—a concept not unlike Bourne's ideal priestly community. Having discussed the notion with Amigo, in 1897 Bourne asked Vaughan to release him to Southwark. Vaughan refused. But Bourne and Amigo continued to discuss the plan, and in 1901 Vaughan gave his consent.

Bishop Bourne immediately appointed Amigo Vicar General of the Southwark Diocese, a signal to his occasionally unco-operative clergy that they were to take the new man seriously. His job was to found what he and Bourne called the Society of Secular Priests. Its programme was radical. The reserved Bourne and the extrovert Amigo came up with 'Fundamental Articles' which included:

- To live, in imitation of Jesus Christ their Master, a simple life, detached from this world, all financial income being contributed to a common fund.
- To live in community either in the seminary or in the presbyteries assigned to them by the local Bishop who would always be the Superior General of the members of the society.
- To take as their guides in the priestly life 'those holy men raised by God, in the seventeenth century especially for the reformation of the clergy', and in particular St Francis de Sales.[5]

As we have seen, the programme was not unprecedented.[6] The difficulty was the creation of what many priests would see as a special caste within the diocesan clergy. Might not a Bishop be accused of favouritism towards these (supposedly) especially holy priests? And how would the society function if the Bishop disapproved of the idea? Events swiftly overtook Bourne and Amigo, and the society was never established, though they made a start.

Fr Amigo travelled to Paris to see the Sulpicians at first hand and was impressed. On his return, Bourne made him parish priest at St Augustine's Walworth, where he began preparations for forming the Society. At this time, Bourne himself was much taken up with mediating between the British War Office and the Vatican on the provision of Catholic military chaplains, a duty which had fallen to the bishops of Southwark since the time of the Crimean War half a century earlier. The seriousness with which he undertook this task, and the time and energy he expended on it—successfully, as it turned out—were typical of the man. But his conscientiousness could also lead to a certain rigidity, as would soon become apparent.

The cost of crossing the Thames

Cardinal Vaughan died in June 1903, aged 71. Two months later, to general surprise, Francis Bourne was chosen to succeed him as Archbishop of Westminster. His name had not been among the six originally submitted to Rome, though in retrospect none of that group was suitable.

Bourne had worked closely with Vaughan when the Cardinal's health was failing, but all of his priestly life had been dedicated to Southwark. He had been born there and had worked so hard on the education of its clergy. It was notable that when he travelled to Rome to receive the pallium from the Pope, his two companions were Southwark priests: Canon St John and Monsignor Charles Coote. In October 1903, he issued a farewell letter to the clergy of his old Diocese of Southwark, paying fulsome tribute to the still-anonymous Frances Ellis:

At this moment, when in ready obedience to the Divine Will, but, nevertheless, with deep sorrow of heart, we are severing the ties which bind us to the Diocese of Southwark, to the service of which, until a very short time ago, we thought that the whole work of our life was to be given, it is a true consolation to us to be able, once again, to ask you to give thanks to God with us for the work which He has accomplished in our midst during the past year. We must speak first of the numberless works which we owe to one benefactress who, while humbly desiring to remain unknown, never ceases to extend more and more the influence of her generosity. The new churches at South Bermondsey, Stockwell, and South Croydon are now ready for the worship of God. In addition to the site between Hither Green and Catford, to which allusion was made last year, we have been able also to secure sites at Nunhead, Peckham Rye, South Walworth, North Brixton, Lorrimore-road (Walworth), Clapham Park, Altenburg Gardens (Clapham), Forest Hill, South Norwood, and Earlsfield. Large rooms in the houses at Clapham Park and Altenburg Gardens have already been converted into temporary chapels, and have been, or will very shortly be, opened for Mass. At Mottingham (near Eltham) the stables adjoining the orphanage have been converted into a chapel for the children, and the faithful in the neighbourhood are admitted to hear Mass.

At Charlton, the Oblates of the Assumption have opened a large room in their new Convent for Mass, and thus have enabled us to begin this mission at once without waiting for the church to be built. Rooms in the house at East Hill, Wandsworth, have been converted into a temporary chapel and the mission has been placed under the care of the Salesian Fathers. Already it is necessary to have three Masses on Sunday and a permanent church is greatly needed. All the above new foundations give us the greatest encouragement. The faithful in these neighbourhoods are most grateful because a church has been placed in their midst, and already we hear of many negligent Catholics who have returned to the practice of their religion. At all the above places our Successor will, we trust, be able to build simple churches and presbyteries during the coming year, if the buildings on the sites cannot be converted into temporary chapels.

We most earnestly beg your prayers that God may abundantly reward, now and hereafter, the giver of all these gifts, whom He sent to console and encourage us when we were weighed down with anxiety at the seeming impossibility of being able to meet in any way the ever-growing spiritual needs of South London and the suburbs.

And now, dear Reverend Fathers and dear children in Jesus Christ, we must take leave of you and of the Diocese of Southwark. From the depth of our heart we thank you all alike, the clergy, the religious communities, and the faithful, for your loyal devotion to us, and for the help and encouragement which you have afforded us during the last seven years, from the day, when as Coadjutor to our beloved Predecessor, we came among you, well-nigh unknown to most of you. May God bless and reward you all ... We shall not be very far away, and the affectionate memory of these years shall not pass from our mind and our heart, and, amid the still larger cares which God is entrusting to us, we shall never fail to watch with the deepest interest the growth, the progress and the development, which are characteristic of the great Diocese of Southwark.[7]

Bourne used the address to his priests to express his deep gratitude to the anonymous Miss Ellis. It shows also that, by late 1903, plans were already in hand for fifteen new churches in south London. Though Bourne does not mention him, Canon Edward St John was the man who invested Miss Ellis' money, and drove forward the church-building programme.

Cardinal Bourne around 1912

A modern reader is struck by Bourne's use of the royal, or perhaps Papal, 'We'. This was a hierarchical and deferential age, and presumably his audience was not surprised. They might have been surprised, though, if they knew the strength of his promise that 'we shall never fail to watch with the deepest interest the growth, the progress and the development, which are characteristic of the great Diocese of Southwark.'

The elevation of Bishop Amigo

In January 1904, Fr Peter Amigo was appointed Bishop of Southwark, Bourne having lobbied on his behalf with the Vatican as well as with the English bishops. This was not really the done thing, especially in Rome, where discretion was valued. That Bourne took this approach demonstrates how highly he rated Amigo and suggests that he saw him as a close ally and collaborator in their episcopal missions. But the work on the Society of Secular Priests was abandoned as too difficult under the new circumstances.

Like Bourne before him, Amigo was not initially a popular choice among the Southwark clergy. More unfortunately, it soon became clear that Archbishop Bourne really did retain a close personal interest in Southwark and especially Wonersh, over which he continued to exert as much influence as he could. This was odd behaviour from the head of the Catholic church in Britain.

If Bourne thought that Amigo would be his compliant protégé, he was mistaken. Their strained relationship had a variety of causes, though overall the balance of blame lay with Bourne. Having planned to work so closely together, they became estranged, even if relations never entirely broke down. Bourne, the senior in age and status, was a highly-strung, socially insecure introvert, Amigo a bluff self-confident extrovert. Both stuck to their guns over the next decade of strange wrangles. Bourne hid his intentions behind a screen of legalistic language, while Amigo, though clearly annoyed, responded to provocations in a polite and straightforward manner that reflected his inner toughness. As time went on, Amigo's position was strengthened by the growing loyalty of his own clergy—though even that encouraged Bourne to believe that Amigo was being manipulated to conspire against him.

The vexed question of Wonersh

Bourne was anxious that Amigo's seminary at Wonersh should maintain the ideals he had learned at St Sulpice. This anxiety manifested itself in a concern for the senior staff at the seminary, some of whom were suspected of Modernism by Amigo (and by the Vatican). During the course of his first two years as Bishop, Amigo removed some of the more radical lecturers and replaced them with men of unimpeachable orthodoxy. Bourne was disturbed by the changes, but at first held his tongue.

When the Rector, Fr Joseph Butt (nephew of the founder Bishop Butt), left in 1907, Bourne desired as his successor Fr Thomas Hooley, the Regent in charge of the juniors. He told a startled Amigo of his wishes in no uncertain terms. Confused, Amigo at first agreed, then a day later thought better of it. Instead, he appointed Fr Arthur Doubleday, who was not an alumnus of Wonersh.

Bourne was upset and warned Amigo that the seminary was a 'delicate organism' that had been built up over many years and could 'be easily disorganised'.

Changes began to be made that did indeed alter the character of Wonersh. The teachers became more remote from the students, and any hint of Modernism was expunged from the syllabus. Extraordinarily, Bourne wrote to Amigo telling him that their friendship was over.

In 1909 Amigo moved Fr Hooley from Wonersh to the new mission at St Bede's, Clapham Park. Hyde House, the palatial presbytery given to the Diocese by Miss Ellis in 1902, had been used since Bourne's day as a prep school for the junior seminary at Wonersh, and later as a school for some of the junior seminarians themselves. With Fr Hooley's arrival, that direct connection with Wonersh ceased. Instead, Hyde House became the presbytery and Archbishop Bourne's unofficial South London resort, an unusual development which is treated at greater length in Chapter 7. He travelled there frequently for many years, if only to make his confession to Fr Hooley. Bourne rarely extended to Amigo the standard courtesy of one Bishop notifying another that he would be operating in his Diocese. Amigo never complained, though he undoubtedly felt shabbily treated. But worse was to come.

Southwark's financial trouble exposed

The new Bishop of Southwark soon learned about the parlous state of diocesan finances. The problem dated back to 1882, when the original Diocese of Southwark had been divided to create the Diocese of Portsmouth. The financial division was an adverse one as far as Southwark was concerned, as 40% of Southwark's assets were then assigned to Portsmouth. This was particularly iniquitous because the largely rural new Diocese contained many wealthy Catholics, while Southwark bore the burden of caring for the poor and rapidly expanding metropolis of South London.

And since 1894, the man principally carrying that burden had been Canon St John. He was trusted by Bishop Butt, who had appointed him treasurer, and by Bourne during his six years at St George's Cathedral. Both men saw his absolute dedication to supporting the work of the Diocese, to finding the cash for churches and schools and orphanages. He worked himself extremely hard, and his health suffered as a result. But he had his own way of doing things, relying on a small group of lay advisors to assist him. The Bishop and a handful of clergy attended monthly meetings of the finance committee, of which St John was secretary, but they seem never to have raised concerns.

An advisor named William Romaine had persuaded St John that the conventional investments held by some of the older and more prosperous Southwark parishes could profitably be sold and reinvested in rental properties. St John followed his advice, and then appointed Romaine his Director of Buildings, to administer the new property portfolio.

According to the late Fr Michael Clifton, Amigo's biographer, Romaine was a 'con man' who paid himself a commission at every stage of proceedings.[8] Fr Clifton's evidence for this assertion does not survive, so cannot be assessed. If true, St John was guilty of a worrying degree of naivety. On the other hand, it is clear from the siting of the Ellis churches that many of them were built on cheap land, usually close to railway lines. That at least is evidence of an attempt to control costs.

St John himself was clear that whatever Romaine's personal qualities, their business relationship was entirely straightforward. In March 1911 he explained that relationship in a letter to an unidentified cleric.

> Archbishop's House, Westminster SW
> March 5th 1911
> Dear Monsignor
> The Archbishop has asked me to reply to you direct about Mr 'Romano'. The man's name was Romain and he was a builder by profession.
> I employed (Romain) for some ten years or more, first in repairing buildings that were the exclusive property of the Diocese and latterly in the erecting of some of the many buildings that were put up, and also in helping me find the necessary land for the new churches and priests' houses that Miss Ellis was enabling the Bishop to build.
> The statement that this man has sold any diocesan property is absolutely untrue. It was impossible that he could have done so, as in all the many sites that were purchased by me on behalf of the Diocese, every single site was purchased in the name of the Bishop and three other Diocesan Trustees and no part even of any land could be sold without the signatures of all the four Trustees.
> In one case a piece of land was purchased at Earlsfield that was larger than the church and house that were to be built upon it. I instructed Mr Romain to try and find a purchaser for the land that was of no use to us and after some months he succeeded in finding a purchaser and a much larger sum was paid for this land than we had given for it. The Diocesan Solicitor (Mr Fooks) especially congratulated me on this transaction. This is the only case I can call to mind when I made use of this man to help me to sell land and this small transaction was carried out

under the Bishop's instruction and the Bishop signed the deed of conveyance.

Some months ago I heard from a third party that the Bishop and Monsignor Brown were saying that many of the sites purchased by me, with Miss Ellis' money, were bought at too high a price. No such complaint has ever been made to me direct. You already know that house property is much cheaper than it was 8 or 10 years ago.

Every single property was bought in the names of four Trustees and the money in settlement was always paid to the vendors by the Diocesan Solicitor and not by Mr Romain.

The greatest care had to be used in the purchase of some of the sites in order that the vendors might not find out until after they had agreed to sell that the purchasers were the Catholic authority. The Diocesan Solicitor himself drew up a form of receipt which Mr Romain always used when acting as my agent he made any purchases on my behalf.

When I found a property that suited us, I sent Mr Romain to see the owners and this man would find out the lowest prices the owners would take for it. I then went to the Diocesan Solicitor and consulted him as to whether the price was reasonable. If it was decided to purchase I then provided my agent Mr Romain with 10% of the purchase money and he took it to the vendor and always used the above-mentioned form of receipt which stipulated that in the event of Mr Fooks the Diocesan Solicitor not being satisfied with the title the vendor would return the 10% acknowledged by the receipt.

Mr Fooks then examined the title, and when all was ready to complete the purchase I provided the

Solicitor with the money and not Mr Romain and the Solicitor paid the vendor. In two or three cases vacant land that had become of no use to the Diocese in the course of time was let to a builder, and I used Mr Romain as my agent to find a builder willing to rent this land for building houses on; but in every case the Diocesan Solicitor made all the legal arrangements with the builder and not Mr Romain.

More than a year ago Mgr Brown told me that it had been discovered after I had left that I had paid a much smaller sum for a Protestant church I had purchased at South Norwood than was first put down in the books of the Diocese. I demanded an immediate inquiry but I have never been able to get an answer from the Bishop as to whether he believed this false statement (nor) have I been able to get this false accusation withdrawn.

I can give a clear statement re any case that is brought before me but my accusers will only for the most part make general statements but will not bring definite cases before me.

Mr Romain left my service about 4 years ago. All the business he did for me was carried out in a strictly business like way and when he left all money was properly accounted for. I discovered after he had left my service this man had been leading an immoral life. I of course told the Bishop of this discovery of mine. His Lordship seems to think that because this man's private life was reprehensible that the business he transacted for me must have been dishonest but this is not the case.

Southwark's financial house of cards exposed

St John's other principal fund-raising technique was to mortgage diocesan property, including churches and the land they stood on. The parishes, missions, schools or other institutions were saddled with the debt, and were required to meet the interest payments, usually out of their relatively meagre income from the faithful. As long as those repayments were made, the overall diocesan debt of £300,000 did not seem dangerous. At the start of the 20th century, interest rates were stable, and with a typical rate of 3–4%, the overall burden on the Diocese, or rather on the parishes, was around £9–12,000 per annum. For instance, a parish whose church was mortgaged for £4,000 would need to find £160 a year.

So long as nothing else happened to upset this financial house of cards, the Diocese could jog along—or so it seemed. But in 1905, the second year of Amigo's tenure as Bishop of Southwark, there came a real disaster. Mr William Henry Bishop, who had been Southwark's chief investment advisor since 1870, declared himself bankrupt, having run up losses of more than £88,000 on the stock exchange. He had been playing the stock market with diocesan money, and particularly with cash from a charity called the Dawes Trust, of which Bourne, Amigo, St John and Canon William Murnane were the Trustees. The Trust administered £86,000 which had been left to the Diocese by a Mr Charles Dawes when Bourne was still Bishop of Southwark. The trustees rarely met, and the day-to-day business was left to Mr Bishop. Canon St John learned in September that £12,000 was missing from the Trust but continued to accept Bishop's evasive justifications. By the end of 1905 total losses to the Diocese, revealed when Bishop filed for bankruptcy, were £36,600.

The financial losses were devastating. But there was a potentially more disastrous aspect of the Dawes Trust affair. Bishop was able to misuse funds on this scale because he had been given power of attorney over the Trust's assets. That meant that the eminent trustees had failed in their fiduciary duty. This was bad for Amigo, St John and Murnane, but for Archbishop Bourne, head of the Catholic church in England, it might prove fatal.

A version of the truth

The bombshell exploded in early 1906, when the radical magazine *Truth* began to publish allegations of financial misconduct at Westminster, Southwark, Portsmouth and other English Catholic dioceses. The source of these stories certainly knew something about William Bishop and the Dawes Trust, and it is likely that he had been briefed by someone at Southwark. It is almost certain that Fr Ethelred Taunton, a disaffected priest, formerly of Southwark but now resident in Rome, had informed the Vatican of the allegations and was also leaking to *Truth*.

The claims continued to appear throughout 1906. The articles themselves were written by the editor and publisher of *Truth*, the flamboyant radical MP Henry Labouchère (1831–1912), known to both friends and enemies as 'Labby'. He penned many forthright articles which hovered somewhere between news, investigation and condemnation. These in turn encouraged Catholics to write in, generally against Bourne, but some in his defence. The Attorney General was thought to be taking an interest, as was the Charity Commission.

Labouchère's original source was William Reed Lewis, a lay busybody of a type familiar on the fringes of the church throughout the ages. He was a businessman who had served as British consul in Algiers before retiring to Dinard in northern Brittany, where there was a well-heeled British expatriate community. But it was clear that he was also in touch with Fr Ethelred Taunton. Once he had managed to publicise the Dawes Trust scandal through the pages of *Truth*—which were repeated in the *Catholic Herald* as well as some Fleet Street titles—Reed Lewis offered his services as a 'candid friend' to Bishop Amigo. In an unctuously phrased letter from Dinard dated 7 November 1906, eight months after the first allegations had appeared in print, he wrote:

> My Lord Bishop
> As I hear that your Lordship is about to go to Rome I ask if I may be allowed to send you *in strictest confidence* a statement on the affairs that have appeared in 'Truth'. I think it is advisable for your own sake that your Lordship should know what I have to say; but I can only write fully on the clear assurance that what I have to tell is received strictly in confidence and not communicated in any way to the Archbishop or to any of the other English bishops. I am induced to do this out of sincere sympathy for your Lordship in the unfortunate position you have found yourself which became evident to me during my recent residence in the Diocese of Southwark.
> Begging your blessing I am my Lord Bishop
> Your faithful and obedient servant
> Wm Reed Lewis

Amigo replied politely that he could give no such undertakings, as the allegations published in *Truth* implicated not only the Archbishop but also himself and at least two other prelates, and that he was not prepared to betray his brother bishops. Reed Lewis responded that he wished to discuss communications with the British government and the Vatican, and that these concerned only Amigo. The Bishop then accepted the conditions.

Reed Lewis's next letter to Amigo was a masterpiece of intrigue, in which he purported to play the role of honest broker between the Charity Commissioners, the Vatican and the Diocese of Southwark. He claimed that the Charity Commission—'evidently animated by no unkind feelings towards the church'—had approached him as a responsible lay Catholic to see whether he could 'devise or suggest any scheme to bring the administration of Church funds into line with English law without that law having to be brought into action.' Reed Lewis was writing in similar terms to a number of leading English Catholic laymen, adding that the Charity Commission had unofficially asked him to approach the Vatican to get Rome to sort out the mess.

Before Amigo could respond, Archbishop Bourne punctured this balloon by sending his own solicitor to speak to the Charity Commissioners, who made it clear that Reed Lewis was not their agent, official or unofficial. They also absolved Bourne of misusing Petworth Trust funds, another of the allegations published in *Truth*. But the Archbishop could not ignore a letter from Cardinal Merry del Val, the Vatican's Secretary of State, who said that the allegations circulated in Rome by Reed Lewis and Fr Taunton must be dealt with. Bourne agreed that the control of church property in England needed reform. But he also claimed to be the victim of a conspiracy of people who opposed his election as Archbishop—including a cabal of Southwark priests who resented having been disciplined by him during his time at St

George's Cathedral. Merry del Val told him not to worry —he was the Archbishop, and he had Rome's support.⁹

There was one further scare in May 1907, when Reed Lewis told Cardinal Merry del Val that he was planning to petition the Attorney General to prosecute Bourne for breaching the terms of the Dawes Trust. Despite the threat, Merry del Val wrote to Bourne that the Holy See entirely accepted his account of events, and that he was at liberty to show this letter to Reed Lewis. Bourne sent Reed Lewis a copy of the letter and invited him to examine the original at Archbishop's House.

Unexpectedly Reed Lewis caved in. 'I have no desire to verify its contents ... I take this opportunity of congratulating Your Grace upon your enjoyment of the full confidence of the Holy See, which I trust you may merit for many years to come.' What caused this change of heart in Reed Lewis is uncertain, but the death of Fr Ethelred Taunton that very month may have had something to do with it.

For Amigo, as for Bourne, Reed Lewis' capitulation was a great relief. But while they, and indeed the whole English Catholic church, had escaped further public humiliation, it was evident that they needed to clear up the financial and fiduciary tangles exposed in *Truth*. However, the two London bishops, who had been friends and collaborators only three years earlier, failed to address the task jointly. Indeed, over the next few years, Bourne proved unco-operative when asked to withdraw from the several Southwark trusts of which he was still a trustee.

Canon St John at bay

Amigo, and the men he had promoted into the Southwark Chapter, faced the yet bigger challenge of putting their own diocesan finances onto a sound footing. At this point, Canon St John remained at the centre of business affairs. He had been appointed originally by Bishop Butt, and had worked closely with Bourne in his six years at St Georges, not least in deploying Frances Ellis' money into the church-building programme. In 1901 Bourne had appointed him a canon of St George's Cathedral. By 1906 he had been running the diocesan finances for twelve years and was, as he himself admitted, exhausted, and wished to reduce his commitments to a more manageable level.

In the summer of 1906, St John sailed to Canada to see for himself the fruits of the Southwark Rescue Society's emigration policy. This policy placed orphans from the Society with Catholic families in Canada, either to be adopted or, if old enough, to work on farms owned by Catholics. He wrote to Amigo from the ship to say that he wished to resign his Canonry, to which he felt unsuited.

> You will know that this title has always been a very great trial to me, but I felt bound to accept it at the time as Bishop Bourne was very anxious to have his Curia in the Chapter.[10] There is now no reason that I should be burdened by attending 12 (to my mind) perfectly useless meetings per annum and surely upsetting the work of 12 days that might be better spent ... I shall hope to return revived by the change and relieved of the office of Canon that has always been a trial to me & quite fit to go on in bringing the work up to date and to pass it on to those that are to come after me as soon as you may desire.

This and other letters demonstrate that St John really did not feel at home at St George's Cathedral, whose canons were supposed to be the bishop's close advisors on pastoral affairs. He wanted to concentrate on the things that mattered to him while he had the strength. These were the Southwark Rescue Society and the administration of Miss Ellis' largesse. He made it clear to Amigo that he served on the finance committee not because he particularly wanted the work, but at the pleasure of the 'Bishop for the time being'. He was 51 years old in 1906 (at the time an Englishman's life expectancy was 47), and his health was suffering.

St John had been named by *Truth* as one of the purportedly guilty men, along with Bourne and Amigo. There is no record of support for St John from Amigo or any of his diocesan colleagues. But he received strong backing from Bourne in a letter to *The Tablet* rebuffing the allegations:

> No diocese has ever had a more loyal, a more devoted, a more self-sacrificing servant than Canon St. John. For nearly twenty years, ever since he was appointed to the task by my venerated predecessor, Bishop Butt, he has been engaged in consolidating the finances of the Diocese. If during the last twenty years the Diocese of Southwark has made quite extraordinary progress, to no one man is that result more distinctly due than to Canon St. John. I have personal knowledge that within the past six years he has been the means of obtaining for various diocesan works benefactions amounting to at least three times the value of the loss incurred through Mr. Bishop's failure. No one can have felt that loss more acutely than he, for it has thrown back many of his hopes, and no one, therefore, has a greater claim to sympathy, to support and to consideration.[11]

At the beginning of 1907, twenty Ellis churches were up and running, two on Thanet and eighteen in South London. There were another sixteen to come in Southwark, as well as three in Plymouth and one in Westminster. The responsibility for finding the Southwark sites, commissioning builders and monitoring construction all fell to St John, as he himself and Archbishop Bourne later testified. It is strange, and perhaps telling, that there are no records of this programme left in the Southwark archives, nor any testament from Amigo or other diocesan officials to his dedicated labour.

Given the financial constraints, and the looming scandal, Frances Ellis' uncomplicated generosity must have seemed heaven-sent. The construction of a new 'Ellis box' usually required little or no financial support from other diocesan funds. Nevertheless, St John, and the officials who succeeded him, often immediately raised mortgages on the new churches to fund other projects not supported by benefactors like Miss Ellis. Under this system, a £3,000 Ellis church provided the Diocese with a further £3,000 borrowed cash, the interest on which would become the responsibility of the rector of the new mission and his parishioners. It was a rough and ready way of doing things, and it was about to come under intense scrutiny.

Trouble ahead: The Duke of Norfolk's Commission

To get a grip on the diocesan finances, Amigo added new members to the Finance Committee and took a closer interest in the meetings himself. There are signs from 1906 of tighter control over expenses at parish level. To restore—or more accurately, to establish—a reputation for financial probity, he needed to cleanse the stables in a public and unimpeachable manner. In December 1908 a Commission was established under the chairmanship of the Duke of Norfolk 'to investigate the general financial position of the Diocese, to have access to all accounts and documents, and the assistance, if necessary, of Chartered Accountants, to ascertain the causes of excess of expenditure over income, and to make such recommendations as they see fit.'

The Commission was constituted of seven laymen and three clerics, including Canon St John. In normal circumstances it should not have taken more than six months to report back, with lawyers and accountants involved to sift the figures. In the event it took two years to issue a majority opinion, with two dissenting minority opinions, the smaller minority being St John himself.

Early in proceedings St John rejected the figures provided by the diocesan accountants, and he continued to argue against them after the Commission's report was finally published in 1911. Away from the Commission he was increasingly at odds with Amigo and the rest of the Chapter.

Much of his dissatisfaction stemmed from the new policy towards Southwark's non-ecclesiastical property. He suspected that his work for children was being undermined. On 1 July 1909 he resigned from the diocesan finance committee, almost certainly at Amigo's request. He asked for and was granted a year's leave.

The Commission's initial findings appeared reassuring. Southwark's overall liabilities amounted to £322,837, while assets in real property were more than £1 million, and other assets exceeded £101,000. That ratio of debt to assets would not normally be regarded as excessive. However, as the property—principally churches—was almost entirely for 'the service of religion' it would be impossible to realise its value without destroying the mission of the Diocese. In the most recent year, the Diocese had shown an excess of expenditure over income of £834. This excess should be addressed at the same time that the Diocese began to pay down the debt.

To this end the Commission recommended the Diocese increase its income, especially by seeking more generous donations from the wealthier parishes, some of which were not pulling their weight. Tighter discipline should be applied to indebted missions to ensure that income exceeded expenditure. But the greater challenge should be addressed by creating a fund to receive, hold and apply money and other assets for the liquidation of the diocesan debt. The Commission also hoped that such a fund would attract legacies.

While deploring the £36,600 stolen and lost by Mr Bishop, the Commission was confident that the Diocese had learned the lessons and needed no advice. It praised the accuracy of the accounts and went out of its way to commend the 'ability, zeal and devotion of the late Treasurer' Canon St John.

If the members of the Commission were trying to be kind to St John, placate him even, it was far too late. Since his resignation as treasurer in 1909, he had been at odds with Bishop Amigo and with the rest of the Southwark Chapter. As he wrote to Amigo:

> From the day of my ordination until now, I have had my ordination promise of obedience and my oath to Southwark's Bishop constantly before me but my dismissal from the Treasurership, during the sitting of a Commission appointed to look into business with which I have been so closely connected for so many years, can have but one meaning.[12]

St John continued to oversee the work of building Ellis churches, with another sixteen begun between 1907 and 1912. This must have become difficult after 1910 because, although he retained a room in the clergy house at St George's, he spent much of his time staying at Hyde House, Clapham Park, or at Archbishop's House Westminster Cathedral, and as far afield as Cornwall, where Miss Ellis records him visiting her and the nuns at Hayle. She certainly knew about his travails, because in early 1911 Bourne sent him down to Cornwall to brief her on the latest dispute with Amigo.

St John retaliates

Stubborn and single-minded, Canon St John was determined to defend his honour. Having tried and failed to get the accounts of the Diocese and the rescue committee revised, in March 1913 he published a 28-page pamphlet setting out his own version of the accounts and attacking the Bishop and the signatories of the Commission majority report. On the first page of the pamphlet, he quoted from scripture:

> I was dumb and was humbled and kept silence from good things; and my sorrow was renewed.[13]

The pamphlet took issue with the accounts published by the Commission and questioned the honesty and good faith of the accountants, the diocesan solicitor Mr Fooks and some of the senior diocesan clergy. It is impossible after more than a century to judge the rights and wrongs of the dispute. St John did however demonstrate that sets of accounts that had been submitted to the Commission early in the process were amended later without reference to him. He also claimed that the Bishop, influenced by newer members of the finance committee, had accused him of taking diocesan money and applying it to the Southwark Rescue Committee. This he denied, pointing out that the Rescue Committee's audited accounts had been published in full every year that he was involved, though the Diocese had ceased publishing them after his departure.

St John also wrote that Amigo had turned against Miss Ellis' programme. 'The Bishop has stopped this work of extension, and is now seeking to destroy some of this lady's good works.' He offered no evidence. However, it is true that Christ Church Eltham, subject of Miss Ellis' last gift to Southwark, opened in 1912.

The reaction was predictably furious. Some advised Amigo that St John was insane, others that his calculations betrayed his financial ineptitude. Amigo himself took a cautious line with St John once he had left both the finance committee and the Rescue Society. The Bishop's real purpose was to gain control of the diocesan finances, not to punish the former treasurer, whether guilty or innocent. He offered him various parishes, starting with Our Lady of La Salette and St Joseph, Melior St, a challenging church near London Bridge, even though St John had never worked on a parish. St John refused them all unless he was exonerated from the charges he believed had been brought against him.

It is evident that through all this conflict St John remained closely in touch with Archbishop—by now Cardinal—Bourne. St John was living at Hyde House, the palatial presbytery of St Bede's Clapham Park, where their mutual friend Fr Hooley was in charge of the mission.[14] On Whit Monday 1912, which that year fell on the Feast of St Bede, Cardinal Bourne attended a High Mass there celebrated by Canon St John.

Then in March 1913 came an unexpected development. Archbishop Thomas Whiteside of Liverpool wrote to Bourne, suggesting that St John might take on the chaplaincy of Walton Prison, Liverpool. He thought it 'would be an honourable and satisfactory way out of a wretched impasse'. Bourne agreed, but asked that Whiteside himself approach Amigo, 'for he always makes difficulties where I am supposed to have any wish in a matter'.

When the offer became known, some Southwark canons strongly advised Amigo to prevent St John taking it up unless he withdrew the charges in his pamphlet and apologised. He was after all still a priest of the Diocese and, despite his efforts to resign, a canon of St George's Cathedral. Wisely, Amigo let St John go, and his former treasurer became an employee of His Majesty's Prison Service.

Walton Gaol was no sinecure. It was a tough prison in a tough city with which St John had no previous connection. He was 58 years old when he accepted it, had been under nervous strain for several years, and was not in the best of health. Yet he flourished there, transferring his previous devotion to poor and orphaned children to the chaotic and often violent inmates of Walton. The prisoners liked this honest, open-hearted, rather upper-class priest from London. He made many converts in his twelve years at Walton, as evidenced in this letter to Amigo in December 1915. Amigo had just written to him on the occasion of his sixtieth birthday.

> My Lord Bishop
> When I saw your letter this morning I thought it was to ask for the deeds. It is difficult to get two witnesses together here but I will send them early next week. With regard to my birthday I thought I must have pretty well broken all records when I served as sub-deacon at a High Mass at the

Cathedral in which I had been ordained 25 years before to the very hour, and when I left the subsequent Chapter meeting without a word from any of my brethren except one 'How do you do' from one Canon. With regard to birthdays I have for a long time thought the keeping of them unCatholic but there is some excuse for the 60th because the Church legislates for it.

I think again Divine Providence has given me an illustration that is a record, as while you were remembering me at 60, the altar for which I am very grateful, I was giving first Communion to a poor Negro whom I had baptised unconditionally the day before and I was taking him to the gallows (with another man) just after his communion. [15]

I don't think many are likely to keep my anniversary as I seem to keep mine, and that a double execution breaks all records.

After all, these things seem to bring one closer to God, and so make one fear to hear that one 'had better not been born.' I doubt that I shall ever get a better offering than my poor friendless Negro will provide for me in his baptismal union before God. With regard to Chapter I will attend when I am able but there is much to be done here and I never take anything like the leave I am entitled to because it means that much of the work has to be left undone if one gets a stranger to supply.

I am very sorry to hear about Scannell and Connolly, I did not know that they were both seriously ill.

Again thanking you for the memento.

I am your Lordship's obedient servant

Edward St John

In addition to its dramatic vignette of prison life and death, St John's letter shows that Amigo was still trying to straighten out some of the Southwark charitable trusts which he had inherited from the days of Bishops Butt and Bourne. St John and Bourne remained trustees of several of these bodies, long after they should have retired, if only because they never attended meetings. The deeds referred to in the first sentence of the letter may have related to the trust governing St Catherine's Hospital in Ramsgate, which Amigo was trying to alter (see Chapter 5).

St John also referred to his canonry at St George's, a position he had been trying to resign since 1906. His duties were to attend 12 meetings a year with his fellow canons, and to celebrate Mass at the Cathedral a dozen times year on a rota drawn up by someone else. As he intimates in the letter, he no longer had friendly relations with his fellow canons, and his duties at Liverpool made it difficult, if not impossible, to attend as expected. It is unclear why Amigo would not let St John resign. Letters preserved in the Southwark archives show that Amigo was regularly reminded by some of the less well-disposed canons how derelict St John was in his duties. On the other hand Bourne strongly advised St John to maintain his canonry.

St John was anything but derelict in his duties as chaplain at Walton Gaol. Apart from a pilgrimage to Lourdes, he laboured full time at the prison for twelve years. He remained there until his 70th birthday, retiring in September 1925. A portrait photograph taken at that time hung in the sacristy of Walton chapel until at least 1993. Alongside it was a brass plaque inscribed:

> Presented to the Very Rev. Canon Edward St John, RC Chaplain, HM Prison Liverpool by the Y.C.W. with their best wishes and regrets on his

retirement. 'His one thought and hope was for the prisoners in his care.' [16]

Canon St John

Canon St John returned to London, but to Westminster Cathedral rather than to St George's. His friend and patron Cardinal Bourne found a room for him at Clergy House, and there he lived in retirement for several years. He was present at the reopening of St Mary's Clapham on 5 April 1930, when Cardinal Bourne paid generous tribute to him and Miss Ellis, who had died a few days earlier.

Thereafter, his health failing, he moved to Twyford Abbey, Ealing, remaining in the care of the Alexian Brothers until his death. Cardinal Bourne and Bishop Amigo both visited him in his final days. He died, wrote the chaplain Fr Barrett, *'in oculo Domini'*, making an effort to kiss the crucifix.

The Tablet of 23 June 1934 published the following obituary:

THE VERY REV. CANON ST. JOHN.

Three dioceses—Southwark, Liverpool, and Westminster—knew Canon Edward St. John, whose collapse, at Twyford Abbey, as the result of a cardiac seizure, was followed by his death last week at the age of seventy-nine. In the Diocese of Southwark he spent his most active years, chiefly in connection with the work of the Southwark Rescue Society and, for upwards of twenty-two years, as Diocesan Treasurer. In 1901 he was made a member of the Cathedral Chapter. From Southwark he removed, in 1913, to Liverpool, where he occupied for twelve years the post of Catholic chaplain at Walton Gaol. He retired from the chaplaincy in 1925; and he then came south once more, and later took up light duty in the Archdiocese of Westminster in connection with the Westminster Diocesan Education Fund. Canon St. John's spare figure gave an impression of frail health which, until a few years ago, his energy belied. Advancing age, however, told upon him rapidly in the last decade of his life. He made his home with the Alexian Brothers at Twyford Abbey, and was there cared for until the end. He died fortified by the Church's consolations, visited in his last illness by Cardinal Bourne and by the Bishop of Southwark.

Monuments to Canon St. John's zeal and ability are the rescue homes at Orpington and other places, and the boys' home—since removed elsewhere—which he established near St. George's Cathedral. In a special way he will be remembered in Southwark as the 'children's friend.' His interest in the welfare of Catholic boys and girls was tireless during the long period of his association with the Rescue Society. In old age he compiled Manning's Work for Children, as a reminder to the faithful that here is a work wherein there is a continuous call.

After a requiem Mass, on the 15th inst., in St. George's Cathedral, Southwark, the interment took place in the Catholic cemetery at Mortlake. —R.I.P.

Notes

1. In 1907, *The Times* observed in its report of the first-ever visit to London by a Papal Nuncio that continental clergy wore traditional wide brimmed soft black hats, but the English Catholic priests wore silk top hats.
2. P. A. Fournet 'The Society of Saint-Sulpice', in *The Catholic Encyclopaedia* (New York: The Encyclopedia Press) 1913.
3. M. Vickers, *By the Thames Divided: Cardinal Bourne in Southwark and Westminster* (Leominster: Gracewing, 2013), p. 44.
4. Ultramontanism developed during the Middle Ages and grew rapidly during the French Revolution. Its supporters criticized the separation of Church and state, as well as what they considered manifestations of modern liberalism. They pushed for the supremacy of the Catholic Church in both civil and religious matters. This school of thought was mainly characterized by its attachment to the Holy See's authority and, as of 1870, by its faith in the Pope's infallibility. The term *ultramontane* meant, literally, "beyond the mountains," because the French Ultramontanes believed in the supremacy of the Vatican—which is located beyond the mountains of the Alps—over the local clergy.
5. M. Vickers, *By the Thames Divided: Cardinal Bourne in Southwark and Westminster* (Leominster: Gracewing, 2013), pp. 89–90.

6. As well as the House of Pastoral Theology, there were similarities with the Oblates of St Charles, established in 1857 by Fr (later Cardinal) Edward Manning at the request of Cardinal Wiseman. The aim was that diocesan priests would live in community and engage in pastoral and domestic mission labours.
7. *The Tablet*, 10 October 1903, p. 581.
8. M. Clifton, *Amigo Friend of the Poor: Bishop of Southwark 1904–1949* (Leominster: Gracewing 2006), p. 56.
9. Rafael Merry del Val (1865–1930) was born the son of a Spanish diplomat in Britain and spent much of his childhood in England. Having trained for the priesthood at Ushaw, he spoke English as a native, and was well known throughout the English Catholic church. His had been one of the names sent to the Vatican as a potential successor to Cardinal Vaughan, but it was felt that his name would unhelpfully remind the English of the Spanish Armada. He was appointed Cardinal at the age of 38 but remained close to the English Church.
10. In other words, Bourne had wanted his own men in the sometimes over-independent Chapter.
11. *The Tablet*, 6 October 1906, p. 537.
12. St John to Amigo, 6 August 1909. Westminster diocesan archives, Box 3/8 No.7
13. Psalm 38:3.
14. Fairly or unfairly, Hyde House had come to be seen as the centre of pro-Bourne sentiment within Southwark.
15. The double execution of John Thornley and Young Hill took place on 1 December 1915. Young Hill was the black man received into the church by St John. He was a seaman who had murdered another sailor on the freighter SS Antillian, apparently during an argument over the cleanliness of a bucket of water.
16. Young Catholic Workers.

5

A Missionary in Cornwall

Around the turn of the century, just as she was preparing to become a Catholic, Frances Ellis decided to move to west Cornwall. The healthy air and milder temperatures of the far southwest of the country were major factors. She was looking for a permanent home for herself and her sister Rose, a home which she proposed to combine with a small community of Daughters of the Cross. She had the agreement and support of Mother Iphigènie, who was planning a separate initiative in Penzance which Frances also promised to finance. Both women relished the challenge of representing the Catholic faith in such a strongly Protestant county.

The move was accomplished in her typically thorough way, beginning by establishing a fruitful relationship with Bishop Charles Graham of Plymouth. In October 1900, at Frances' request, Abbot Bergh of Ramsgate wrote to Graham, introducing her business manager, James Lee. There followed an unencumbered offer to the Diocese of £3,000. In his reply to Mr Lee, the Bishop wondered whether instead Miss Ellis might consider supporting a new church planned at Plymouth to cater for naval personnel and their families. The Diocese had the land and the plans, but no money for construction. Via James Lee, Frances immediately gave £5,000 which covered the entire cost of building the church of Our Most Holy Redeemer, Keyham.

James Lee asked the Bishop not to mention Miss Ellis in his pastoral letter as she was 'merely assisting in the efforts of the people to build the church'. This was before she was formally received into the Catholic Church.

Frances was also in contact with the Canons Regular of St John Lateran (CRL) at Bodmin. They were the largest community of priests in Cornwall, and important potential allies. In mid-January 1901 Canon Bernard Wade CRL advised Bishop Graham that he had found a site at St Ives for Miss Ellis and Mr Lee 'to consider'. This was a vacant shop in Street-an-Pol, opposite the St Ives Guildhall, which could be used as a temporary chapel in this staunchly anti-Catholic town. Frances duly purchased the building, and a chapel was dedicated to the Sacred Heart & St Gertrude. The first Mass was celebrated there in February 1902, and the numbers of the faithful grew over the next few years. The Canons Regular would supply the priest.

Frances is recorded in the 1901 census—taken on 31st March—as head of the household at Rosevale, Alexandra Rd, Penzance. Rosevale is a pleasant Regency villa with a southerly aspect, set back a quarter mile from the beach.[1] The other members of the household were a married couple, James and Fanny Lee, described as boarders, and two female servants, Myra Collins and Dolly Windsor. James Lee of course was her business manager. Unlike the previous census of 1891, there is no mention of Rose Ellis, who perhaps had been left temporarily in the care of the nuns in Thanet or Carshalton. Frances was in Penzance looking to purchase a suitable property.

Later that year she found the right house, called the Downes, on an elevated site outside Hayle, and bought it from a Mr Rawlings. Seven miles from Penzance and three miles east of St Ives, Hayle is on the north coast of Penwith, as the far west of Cornwall is known. Architecturally, there is some similarity between the

Downes and Waltham Place, though the new house, built about 1880, was smaller. The Downes enjoyed an established formal garden of five acres, facing west across the Hayle river and with views extending out to sea. The garden was to play an important part in the life of the community as it grew over the next thirty years.

The Downes in 2021

The cost of the Downes is not shown in the record of Frances' benefactions kept, otherwise scrupulously, by the Daughters of the Cross. It was to be a home for Rose and herself, and to be a small convent and nursing home for invalid nuns. The convent (though not the house it largely occupied) was named St Teresa's, in honour of the founder of the Carmelites, the order which had trained Mother Marie-Thérèse Haze and her first companions for the religious life. It was formally established on 12 July 1902.

At first the drawing room of the Downes was used as the chapel of St Teresa's, but in 1903 Frances built a small extension which included a purpose-built chapel. Although she had given the house to the order, and the convent was under its own Sister Superior, Frances was clearly its chatelaine. She paid all the household bills, as well as the chaplain's salary of £100 a year. From her correspondence it seems that the chaplain was usually resident, and in some cases was himself a patient of the nursing home.

The interior of the old chapel at the Downes

A handful of local Catholics began to attend Mass in the chapel at St Teresa's. In addition, instruction in the faith was given at the convent on Sunday afternoons before Benediction.

As her friendship and co-operation with the Daughters of the Cross deepened, the nuns decided to give her the rare privilege of wearing the special cross of the order. There is a note in the archives that Frances received the cross on 6 January 1904.

Frances' letters record the gentle tenor of life at the Downes, punctuated at times by visits from bishops or crises in the health of patients, particularly the chronically sick nuns who were cared for by the nursing sisters. On 10 May 1908 she wrote:

> There is something in sea air, for those who live inland, especially in summer time, wonderfully reviving and here the addition of shade is a wonderful benefit ... Our little chapel looked beautiful this morning. We are certainly wonderfully well off for flowers, and now we have the benefit of the June crop, and the Holy Face in a copper frame and a little lamp burning under it, at the side of the altar—all adds very much to devotion. Sister Jeanne de la Croix is still very weak. I am going to try what little drives will do for her. We went to St Ives on Friday and looked at the new church building. I took over some flowers for Miss Pagalt. Be sure you go on getting all you can that would do Rev Mother good, and put all expenses for her down to me. As you know what a strong satisfaction that is to me.

This letter from Frances to Sister Honorine is typical of the hundreds of her letters from Hayle preserved by the Daughters of the Cross in their archives at Cheam. They reflect her loving care for the sisters she knew, her interest in the weather, health and good food, her generosity of spirit and her intense religious devotion. They testify to the close and constant relationship between Frances in Cornwall and the leading nuns of the Daughters of the Cross, especially Mother Iphigènie. Although she was 300 miles away, she was involved in all their major projects.

Frances Ellis had lived all her life in communities over which she wielded authority. For the first part of her life, she and her family had lived in large houses with up to 20 servants. With the death of her parents, she had, at the age of 44, become the undisputed mistress of Waltham Place. In her mid-fifties she had swapped that life for the Downes, a small religious community which depended on her to meet most of its running costs. She cared deeply and held strong views, but was keen to remain as far as possible in the background.

At the Downes Frances took as full a part as she could in the nuns' devotional life, praying the office with them in the chapel and of course attending Mass. She maintained contacts for them with the outside world, especially with the clergy. She had a warm friendship with Canon Wade CRL, the superior of the Augustinian priory at Bodmin, which then and for many years afterwards supplied the west of Cornwall with badly needed priests. She also worked closely with the bishops of Plymouth, especially Bishop Graham (1834–1912). Abbot Thomas Bergh OSB of Ramsgate was a regular visitor and a wise counsellor.

There were some tensions between Frances and the sisters at Hayle. In her correspondence with senior nuns at Carshalton she makes the occasional, self-deprecating reference to these. Writing to the order's Superior in 1915 she alludes to a disagreement with Sister Superior at the Downes over the best way to treat the much-loved Sr Jeanne de la Croix Price, who suffered with tuberculosis. Frances had wanted her to be allowed out in the garden in a bathchair, Sister Superior wanted her to stay indoors. She reflected:

> We are now getting on quite smoothly and happily. I know that a little friction is very good for

me, if it were not for that I should be spoiled altogether.

Part of her generosity was put into practical gifts to support the sisters and their work at Carshalton, Cheam and elsewhere. A partial list gleaned from her letters includes:

- Weekly shipments of fish from St Ives in large quantities (one mishap is recorded, with baskets of rotten fish delivered due to railway delays). The consignments of fish—mostly herring—were widely distributed to half a dozen different DoC houses in addition to Carshalton.
- A crate of 5-dozen broccoli, once a week in season
- Flowers ('all from the garden. I picked them for Revd Mother')
- Grapes from the greenhouse
- Peaches and nectarines from the garden
- Two 12-pound turkeys to Carshalton every Christmas
- A pair of large ornate flower stands for the chapel at Carshalton
- A therapeutic waterbed for Cheam (acquired in a sale)
- A full-sized billiard table (Cheam)
- A clock (Cheam)
- A water hose (Cheam)
- Quilts which she herself had made (Cheam)
- Regular gifts of wine (Berncasteler and champagne)
- New Jaeger wool-jersey underclothing for Revd Mother (highly fashionable at the time)
- Organ music
- A gas stove (acquired by Mr Lee)
- A gilt copper plate ('sure to be useful in some of your ceremonies')
- A carpet
- A tea urn

This last item was obtained at some trouble:

> Yesterday I went to Penzance to wait on the urn at a sale, and I had to wait five hours for it, but at last secured it ... I am beginning to think of furnishing Mrs Boulder's house at the gate, and have laid in a bed and 12 chairs at this sale, and some carpet and oil cloth. People say she is by no means an object of charity ...

The instruction in the letter quoted above 'put all expenses for her down to me' demonstrates her determination at all times to support the DoC financially. Between 1902 and 1914 Frances is recorded as giving the Daughters £50,746, an average of nearly £4,000 a year.[2] To get an idea of what this means in modern terms, it should be remembered that the average wage in 1910 was £62 per year, whereas the average wage in 2018 was £29,000. On this measure of inflation, Frances' *annual* benefactions were worth nearly £1.9 million in the pre-war years. The total for those twelve years was the equivalent of £23.7 million today.

Property at Penzance and St Ives

The Daughters of the Cross had sent four sisters under Sister Antonia Storey to Penzance in December 1900. Their task was to take over St Mary's school, which had been built in 1892, and run initially by a French order, the Company of Mary, Our Lady. St Mary's was the only Catholic school in Penzance, and also took in some orphan girls on an informal basis. The French sisters decided after some years that they were not suited to the work, which left too little time for prayer and contemplation.

Initially the Daughters lived near the school at Albert House, the rent being paid by Frances Ellis. But the house was not suitable, and in July 1902, encouraged by Canon Wade, Frances spent £1,506.50 on a property for a small convent. Of this sum, £1,150 went to purchase Lescinnick House, which would be the nuns' home for the next 45 years. They also ran a commercial laundry. Later they formally established a girls' orphanage.[3]

The Penzance nuns encountered a degree of hostility from the town council and some residents that reflected the very Protestant views of most Cornishmen. When the girls in the orphanage contracted measles, the sisters had to conceal the fact from the authorities who could have used the outbreak as an excuse to close the home. There was also local resentment of the laundry, which was able to undercut its commercial competitors in the town because its workforce of nuns was unpaid.

Despite the hostility, the sisters took the Cornish to their hearts. An anonymous nun, writing some years later, put it like this:

> The Cornish people are ... a race apart, a gifted vivacious people. Conversions are rare, a genuine one rarer still. The people are clannish to a degree: but withal there is something in this people that is very loveable, one cannot help liking them and this makes us look forward to better days.

Having purchased a shop in St Ives for use as a temporary Mass centre, Frances went on to buy a site in the town centre to build a new Catholic parish church—another bold challenge to local prejudices. Planning and building the church of the Sacred Heart and St Ia took five years, all the costs of which she bore.

Nursing at Hayle, Torquay and Much Hadham

The status of the Downes as a nursing establishment seems at first to have been at variance with Mother Iphigènie's plans. She was interested in establishing a nursing home for invalid nuns at Torquay, ninety miles away in south Devon, and that much closer to the Order's headquarters at Carshalton in Surrey. Nevertheless, Frances supported her Godmother, purchasing Conway House, Torquay for a substantial sum, and plunging into the business of furnishing and equipping it. In May 1903, she gave the DoC £3,942 *'pour un future couvent au sud'*—for a future convent in the south. It is probable, though not entirely sure, that this was the money for Conway House, because there were also plans at this time for a convent at Bournemouth and another at Great Yarmouth on the east coast of England.

Convent and High School of Daughters of the Cross, Great Yarmouth

The history of the Daughters of the Cross records that in 1903 Frances Ellis established on their behalf a primary school attached to the Jesuit-run Catholic parish at Great Yarmouth. Later a secondary school was added. Other than this statement, little documentary evidence survives. Miss Ellis refers sporadically to Yarmouth in her letters, including one dated 9 March 1909 which mentions that she has been there. A small community of nuns ran it. The school was damaged by German naval bombardment during the First World War, and in 1919 the DoC gave it up to the Sisters of St Mary of Namur.

In one letter Frances refers without further explanation to 'the Bishop', Canon St John and Mr Lee visiting a site to assess the prospects, but in the context of the letter it is unclear whether they are investigating Bournemouth or Cheam.

Conway House operated for only a year, when it became apparent to Sister Iphigènie that it was duplicating the effort made by the order elsewhere. Early in 1905, the invalid sisters were transferred from Torquay to the Downes at Hayle, which from then on was their main private sanatorium.

Altogether in 1903 Frances spent £5,347 on behalf of the order. Apart from the money for a 'future southern convent', she spent £1,250 on the Downes, and £100 on the order's house at Much Hadham, Herts.

Much Hadham, 25 miles north of London, was the location of St Elizabeth's home and school for people with epilepsy, the first of its kind in the UK. In 1899, Cardinal Vaughan had asked the Daughters of the Cross to find a way to care for young epileptics. Sister Iphigènie bought the land in 1901, and the building was started in 1903. Miss Ellis gave £100 in that year. No other donations are recorded. Today, St Elizabeth's remains the only UK charity providing specialist care, education and living facilities for people of all ages with severe epilepsy and other complex needs. Although the nuns are no longer involved in running it, they remain as trustees, and St Elizabeth's retains its Catholic ethos.

Oxford: Nuns' education (1910)

In 1909 the Daughters of the Cross realised that the expansion of their schools required more formal training for teaching nuns. This would not be possible 'in-house', and Mother Iphigènie looked for somewhere for nuns to stay while they worked for their teaching diplomas.

In 1910, Frances Ellis gave £3,000 to acquire and adapt a House of Studies at Oxford. It opened in 1911. Over the next decade there were usually two or three nuns living at Alexandra House, as it was called. But after the First World War sisters began studying as extern students at the University of London, and the Oxford property was sold.

In later years, sisters trained as full-time students at London, Manchester, Belfast and Dublin universities, as well as various teacher training colleges.

St Anthony's Hospital, Cheam (1904–2014)

St Anthony's Hospital at Cheam, Surrey (now in the borough of Sutton) was the most ambitious individual project undertaken in Britain by the Daughters of the Cross. A success, in medical terms, right from the beginning, it grew throughout the twentieth century. Primarily a TB clinic at the start, by the later twentieth century it had become a highly specialised cardiology hospital. It remains a functioning private hospital to this day, though the DoC withdrew in 2012.

Fresh Air TB Ward, St Anthony's, Cheam c.1910

It began in 1904 when Frances purchased for £4,625 a former coaching inn at Cheam. This had been the family home of the Macaskies, one of whose daughters was Sister Mary Alban of the order. The site was three miles from the school and novitiate at Carshalton, in an area of southwest London that was expanding rapidly.

It is not clear how much Frances gave altogether for St Anthony's, but in the period 1904–1906 donations from her totalling nearly £20,000 were recorded by the DoC without specifying what they were used for. It seems probable that much, if not all, of this was for St Anthony's: the hospital would not have got off the ground without her unstinting support. In 1906, for instance, Frances gave £13,200 in three separate tranches, none of them identified for a particular cause. It is possible that all of this money was intended to support St Anthony's; or some may have been given to support the Daughters' general needs.

The first patients to be admitted to St Anthony's were a woman and her three-year-old son, both suffering from TB. By 1907 the old house had been extended, and the Hospital then had forty beds in five wards. An open-air shelter for children with TB was built to the north of the hospital, and a chapel to the south of it. All patients paid for treatment according to their means; contributions varied from a few shillings to 2 guineas (£2.10p) a week, but many received free care. This was a pattern common to all of the DoC's medical institutions, which charged what they could to patients with the means to pay so that they could also care for the poor and destitute.

In 1914 a new three-storey hospital was erected close by the existing building, expanding the number of patients and the range of conditions that could be treated. It is clear from her letters in the three or four years prior to its opening that Frances Ellis was involved in the discussions within the order, and that she was giving money to the development programme. In late 1912 the nuns recorded specifically that she gave £1,000 for the new hospital chapel.[4]

Opened in September 1914, the new building also enabled the DoC to transfer their nurse training facilities from Whitechapel to Cheam. Three years later the male TB patients from St Catherine's in Ramsgate were transferred to St Anthony's. The hospital flourished over the next few decades.

With the establishment of the National Health Service in 1948, it began to accept NHS patients. The NHS contract was withdrawn in the early 1970's, and St Anthony's returned to the private sector, developing a cardiology speciality. During the 1980's, the DoC established St Raphael's Hospice nearby, and this became an important part of their mission.

In 2014, after 110 years, the Daughters of the Cross withdrew entirely from St Anthony's hospital, selling it to the Spires Health Group. They continued to run the nearby St Raphael's Hospice under the umbrella of a new charity. They also opened St Joseph's convent to which the remaining nuns from St Wilfrid's moved when Tite St Chelsea was sold in 2022.

St Michael's Hospital, Hayle (extension of the Downes) 1913-onwards

In 1905 the Daughters of the Cross abandoned their short-lived Torquay nursing home for invalid nuns and transferred their West Country effort to St Teresa's Convent at the Downes. As a medical facility, Hayle was successful, but necessarily on a small scale. It catered primarily for invalid nuns of the DoC although it was also available for priests and lay patients when rooms were free. The house was very much the Ellis sisters' home as well as a convent, with a warm domestic atmosphere. Like other DoC hospitals and nursing homes, there was a scale of charges, although whenever possible poor patients were treated for free.

As Frances' first decade at the Downes drew to a close, it was apparent that there was a need for a more ambitious, less domestic medical facility. This also coincided with the end of her south London church-building programme, Canon St John having been cast adrift by the Diocese of Southwark. In addition, Frances had by now spent most of her fortune, and had just made a substantial gift to the Pope.

One of the last major Ellis donations recorded by the Daughters of the Cross was £5,320 in the second half of 1913. There is an undated letter to 'My dear Revd S Provincial' informing her of an imminent gift of £5,000. The formality of the address shows that Frances was writing to Mother Iphigènie's successor Mother M. Theophile; Mother Iphigènie had died the previous year.

> I am writing to my Bankers to pay into your Bank £5000. It will be probably the last big sum I can give away, without stopping my usual payments but I feel justified in doing this against advice as there is no one in whom I trust now as I do you. Do not thank me, I shall be happier if I think no more about it—it is the result of daily prayer to Our Lady of Good Counsel.
> Best love—I hope you keep better
> Yrs very affectionately
> FE. Ellis.

In 1904 Frances had purchased a house and garden across the lane from the Downes called Bank's Croft. This was done with an eye to the future, though it is likely that for some years she rented it out. Having reached agreement with the DoC, Bank's Croft was demolished to make way for the new hospital. The Foundation Stone was laid with great ceremony by the chaplain, Fr Alphonsus McElroy CRL, on 20 August 1913. As the hospital was intended for the service of the Cornish people, the nuns had decided it would be under the protection of St Michael, the patron saint of Cornwall. St Michael's was formally opened in September 1914, just as the First World War was getting under way. It is a remarkable coincidence that St Michael's and the new St Anthony's were both opened in that same, ominous month.

At first a two-storey building was the plan, but in a letter to Mother Theophile Frances recounts that Fr Riley, the chaplain at St Teresa's, had prevailed on the builder to add a third floor without consulting the architect, a Mr Tappley. The latter was not best pleased when he returned from his holiday to find the work of adding a new floor actually going on. Might Miss Ellis herself have been involved in this escapade, which must have driven up the costs? But Mr Tappley acquiesced—he had little choice—and it turned out to be a good decision.

The new hospital was constructed of Cornish granite, while all the internal floors were polished terrazzo tiling. On the ground floor was a ten-bed ward, a consulting room and a medicine room. A lift led to the first floor where there was another ten-bed ward, a private room, a private ward and the operating theatre. The top floor held a nurses' room and storage.

St Michael's was advertised as being in all respects a modern hospital, and it was certainly a substantial addition to early 20th century medical provision in Penwith. It was intended to be self-financing.[5] The standard fee, for those who could afford it, was two guineas (£2.10p) a week. That was twice a Cornish agricultural labourer's weekly wage, but less than the national average working-class man's wage of about £3. Where possible, the nuns treated poor patients for free. Donations were solicited, while, for £30, a person had full access to the hospital and all of its services, for a full year. According to a later history of the Daughters of the Cross in Cornwall, Frances Ellis ensured St Michael's was always solvent.

St Michaels was open to all, irrespective of religion. Unfortunately, it was hard at first to overcome the native Cornish suspicion of Catholicism, and for a couple of years the hospital operated below capacity. Thankfully the distrust of Rome, and of Catholic nursing sisters, evaporated during the course of the war. The terrible conflict across the Channel may have helped with that—

people realised that Catholics fought and died with as much bravery and dedication as Protestants—but so did the excellence and professionalism of the care at St Michael's. In fact, during the war St Michael's treated children from London suffering from what in those days was called shell-shock (post-traumatic stress) as a result of bombing by German zeppelins.

Once the hospital was up and running Frances Ellis stepped back from any possible limelight, as was her wont. It continued to expand throughout the 20th century, with two major enlargements in 1927 and 1932 bringing bed capacity up to 75.

The Daughters of the Cross ran St Michael's until 2003, when it was taken over by the Royal Cornwall Hospitals NHS Trust. It is now used as a specialist surgical unit treating 5,000 cases a year of breast cancer and various orthopaedic conditions. The hospital also provides a wide range of outpatient services including pre-assessment clinics allowing suitable patients to be fast-tracked for orthopaedic operations. It is also home to the specialist rehabilitation unit, Marie Thérèse House, which provides in- and outpatient care for patients with neurological conditions and brain injuries. Services such as physiotherapy, occupational therapy and x-ray provide essential support in the diagnosis and treatment of in- and outpatients at the hospital. The work begun over a century ago endures.

Notes

1. Today the house is listed Grade 2.
2. Her total benefactions certainly exceeded the sum recorded by the DoC.
3. The orphanage was replaced in 1938 by St Gertrude's High School for Girls.
4. The first Mass was celebrated there on 21 September 1914, the Feast day of St Iphigènie of Ethiopia.
5. This was more than thirty years before the establishment of the National Health Service.

6

Letters from Hayle

Frances Ellis wrote many letters from Hayle to nuns of the Daughters of the Cross. Mostly they were addressed to Sister Honorine, the Superior at Carshalton, sometimes directly to Mother Iphigènie, though she nearly always began her letters to Sr Honorine by inquiring after 'dear Mother's' health. The letters are chatty and warm, with detailed information about the health of the various invalid nuns at Hayle—especially the consumptive Sr Jeanne de la Croix, who was a great favourite of Frances'—and accounts of visiting priests and the occasional bishop. In among the chat were business messages, confirming that she remained fully involved in the affairs of the order.

Dating individual letters is a challenge. Frances wrote only the day and month, never the year. Some can be dated from references she makes to particular events, such as the opening of the new church at St Ives in 1908. But in most cases, precise dating is impossible, and their contents must be used more broadly to build up a picture of life at the Downes.

One letter to Mother Iphigènie gives a lively account of the activities (or otherwise) of the convalescent sisters, including gardening (much approved by Frances for getting them out into the fresh Cornish air). There is also a priceless glimpse of Frances' plans for playing the concertina in the children's procession on the Feast of Corpus Christi:

1st May 1904
My dear Godmother
… Sister Gertrude Mary has not been down yet, but she has seen her sister in M Superior's room, and she is hoping to be carried down to Mass on Friday for the Feast of the Cross. When the wild weather comes I shall be all right. All who can now work in the garden, and it is beginning to improve. Sister Lavinia is an excellent worker, and she can do that without hurting herself. In fact the fresh air does her good. Your building must be grand, I shall look forward to seeing it, though not just yet.[1] I am actually learning my notes on the concertina that I may walk with the children in the procession at Corpus Christi and play the Lauda Zion. S. Jeanne will take the organ, and if I can do it, outside will suit me

The garden contributed greatly to the life of the Downes, as well as providing paid work for boys who had left the Daughter's orphanages. It was a beautiful resort for both the well and the invalids, especially in good weather. It provided fresh fruit, vegetables and flowers, while sales to the public contributed to the running costs of the house and garden. It was a source of great joy and satisfaction to Frances, and her appreciation of the work of the gardeners, as well as those nuns who took an interest, is warm and personal:

The garden here is beginning to look very nice. We have a real spring garden on the terrace, and shrubs have walked about and settled themselves in new homes, and peach trees which had run into all manner of shapes have turned into neatly trimmed rows, paths newly gravelled, trees pollarded, and beds all being dug up and filled—it is a new place and all through Sr Jeanne de la Croix though looking as though she had not an atom of strength left, yet able to hold and guide gardeners Henry, William, Alfred and John.

In one letter to Carshalton, she reported:

> Sister Mary Aloyse and Sister Mary Ursula are a little better. Also their rooms are downstairs, and I hope they will go out for a few minutes in the donkey-chair down our own avenue and to Gardner's cottage and round the island. The donkey is to take the 4—2 at a time—Sisters Gertrude Mary and Mary Stanislaus making the 4.

Medicines were also always of interest:

> October 25, 1909?
>
> My dear Revd Sister
>
> I return the book with many thanks. I have read it carefully and kept the address—for though Sister Josepha is trying some powders from Harrogate sulphur springs, I am very doubtful if they will suit her, and then if she likes she may have these powders. Hers being rheumatism, not gout, they might not suit...Sister Jeanne de la Croix has gone thoroughly into her new charge. She has good help, as now we have three more sisters and the boys can be entirely out in the garden and Sister Monica & Divina & Micheline can go there part of the afternoon—she directs Henry & William & the boys in everything they do, watches them at work & rests between on the sofa, studying garden books & the neighbouring gardener comes over once a week & looks over the work that has been done & instructs her as to pruning the fruit trees & all she wants to know. The result so far as the garden is concerned is excellent, we are watchful & anxious about how far her strength & health will stand it, but so far ... I do not think she is

much the worse, her lung does hurt her, but so it did this time last year.

Henry and William were two orphans from Ramsgate who had been moved to Hayle once they were old enough to work in the gardens, probably when they reached 13 or 14. In due course they became professional gardeners, and settled at Hayle, with the exception of the war years, when they served together as soldiers in Egypt and Palestine. Frances took a close interest in their education and welfare, and their wartime letters to her attest to their affection for her and the nuns.

Fr Mullins, the chaplain, was also a gardener with an entrepreneurial spirit, in partnership with another of the orphans.

> Fr Mullins is trying some marketing on his own account. I suppose he is tired of making presents of his lettuce. He now sends Johnny FitzGerald to Penzance on Saturdays with a basketful of radishes and cress, penny bunches. Johnny has his school ticket and gets 4d in the shilling for what he sells. Fr M takes Alfred Friday nights to hold a light whilst he cuts cress—he got 1/4 last week. I have not heard the result this week.

The Alfred holding the light for Fr Mullins was another orphan, Alfred Holland, for whom Frances stood *in loco parentis*. He may also have come from Thanet, but it seems more likely that he was from the little orphanage run by the nuns at Penzance. She made sure he received a proper education, and when he got married, she bought him and his wife a cottage.

In addition to the handful of Catholics in Hayle who attended Sunday Mass at the convent chapel, there were also Catholics who rented rooms at the Downes or its adjacent cottage. Their presence contributed to a growing sense of community.

Rear view of the Downes, with extension and new chapel, 2021

September 10, 1909

My dear Revd Sister

Thank you very much for the Philomena & your letter.[2] I only hope dear Revd Mother will escape cold, for this is a most trying time, so windy and changeable—but you will take all the care possible, and she will too, I know, when you tell her. We had a beautiful Feast on Wednesday—Exposition and our two new Catholic ladies were very devout, Mrs Alexander praying in the Chapel for 3 hours—and in the evening the grotto of Lourdes was illuminated, and the Sisters and children sang hymns.[3] Sister Jeanne de la Croix was wonderful before, in superintending the

> illumination of the grotto, and even was out in the evening listening to the singing, but she is not the worse for it, only tired. She is certainly regaining strength, and takes great interest in the garden which has been very much more satisfactory this year—I hope you may see it still.

Frances Ellis was assiduous in her work of supplying the DoC houses in and around London with freshly caught fish from St Ives or Penzance. She sent Mr Gardner the gardener with the dog cart to purchase them.[4] One presumes the recipients appreciated this regular supply of healthy food, transported by train in wicker baskets. And of course, the health of the nuns, including their dental health, was never far from her mind.

> I have also marked what seems a useful lot for Cheam—a clock and a water hose.... you must let me know what you pay for these things, and air bed (sic), and anything else that I can put on to the Hayle chaplain's cheque, which will soon be done.[5] We were fortunate with the fish this morning & were able to send to St Wilfrid's, Totteridge & Brook Green, besides you & Cheam & Penzance & our own—nearly all herrings, but good. S. M. Aloysia went too with S. Superior and had her teeth out. It was quite time, the Dentist said, as there was an abscess already.... Tomorrow you will have your grand guest, and I hope Revd Mother is well enough, and will not catch cold looking after him.[6]
> With best love, yours very affectionately
> F. E. Ellis
> (PS) I have just met S. Florentine, and she said how she wished Revd Mother would come for 5 or 6 days in the summer, and let her pull her round the garden in the chair. If you see or write to St

> Wilfrid or Brook Green, you might ask them to let us have empties back—I wired to Totteridge to make sure of their getting the fish & mentioned it.

Although she generally makes little of her own health, preferring always to report on the state of the nuns at Hayle, Frances did shed light on her condition when promising to go herself to buy the fish for the Daughters of the Cross.

> It does not hurt me going to Penzance. I cannot get warm without going out, being obliged to be nearly always by an open window to be able to breathe, and I am always very cold until I have been out. But I am wearing those beautiful warm socks under my stockings, and they are delicious.

In another letter, she reveals her sleeping arrangements.

> I am thankful to say I am well, except for one of my usual colds, which I think is beginning to go off, but it is impossible to prevent colds, sleeping with my balcony windows open close to the bed, and yet I cannot breathe without it. I enjoy it.

The convert Mrs Alexander became a paying resident of a cottage in the grounds of the Downes. She had several prints made of a photograph of the house which Frances sent to Sister Honorine at Carshalton.

> Mrs Alexander had it taken as a parting gift for her husband, now returned to India and I bought this copy of her—Revd Mother has never really seen the house, and Sr M. Domini may like to look at it in its improved aspect. Mrs A. the tenant continues to be perfectly satisfied with it and occupies her time in doing church work, for a church she hopes will be opened in India. She has no fear of burglars, windows open whether she is

> there or not, as there is nothing to steal but fruit always on her table—on which she subsists, along with bread and milk.

Retreats given by visiting priests were a regular feature of life at the Downes. Sometimes these were led by priests who were temporary in-patients.

> Fr Healley has just left us on the long journey to the Hospital at Ramsgate to try inhalation for his asthma. He suffered much less here, from the softer air, and care of the Sisters, but he is still full of asthma and far from well. We could not have had a better, kinder Father. Though he has been over to Lands End and St Ives, he has given three organ lessons to Sr M Edwin, and done all he could for us, gave us a beautiful retreat, amused us, played to us, and in a gentle way called Fr Mullins to order on many points which were beyond us.

Gifts flowed in two directions. Just before Palm Sunday 1905, Frances wrote to thank Sr Iphigènie for the presents she had just received:

> My dear Godmother
> What beautiful presents you have given me with your own writing on the box. The Rosary that has touched the Holy Sepulchre, the Scapular from Mount Carmel, & Our Lady of Lourdes, and all so beautifully packed in the Easter eggs, with such taste and skill as only religious could do... I think it would give you great satisfaction to see how all is carried on here... Sr J de la Croix is hoping to finish the gilding for the altar before Easter. Though the close work is trying her considerably, she has borne it better than we had dared to hope. She is all energy and courage, too much some-

times and wants holding back. I am hoping that when I am able to go to you for a little visit, you will let her accompany me. I must tell you about our well—Last year Gardner was doing something to the roots of the vines in the vinery, and his foot went through a hole in the ground. He drew it back luckily and investigated & found it was the opening of a well about 70 feet deep—20 feet of water, an iron ladder going halfway down to a platform (with) an iron chain.

The discovery of the well—which Frances thought might be 'prehistoric'—led to further investigations, and a Mr Vivian, who had been around in 1880 when the Downes was being built, remembered it being covered up. It was decided to find a way of supplying the very good water to the house. Frances told Mother Iphigènie that she regarded it as 'God's present to the Daughters of the Cross'. From the Downes there was a clear view of St Ives Bay a mile and a half to the north. This allowed Frances to observe the weather and the condition of the sea, which afforded constant interest. She was also able to monitor the local fishing fleet, and to know in advance whether or not there would be plentiful fish supplies for the Daughters of the Cross.

> We had some wind the night before last, which sent the herring boats in. On that night I never saw such a great glare of light from the sea, there must have been a hundred boats. Again last night and this morning we had a fine day and it appears likely today there will be fish.

Frances' many letters to Iphigènie are tenderly solicitous of her health—which was poor—but mostly they encourage her in the great work of building the ministries of the Daughters of the Cross in England. At Christmas 1906 she wrote to the Superior at Carshalton, closing with medical advice for her Godmother that seems comic in modern terms but was probably sensible enough at the time:

> May I now give warning advice about Revd Mother? This weather is particularly depressing and she ought to drink much more stimulants than at ordinary times—do not spare the whisky or the wine—let her take all she can. And be sure and tell me anything I can get or do of any sort.

In a letter to Iphigènie which begins with Frances turning down an invitation to travel to Liège for a DoC conference, she writes:

> Between ourselves, if I wanted to go anywhere, it would be to you, but I had better stop where I am for the present and look after my Sr J X, my daisies, my dog and my crochet. I am so thankful the doctor is minding you and not allowing you to over exert yourself. What you are doing is very great and shows us all that Our Lord chooses the weak to do His work and I am sure it will prosper, particularly if you will continue to take care of yourself. I hope when warm weather comes and you can be more out it will suit you. The old queen did all her writing in summer houses, and even had her breakfast out, she knew what she was about. [7]

In January 1912 she wrote to the Superior at Carshalton about Iphigènie who was dying and whom she did not wish to disturb. She probably also feared that her Godmother might refuse the help Frances was offering, including a new horse for the nuns' carriage.

> Dear Revd Sister
>
> I send a cheque for the horse and a new collar, though give it a good trial before you pay for it, how does it pass muster etc. It must be proof against all the dangers of the road before Revd Mother can be safe with it. How I do hope the Doctor will find where with to get back her strength and stop the pain which wears her out. But keep him on, whatever you do, and I will gladly pay, for I know she grudges it for herself. If she could be quite free from pain, and be able to get air and exercise, I believe she would still recover strength... You ask about me, my asthma is not yet better, and I cough and wheeze a great deal from the time I go into the chapel until dinner if in the house but always get better in my own beautifully ventilated room and whenever I can go out. The gas radiators are excellent—the Bishop likes them too.[8]

Frances took as full a part in the spiritual life of St Teresa's as she could, praying and singing the office with the nuns, as well as supervising the household and garden and monitoring the health of the invalid sisters. Sometimes she deputised for Sister Superior, as in this affecting letter written 22 February 1911, about the death of one of the invalid nuns:

> Sister Superior has had so much to attend to today that she was unable to write and I have offered to write for her as you would want to hear particulars of good Sr M. Cyprian's last days. She gradually got weaker & falling away, she had occasionally a spoonful of milk or cyder or coffee, but it was all very painful to swallow. She tried to do all she was told, making never any difficulties, and always contented, never a murmur, not even a

groan when in pain, and the whole time would not even have someone sitting up with her—but they saw the end could not be far off, and on Monday afternoon Sr Superior saw Father Riley and asked him to hear her make her perpetual vows when he gave her Holy Communion, so yesterday morning he went up to her, and she made her confession distinctly made her perpetual vows and had H. Communion. She asked them afterwards not to leave her, as she felt faint so they took it in turn to be with her, and Sister Josepha had made her comfortable for the night and left Sr Julia with her. She felt again faint and asked for a spoon of wine or brandy then Sister Superior went in and saw on her face death, she called the other sisters and prayed over her. She spoke to them all so nicely during the day, said goodbye to Sr Veritas, and told S Michelina that her only wish was to go to heaven and that she hoped our Lord would take her that day—she had made her vows and He did. She died so peacefully that they hardly knew when it was exactly. Of course everyone feels it. F Riley said to S Vivinia 'You ought to rejoice for another angel is gone to Heaven.' I believe she will be buried on Saturday. Sister Jeanne de la Croix has been this morning in her chair in the little cemetery superintending the digging.

Photography at the Downes

Preserved in the archives of the Daughters of the Cross are a number of fine interior and exterior views of the Downes. These were taken in May 1908 by the fashionable photographer David Knights-Whittome, commissioned by Frances. Around this time, he took views of a number of Daughters of the Cross establishments, including the girls' orphanage at Totteridge, the home for epileptics at Much Hadham and the convent at Brook Green. He had travelled from London in the mistaken belief that he would make a portrait of Mother Iphigènie. She of course was in Carshalton, and, despite Frances' constant urging, there is no evidence that she visited the Downes after her first trip in 1905.

The photographer David Knights-Whittome, c. 1908

There may have been an element of subterfuge; the photographer was based at Sutton, only a mile from Carshalton, and it seems quite likely that Frances was underwriting his working tour of DoC establishments. Perhaps Frances had lured him down to take pictures of the Downes with the promise of a portrait of one of Britain's leading religious. Knights-Whittome was building his reputation as a chronicler of the great and good, including royalty and aristocracy, though his bread and butter was weddings, schools and country houses in Surrey. He also cultivated an image of himself as a somewhat bohemian artist, which probably tickled Frances and secretly excited the sisters.

Despite the absence of Mother Iphigènie, Knights-Whittome's visit was a success, especially with Frances' favourite, Sr Jeanne de la Croix. She, it transpired, was a keen photographer—an unusual hobby for a nun.

> He was very disappointed that Revd Mother was not here, having brought his proofs to show her. He came by the night train arriving Hayle 7:11 Ascension Day. We had Mass at 730. Gardner and William being at Penzance, we sent Henry to meet him and take him to the hotel and leave him there for breakfast so he got here at 9 o'clock and began work. He took several views and went on Friday to Penzance and left for Plymouth yesterday evening. S Jeanne de la Croix has profited by her opportunities to the greatest degree, she had luckily received a new half-plate camera through the Exchange & Mart only two days before, with a tripod exactly the height of his, so she copied him in nearly all he did. She and I met him at Penzance, and Sr Antonia was only too glad to have her to look after him, being busy preparing for a religious examination herself, and the result

> S Jeanne learned a great deal. Yesterday he took more of a holiday and we sent him in the pony carriage with Fr Mullins for a drive, and he expressed himself having enjoyed his stay. He slept at the Hotel, where I took a room for him, and had all his meals here after the first breakfast. He is now at Plymouth and hopes to photo (sic) the Bishop tomorrow afternoon, who has been away some time after an illness and returns tomorrow.

So ended a brief but stimulating episode in the life of the Downes. Frances appreciated art, and, as can be seen from her works, had excellent taste and a discerning eye. She and Sr Jeanne derived great enjoyment from Knight-Whittome's visit, and one suspects that the photographer too was rather tickled by the whole affair.

Although the letters are nearly entirely concerned with affairs at the Downes or with the Daughters of the Cross at Carshalton and elsewhere, Frances occasionally mentions family members and friends from her past life in Berkshire.

> A cousin of mine has been here today quite unexpectedly, motored from London and called on the chance, Mr Dover Edgell. He was very much pleased with the place and had luncheon here. I had not seen him for 10 years. He met Canon Wade and Fr Healley at lunch.

A snapshot of the community at Hayle

The census taken on Sunday, 2 April 1911, gives an accurate picture of the community at the Downes. In addition to the two Misses Ellis, there were eight working nuns, four invalid nuns and three boys, all employed in the garden. The nuns are recorded by their birth names rather than their names in religion. Thus, the dramatically named Sr Jeanne de la Croix is revealed as the very English Edith Price, born in Kensington.

Of the working nuns, there were four Germans, two Austrians and two Belgians. All four of the invalid nuns were English. What the census recorded as 'household duties' would have covered a full range of activities, from cooking and cleaning to nursing the sick. Sr Josepha, described as a 'sick nurse', was the head nurse, or matron.

A Daughter of the Cross, c. 1910

Birth Name	Religious Name	Age	Born	Occupation	Place of Birth
Eva Zimmerman	Marie Camilla	38	1873	Sr Superior	Germany
Gertrude Breuer	Josepha	57	1854	Sick nurse	Germany
Gertrude Terodde	Julia	77	1834	Household duties	Germany
Ida Hermans	Florentine	45	1866	Household duties	Belgium
Theresa Bodson	Wivina	61	1850	Household duties	Belgium
Maria Maurer	Micheline	42	1869	Household duties	Germany
Maria Unterthiner	Charitas	29	1882	Household duties	Austria
Maria Morkerk	Monica	27	1884	Household duties	Austria
Edith Price	Jeanne de la Croix	44	1867	Invalid teacher	England
Ellen Day	Stanislaus Mary	40	1871	Invalid teacher	England
Annie Neylan	M Aloyse	29	1882	Invalid teacher	England
Winifred Scott	Gertrude Mary	25	1886	Invalid nurse	England
Francis Elizabeth Ellis		64	1846	Private means	England
Rose Catherine Ellis		69	1842	Private means	Italy
Alfred Holland		19	1892	Garden worker	England
Laurence Kappenberg		16	1895	Garden worker	England
Martin Maher		14	1897		England

The census does not mention a chaplain, who may have been recorded either at Penzance or St Ives, or, if a Canon of St John Lateran, at their house at Bodmin. Nor does it appear that the retired bishop of Plymouth, the Most Revd Charles Graham, was yet in residence (although he was certainly living at the Downes by the end of the month).

The hierarchy descends on Hayle

There was usually a young priest in residence at the Downes, either as a chaplain to the little community or as a patient, or in both roles. The Canons Regular at Bodmin were often the source of these clergy. A letter written between 1910 and 1913 gives a flavour of priestly life at the Downes:

> Father Chew arrived on Monday, and cannot say enough about the beauty and comforts of the garden ... He has been for a few bicycle rides with Father Riley. I think we ought to keep him a bit longer, if his room is not wanted. I think he would appreciate it, he is on a strict diet

Frances, like many devout ladies, was a great priest-watcher:

> We like our new priest Father Riley very much. He speaks very little and is reserved altogether, which no doubt is preferable for a young priest. He preaches excellent sermons and sings well and understands plain chant and I wish I had Sr Mary Mildred behind me to help me to harmonise.

Remote though it was, the hospitality and comfort of the Downes also became known among the Catholic hierarchy. In particular, Archbishop, later Cardinal, Francis Bourne stayed there twice.

The first time was in March 1907, when he arrived on a Saturday and stayed till Monday. Bourne was accompanied on this occasion by the indefatigable traveller, Dom Thomas Bergh OSB, Abbot-emeritus of Ramsgate. Frances had been friend and supporter of both men since her early days at Ramsgate: as Bishop of Southwark, Bourne had been the beneficiary of her extraordinary church building programme. She and the excited nuns worked hard to get the house ready for the Archbishop. As she wrote subsequently to Mother Iphigènie:

> The weather so far has been most propitious, and both archbishop and abbot expressed themselves exhilarated by the Cornish air. Gardner on a fly met them at St Erth station at 4.50 on Saturday.[9] The sisters having cleaned and polished the house from top to bottom all last week, were assembled in the hall, the inner front door was ornamented with greenery and a scroll 'Ecce Sacerdos Magnus'.[10] Fr Mullins met them at the gates, and all including myself knelt for the blessing as they entered and were shown into the drawing room where the library table had been placed in the middle to make a double writing table and after that they went to the chapel, walked round the garden with Sr Superior and me (we had not much to show them besides new potatoes in the greenhouse, the flowers are coming later), then we said good night and they had their dinner.
> Sunday morning first Mass at 6.30, Archbishop at 7.30 served by the Abbot, Fr Mullins as usual 10. Archbishop and Abbot writing letters all the morning. The Canons Lateran Fr Sankey and Brighton from St Ives, and Fr Sandling came to lunch. The archbishop was very kind and gentle and courteous to everybody, and after luncheon

took the young canons for a walk. They went over the ferry to the sands and returned at 5. The abbot took a rest. They came in to Benediction quietly through the sacristy door, and dined again alone.

Bishop Graham joined the party for lunch on the first day, though he did not stay, preferring instead to go to St Ives for a few days. Bourne stood in for him at Plymouth cathedral on the Sunday. He and Abbot Bergh then toured extensively in the Diocese of Plymouth. Frances went with them to Falmouth and Truro. In a letter to her godmother, Frances wrote of Bourne:

> The Archbishop and Fr Abbot have been on the move the whole week. The Archbishop impresses me more every day.

Five years later Archbishop Bourne, now at last a cardinal, graced St Teresa's with his presence for a second time. In a letter to Carshalton dated 19 April 1912, Frances writes:

> Now we are talking of the Cardinal's coming and we must get the rooms in order. He and Mgr Jackman are coming on Thursday till Saturday, and then they go to Clifton and Downside.[11] I must say, that I feel a little alarmed that we may not receive the Cardinal properly, though it is a great honour.[12] Our Bishop is pretty well, but still confined to the house, having a tendency to bronchitis and rheumatism.

The visit was over 28–30 April. It may be coincidental, but only a month before his visit Frances Ellis had revoked her previous will and written a new one which bequeathed all her worldly goods to Cardinal Bourne.

By 'Our Bishop' Frances was referring in this letter to Bishop Graham, who had retired to the Downes after giving up the See of Plymouth in March 1911. He had been a regular visitor over the previous eight years. She and the Bishop enjoyed one another's company, and he periodically came for rest and recreation away from the travails of running a far-flung diocese. Frances always ensured that there was good food and drink for him and his companions. He travelled with at least one chaplain. And of course, the nuns were always solicitous of Graham's comfort.

Graham's most notable visit was in September 1908 for the opening of the new church of the Sacred Heart and St Ia at St Ives. This was a grand occasion, with many priests and dignitaries in attendance. It was also probably only the third occasion when Frances Ellis was present at the opening of a church she had built. A letter to Carshalton on Sunday 27 September gives some idea of the upheaval and the challenge of catering for the clergy, who numbered at least ten.

> This is the last of the three days of Jubilee here. The Bishop arrived on Thursday evening accompanied by 5 priests who all stayed here. Prior Smith, Frs Bruno, Hannigan, Bovenizer and Mullins, and next morning came Abbot White, Frs Scully, Brighton and McKinstry. So we had for the Mass Prior Smith celebrating, Bovenizer at the organ, and the others singing, including the Bishop, who has a very nice voice—10 altogether. I had to go to Penzance to see to the fish dinner, and we managed cod and oyster sauce, fried soles and lobster salad. Most of the priests left in the afternoon and evening. The Bishop gave us Benediction Friday and Saturday. This morning he has given us Holy Communion and goes to St Ives after Benediction to give Confirmation and returns to sleep and leaves after luncheon

tomorrow. Yesterday he had to go to St Ives, so I went with him in the carriage and looked at the new church, which is really very pretty, a stone altar something after yours, a little Lady shrine of the same style. They have 75 Catholics now. Over the door there is a stone carving of St Eia holding the parish church in her hands.

Now I must tell you about the speeches after dinner on Friday. Prior Smith proposed the health of the Bishop, being the anniversary of his election. The Bishop responded proposing the health of the Daughters of the Cross, saying that until they came into his Diocese he had not known anything of them, but he appreciates their zeal, not only in the bodily welfare of those in their care but their great zeal for the spiritual welfare. He considered them second to none in his Diocese and he called upon Fr Mullins to respond for them—the latter pulled a long face and asked his Prior if he need make a speech. Being told yes, he got up and said—it was a good thing the Reverend Mother was not present, or what his Lordship had said would have tried even her humility....

On one of Graham's visits, he brought an unexpected gift. As Frances wrote to Sr Honorine, perhaps slightly tongue in cheek:

> Did you hear about the Bishop's present? Such a nice portrait of himself, he looks so well over the sideboard in the dining room. A really good likeness in oils, in a large gold frame, it gives a sort of dignity to the room. Poor man, he was very ill again in September and is only allowed out of his rooms in the middle of the day.

By 1910 Graham's health was failing, and Frances suggested that he stay at the Downes to recover his strength. A reply to her dated 31 March 1910 from the Bishop's secretary Fr Thomas Courtenay goes into great detail:

> Our dear Bishop is very low indeed and can hardly be spoken to except for remedies and food. He has to be tended assiduously and is really at death's door the last week. But now after a slight improvement he has had a relapse. He has to have oxygen and brandy at intervals and of course whatever nourishment he can take in the way of soups, beef-tea, eggs, fruit etc day and night. I fear port wine would not be allowed. But the Dr did speak of champagne in a few days, I suppose, when the oxygen will have to be discontinued... I know no better place for a convalescent home than the Downes Hayle, so I shall urge him when, please God, he can go away, to accept your kind invitation.

Graham resumed his episcopal duties, but his strength failed again, and he formally resigned the see of Plymouth on 11 March 1911, taking the title Bishop of Tiberias *in partibus*.[13] He then retired to the Downes, where the nuns were glad to care for him, and where for a time he enjoyed a new lease of life. He became in fact, if not in title, a sort of episcopal chaplain. At Whitsun 1911 Frances wrote:

> We had it very grand in our little Chapel yesterday with the Bishop and two priests. The Bishop in the evening gave Pontifical Benediction in his mitre and looked so dignified, with the two priests in St Ives dalmatics. He told me that today he had been 4 months here, and feels very much better. He is so happy with his brother, whom Father Riley has asked to stay as long as he could to prolong his

own holiday. He goes on Friday... I do not like depriving the Bishop of more than one of his drives in the week, he enjoys them so much.

Bishop Graham died at the Downes on 2 September 1912, aged 77, and was buried at Plymouth Cathedral.

Frances Ellis, Mother Iphigènie and a unique brand of charity

Mother Iphigènie was Frances' Godmother, but she was also her close friend and a model of dedicated practical Christianity. Even if she had wanted to, Frances would not have been eligible to become a nun. According to the Constitutions of the Daughters of the Cross, candidates had to be between the ages of 16 and 30. In any case, canon law did not permit entry of those who had dependents, as Kate would have been deemed.

Instead, Frances, with Iphigènie's approval, created at Hayle a unique brand of practical charity combining family home, convent and sanatorium. From there she dispensed her philanthropy to the Daughters of the Cross and the Diocese of Southwark, as well as to others whose needs might otherwise have been overlooked.

Despite her devoted friendship, Frances' letters to the Daughter's British headquarters were nearly always addressed to other senior nuns, because she did not wish to burden Iphigènie with the duty of replying. Nearly every letter began with anxious enquiry after Mother's health, and earnest entreaties to the sisters to take care of her. But occasionally she wrote directly, in letters which reveal her deep love and appreciation. Especially, she wrote to Iphigènie every Christmas Day, as in this example:

My dear Godmother,

What can I write to express my gratitude to you for all your loving thoughts and care of me? First I had a letter from Sr Mary Theophile, then one in your own beautiful handwriting, putting everything the reverse way from what it really is, for you and yours are taking the tenderest care of Kate and me, always, and all I can do is give you more work, which you undertake so willingly. However, what I have got to do is to try, if God spares me, and be more worthy of all you do. Then this morning arrive ever so many presents, all delightful in their different ways—such a handsome bedspread, which must have taken a great number of hours, and a great deal of patience to make, then a book which I long to begin at once, and full of pretty Christmas markers, then the bear full of good things and looking so like Cap when he has had one dinner and wants another, then the two boxes full of German cakes.[14] You have lavished good things on me, then I must add that I had yesterday such a nice little letter from the little girls, with a card of their own drawing and a book of views of Carshalton and another from the Aloysians, and I feel guilty for I have done nothing for any of them.[15] All this has given me a large taste of Carshalton and reminded me of how happy you always made me there. Now as it is of no use wishing I could have just one look at you, I will tell you about our doings here. Sister Superior has been praying very hard that all the Sisters might be well enough to assemble today—and her prayer has been granted. Last night 12 were in the Chapel for the Midnight Mass, and the 13th Sister Mary Aloyse was allowed by the doctor to come down to the green room, where she heard Mass through the window in the wall and received Holy Communion. All the outsiders came who could, and we had some offertory pieces very well sung by the new choir, and the Chapel looked as beautiful as could be, I think. Sister Jeanne de la Croix had managed to save a good many fine white chrysanthemums for the altar. I can only say thank you again and again, how with all your suffering, and all your million cares you can set yourself to think of all these things for me, is a marvel—there is one thing you could not do and that is to let me have a peep at you.

The friendship between Frances and Iphigènie had begun at Ramsgate in the last years of the 19th century when Frances was turning to the Catholic faith. It seems likely that when she was under instruction Frances spent periods of time at the convent in Carshalton. They were both strong practical women of a similar age, born to wealth and accustomed to command. Frances had led a life of quietly respectable luxury until the age of 50. Iphigènie had given her life to God aged twenty and devoted her considerable powers to the works of charity undertaken by the Daughters of the Cross, in Germany and then, decisively, in Britain. Frances saw her Godmother as a model of Christian womanhood, and, once she had discovered her own vocation, unstintingly gave Iphigènie her money, love and support.

Appeal to the Pope

In January 1913, a few months after the deaths of her Godmother Mother Iphigènie and her friend Bishop Graham, Frances felt moved to appeal to Pope Pius X on behalf of two of the most invalid nuns at Hayle. Sister

Jeanne de la Croix, she wrote, was 47 and in the last stages of consumption; Sister Mary Raphael Day was 46 and suffering an unspecified form of spinal paralysis. Both had worked devotedly for more than twenty years and would if they could work many more years. Remarkably the Holy Father replied by return of post. Frances' translation from the Italian:

> I will remember particularly in the Holy Mass the two poor invalids with the most ardent wish that the Lord will hear their prayers and will give them perfect cures. In the mean time I grant them from my heart the Apostolic Blessing.
> January 17, 1913
> Pius PP X

The lively, artistic Sr Jeanne de la Croix lived another 17 years, surviving Frances herself by four days, a testament to the Pope's blessing and prayers, as well as the good care and fresh air she enjoyed at Hayle.

The Downes in wartime

The First World War brought change and upheaval to the Downes. Most dramatic was the arrival in Cornwall of large numbers of Belgian refugees after most of their country was occupied by the German invaders in the late summer and autumn of 1914. Some 250,000 Belgians, men, women and children—nearly all Catholics—appeared on the south coast of England in 1914. The large majority were civilians, though there were also many wounded soldiers. They brought with them terrible accounts of German atrocities. Some of these stories were exaggerated—though there is little doubt that the German army often behaved abominably in Belgium—but true or false they were amplified by the British press and believed by the British public. The Belgian Army, hugely outnumbered, had fought heroically and held up the Germans for several weeks. The legend of 'Plucky Little Belgium' was born, and the British took the refugees to their hearts.

The majority of the Belgians arrived first in Kentish channel ports like Dover and Ramsgate. Belgian refugee committees were swiftly established in many counties, including Cornwall. The policy was to settle the refugees and care for all their needs, especially housing and education for the children. In Cornwall most of the refugees were accommodated further east, but several dozen arrived, destitute, in Penzance. They were brought by Belgian fishing boats whose crews knew the waters well and often knew Cornish fishermen.

At Penzance and Hayle, the Daughters of the Cross (some of whom were themselves Belgian) did all they could for the refugees, particularly the youngsters. Frances Ellis arranged for a new schoolroom to be built so that the refugee children could be educated in their own language by the nuns.

The Downes also played its part, with the chapel serving as an unofficial parish church. There were, according to Frances, 27 Belgians in Hayle, along with 25 English Catholics, the priests, sisters, Kate and herself, more than 60 all told. That meant that two Masses had to be said on Sundays. Frances mentions in a letter to Carshalton that:

> We have now here a young mother to console. One of the Belgians at St Ives has lost her little girl of 3 from dysentery, and Father Scully asked us whether she and the remaining little girl of 5 might come over here (as both were ill) for a rest and change. They arrived yesterday, the husband

went to our Presbytery & there is a nice young maid who came from Belgium with them & who does all their work for them—they will only remain two or three weeks. They are very sad, but quite resigned & very anxious not to put us to any inconvenience.

Here were also musical contributions. In an undated letter to the new Provincial, Mother Théophile Conzen, Frances wrote about the success of

... our little Belgian concert ... we are trying to get up another for the relief committee, who have helped us so much in our support of the Belgians. It seems to me a grand opportunity to show our good will and appreciation.

Frances continued to travel during the war. In June 1915 she visited Carshalton. This was partly in order to become better acquainted with the new Provincial of the Daughters of the Cross, Mother Théophile Conzen. Like Iphigènie, Mother Théophile was a German, born in the town of Jüllich which is halfway between Köln and Aachen. This would not have seemed strange when her predecessor had died in 1913, but a year into the war anti-German feeling was intense in Britain. That might have been an added reason that Bishop Amigo would be there as well, though as he wrote to Frances:

I can only manage to get down for one afternoon, returning here as soon as I have had my interview and given her the crucifix. A lady will lend me her motor for both going and returning.

Frances Ellis with her diary

The meeting with Frances was evidently important to Amigo, who disliked travelling by car, and always preferred to use public transport. The loan of the car included the anonymous lady's chauffeur.

Most of the young men who worked at the Downes were away with the forces during the war. Frances endeavoured to keep in touch with them. Her protégé Alfred Holland, serving in the army in Mesopotamia, wrote to her on 24 May 1917.[16] This was two months after the British had captured Baghdad from the Turkish army. Due to military censorship, the letter is short on information, but full of good will.

> Just a line hoping to find you in the best of health and all the sisters as well. I am keeping very well myself. We are having very hot weather just now, and are unable to work outside during the greater part of the day, we rise early so as to be able to do a few hours work before it gets too hot, and we turn out again in the evening when it gets cooler to do a bit more. We had a very severe sand storm a few days ago. It looked a splendid sight to watch it coming, you could see it for miles and it passed right over our camp, it took nearly an hour to pass a given spot, and I was glad when it was over for we were smothered with sand. Kindly remember me to Sister Mary Camilla and Sister Waltera. Good bye for the time. Best wishes to all.
> From
> Yours sincerely
> Alfred

At Christmas 1917 Frances wrote Alfred a characteristically generous and chatty letter full of real news.

> I find it is time to send you what I want you to have at Christmas, though I always hope you may be back here any day. I sent off a parcel containing a tin of tongue, ditto of herring with tomatoes, ditto of chocolates and sweets. I am now sending a few magazines which I have pulled to pieces to save weight in taking out the advertisements. Where ever you are, we all wish you a very happy Christmas & a speedy safe return. How happy we shall be to see you again. Anthony has written that he is in a hospital in London, not seriously ill, but

bad enough to be sent home. The poor Priors are in sad trouble, having lost their only son, he was killed almost at once. Leslie is getting on well, he ought to make a good sailor. Willie Gardner still continues working in England near Swindon. Mr Rowe our butcher is gone to Salonica, I hope he will get on well. He remains in his trade. The Sisters are much as usual, keeping going & the garden has done well with potatoes and fruit, we can use any amount. Mr Philip Henry who was ill in the hospital since May twelvemonth is now dead, within two days of his old father's death. A parcel is come for you from Mesopotamia or India, the contents are described as 'imitation of a brass Indian knife' & signed Hunter. We think he must be a Priest who sent it. We will keep it for you. Hoping that you are keeping well, and that we may soon see you again.

Yrs sincerely

F. E. Ellis

By the time the First World War had broken out, Frances had completed her major benefactions. Of her closest associates, Mother Iphigènie was dead, and Canon St John was effectively exiled, a prison chaplain in Liverpool, and in no position to continue their joint programme of church-building. Her own health was poor, breathing becoming more difficult and eyesight slowly deteriorating. But she remained active, contributing strongly to the life of the Downes and maintaining a vigorous correspondence with friends throughout the country. Although she was no longer actively contributing to the expansion of Southwark, Bishop Amigo occasionally asked for her assistance in solving administrative problems.

Back in Ramsgate, Trust is hard to establish

Astonishingly, the wrangle between the Cardinal and Bishop Amigo dragged on into the First World War, when both men had more important things to think about. Again, the difficulty must be laid largely at Bourne's door. For years Amigo had wanted to remove Bourne and other former Southwark officials (including St John) from various trusts that had been established before his accession in 1903. His reasons for doing so were legitimate as well as sensible: the terms required trustees who represented Southwark. Amigo reasoned that Bourne and his associates would not want to be legally responsible for organisations over which they had no practical control.

But Bourne refused to co-operate, employing a range of delaying tactics, and forcing Amigo to negotiate with Westminster's lawyers. In 1915 Amigo turned to the trust governing St Catherine's Hospital, which Frances had given to the Daughters of the Cross in Ramsgate in 1901 at the time of her reception into the Church. Sorting out the trust had become urgent because the DoC needed to sell the existing buildings and move the hospital to a better site. The local council wanted to remove TB patients from the town, and German Zeppelin raids made Ramsgate, with its naval port, a dangerous place for civilians.

In the summer of 1915 Bourne told Amigo that he would only agree to resign from the St Catherine's Trust under certain conditions.

First, Miss Ellis would have to agree. Her agreement was more or less automatic, so this was not a particularly onerous condition. But it rather implied that Bourne thought Frances more important than the Bishop of Southwark.

Second, the deed should stipulate that St Catherine's must remain exclusively a TB hospital. Frances Ellis' original purpose was to build and endow a TB hospital—but only because that was the DoC's intention at the time. Amigo objected to this because it prevented the Daughters of the Cross using the hospital for such other purposes as might be necessary in future.

Third, he wanted no reference in the trust to the Diocese of Southwark, a calculated insult to Amigo. As the bishop wrote to his solicitor: 'To this I object as Miss Ellis has stated that she all along intended to help our Diocese. The Daughters of the Cross are to have it (the hospital), but if one day it suited them to give it up, it ought to revert to us.'

These conditions all referred to Frances Ellis. Yet Bourne must have known that in this case she would have supported Amigo and Southwark. In one letter to his lawyer, Amigo observed that it was three years since the Pope had instructed the Cardinal to resign from all the Southwark trusts without delay or preconditions. And yet here he was, prevaricating and imposing conditions.

Negotiations dragged on for more than a year at significant cost. At one stage Abbot Bergh offered his services as a mediator, and produced several potential settlements, most of which were rejected either by Westminster, Southwark or the Daughters of the Cross. Frances Ellis was also consulted. Her responses have not survived, but the references to her in others' correspondence suggest—unsurprisingly—that she supported the views taken by the nuns. She does mention, in passing, that Canon St John was in favour of the changes as long as the hospital was solvent.

The final settlement, dated 20 September 1916, was so worded as to suggest that the original trustees,

Archbishop Bourne and Canon St John, were only resigning at the request of Frances Ellis. There was no mention in the recitals of Southwark or Bishop Amigo. The 'indenture'—an archaic name for a property contract—stated that Bourne was appointing new trustees 'with the approbation of the said Frances Elizabeth Ellis'. Those new trustees were four English nuns listed under their birth names: Theresa Kent (M Marcellus), Rosa Morris (Carola Mary), Mary Wheeler (M Cecilia) and Norah Hurley (M Bede).

Bourne failed to get his way in restricting the hospital to care of TB patients, and he also had to give in on the Southwark connection: 'All the said hereditaments are vested in the parties on trust to sell the same at such time and in such manner as they think fit and to apply the proceeds both as to capital and income for the purposes of a Hospital, Sanatorium or House of Rest within the Roman Catholic Diocese of Southwark.' The expensive legal wrangling and consequent delays seem to have been entirely pointless.

On a happier, more harmonious note, the day after the agreement was signed, Frances gave the DoC £1,112 9s. 8d. in memory of Mother Iphigènie, whose Feast Day it was. Frances Ellis had celebrated her 70th birthday during the prolonged negotiations over St Catherine's future. The Daughters of the Cross rejoiced with her, one of them writing a long laudatory poem.[17]

Despite her advancing years, Frances continued to travel. She visited the DoC's mother house at Carshalton in May 1917. She liked to stay in touch with the leadership of the order, to inspect the institutions she had funded, and to see if there were further ways in which she could help. Carshalton was close to St Anthony's Cheam, another hospital that owed its existence to Frances. Its success was leading to further expansion, even in the middle of a world war. At the conclusion of this visit she returned to Hayle with two sisters who were being transferred there. The following year she showed up unannounced at Ramsgate, which, from their diary notes, ruffled some nunnish feathers.

Finale: A new boarding school in Northern Ireland

Miss Ellis made almost her last substantial benefaction to the DoC two years after the end of the First World War, but during the height of the independence struggle in Ireland. Although the Order had expanded across England and in challenging countries like India, it had not previously opened an institution in Ireland. This was strange, the official history comments, because over the years many Irish girls had travelled to England to enter the order.

The opportunity arose when the nuns were asked by Canon Joseph O'Neill, the parish priest of Donaghmore in County Tyrone, to consider starting a hospital in a semi-derelict country house he had acquired. In this very rural region, Catholics had been persecuted for more than 300 years, and had only started building churches within living memory.

A modest classical mansion, Donaghmore House, had been built about 1820 by the McKenzie-Lyle family, who abandoned it in 1913.[18] It lay empty for a time and was then bought by a horse dealer called John Laverty on the strength of a large order for horses from the Greek government. The Greek deal fell through, and Laverty was forced to sell the house at a knockdown price to Canon O'Neill. He in turn offered it to the Daughters of the Cross. Once the order had accepted the challenge, Frances Ellis provided the purchase cost of £987.

It is unlikely that she ever visited the site, and it would have been dangerous for her to have done so. Although ultimately Co. Tyrone remained in the United Kingdom, there was savage fighting across the county, with the IRA attacking police targets, and the security forces taking reprisals, and there were many deaths. Ireland was partitioned by the British government in May 1921, and a ceasefire was agreed in July.

But in September 1920, long before the ceasefire, two Daughters of the Cross arrived at Donaghmore House, with two suitcases of cleaning materials and two chairs. They set to work scrubbing the filthy house and outbuildings and were joined after some weeks by two more nuns. The fighting came closer: one night the police station up the road in Donaghmore was burned down, and the following day the IRA and the police fought a running battle in the grounds of the house. Bravely, the indomitable sisters kept their heads down and got on with their work.

The hospital functioned for only a few months, with six beds donated by a nearby convent and the assistance of the local GP. However, it soon became clear that the site was not suited to a medical institution. After further discussion with Canon O'Neill, the Daughters of the Cross decided to convert it to a boarding school for girls. Opened in September 1922, St Joseph's Grammar School was an immediate success.

Like St Michael's Hospital and many other institutions founded as a result of Frances Ellis' generosity, the school expanded throughout the 20th century. It became co-educational in 1973. As elsewhere in Britain and Ireland, the Daughters of the Cross began to face a shortage of vocations, and their numbers inevitably dwindled. The last nuns left St Joseph's in 2005, but their spirit remains strong. As the principal, Geraldine Donnelly, wrote in 2020:

> Visitors to St Joseph's often comment on the distinctive school ethos which has been the legacy left to us by the Daughters of the Cross, the school's founding Order. As we approach the centenary of the foundation of the school in 2022, we continue to hold true to our role as educators whose work is based on Gospel values and the teaching of Christ. We warmly welcome pupils of all faiths to join us in an inclusive and welcoming environment where every person is valued as a child of God.

Frances Ellis would have regarded that as a most acceptable return on her modest investment.

Later years

Rose Ellis died in 1925 aged 84, loved and cared for by her sister. She was buried in the nuns' cemetery at the Downes.

By now, Frances herself was in poor health, her chronic breathing difficulties worsening as the years went by, but she was well cared for by the sisters. However, in the new year following Rose's death she lost her sight. This was a particularly terrible affliction for a voracious reader and dedicated letter writer, and one who took such delight in the natural world. Perhaps she was helped to bear this new and heavy blow by the memory of her mother Catherine, who had also been blind.

The news of her blindness spread swiftly. The nuns have preserved a note from Cardinal Bourne to their Mother Provincial:

> I am grateful for your kindness in letting me know of the heavy cross which has fallen on Miss Ellis. I am writing to her by this post. May God bless you and all your sisters.
> Yours in J.C.
> F. Card. Bourne

On 28 February, Frances replied to the Cardinal's letter with the secretarial assistance of one of the sisters.

> Your most consoling letter has cheered me much, particularly your promise of prayer, for though I feel very thankful to Almighty God for having given me my sight for 80 years, I want to take what he has now sent me as a means of entire union with Him, and prayers will help me to do so. I need not say how well and tenderly I am looked after. This sudden loss of sight has been a warning that my life may go the same way.... I should much like to see (Canon St John) here if he could come for a few days just to understand matters. Would you be so kind as to arrange this for me on his return?

One of the matters she wished to discuss with St John was her will. He arrived in Hayle within a week of her letter and reported to Cardinal Bourne on 4 March.

> I found dear old Miss Ellis just the same as ever and 'thanking God for having given her sight for 80 years'. She tells me she does not expect to last much longer and that her life may end as suddenly as her sight left her. She said she made her will in 1911 and that it is at her Bankers and that in that year she thoroughly made up her mind, with Mr Lee, that she would leave all she had, except what is in this house to you absolutely. She has never

altered her will since and has no intention of doing so.

The poor old soul has a bandage over her eyes but looks much the same. (Although) the ... doctor says her heart is very tired ... she is a little better today. She insists on getting up for Mass each day and walks up and down stairs to her bedroom but I expect she is right and that the end is not far off. She tells me that Mr Lee is living at Penzance and is delighted to hear that I am going to visit him tomorrow. Mr Lee and his wife are very old and feeble. He managed to come over to see Miss E since she lost her sight but he could hardly manage it. He has nothing to do with her affairs she says because she really settled them in 1911 and she thought it best to leave it at that. Her cousin, a Colonel Davidson I think is his name, has been to see her yesterday and she seems prepared in every way for the end. We had an hours talk alone tonight and of course we shall have other talks before Monday. She is very very pleased that I am going to Harrow. I think she said she had 3 friends there as nuns.

So far not a word has passed between us re Southwark. She told me in some detail her wishes with regard to the Daughters of the Cross and Masses for her soul, but I assured her that I felt sure that you would of your own accord have done what she wished, and she said she felt sure of that but thought she would like to tell me as I was an executor.

The Sisters say she had a personal letter from Pius XI which she has given to them and which they wanted to apply to her eyes but she refused and blessed God for giving her sight for 80 years.

Despite her afflictions, Frances carried on as well as she could, availing herself of the services of one of the nuns to write her letters from dictation. One of these, addressed to Mother Superior and dated 9 October 1926, concerned in part her donation of £1,000 worth of stock for the costs of the new chapel at St Michael's Hayle. Related to this is a letter to her at Hayle from Lloyds Bank in St James's St London, dated 26 October 1926, confirming that Canada 3½ percent stock was redeemable at par any time up to 1934. This does seem to have been her final donation to the Daughters of the Cross.

In her last years, Frances had a companion, remembered by Sister Patricia Ainsworth as the wonderfully named Miss Treadgold, a local woman. She assisted Frances round the house and chapel and took her for jaunts in her wheelchair.

Frances Ellis died at Hayle on 23 March 1930, the cause being given as myocardial degeneration and chronic bronchitis. She was 84 years of age. Coincidentally, it was the Feast day of St Gwinear, an Irish missionary who, with a number of companions, travelled to Cornwall and was martyred at Hayle around 600 AD.

Poignantly, her friend Sr Jeanne de la Croix, who had lived at Hayle for many years, died four days after Frances, aged 65. Sr Jeanne's longevity, despite her tuberculosis, was a testament not only to the care she received from her fellow nuns, but to the restorative power of the fresh Cornish weather, and to her courage and lively spirit so often noted by Frances in her letters.

By her will, dated 1 March 1911, Frances Ellis appointed Cardinal Bourne and Canon St John her executors, and left her entire estate to Cardinal Bourne. However, when the will was proved a couple of months later, the estate was granted to Canon St John alone.

Presumably this was done at the Cardinal's request, although his power as executor was reserved to him.

The net value of Frances' estate in 1930 was £14,866, equivalent to several million pounds today. Such comparisons become less reliable the longer the period of time elapsed, and the real equivalent may be two or three times that given by (in this case) the Bank of England's Inflation Calculator. In his tribute to Frances at the rededication of St Mary's Clapham Common, Cardinal Bourne said she had given at least £200,000 to Southwark, to other dioceses and to religious orders. In addition, he had been entrusted with 'a large gift' made on her behalf to Pope Pius XI in 1913. It is thought that Canon St John and Cardinal Bourne passed her final legacy on to the Vatican.

Frances had also made provision for her Cornish friends, especially the gardeners at Hayle, some of whom she had nurtured since their boyhoods. A £100 War Bond that had yielded £20 interest was divided between the six gardeners, with £20 residue to be reserved for their eventual funeral expenses.

The following month, *The Tablet* reported:

> A solemn requiem Mass was sung at St Ethelbert's, Ramsgate, on April 9 for the soul of Miss Frances Elizabeth Ellis, to whose generosity the foundation of that mission, and the erection of its beautiful church in 1902, was directly due. Miss Ellis not only built the church but also gave the presbytery, and the large plot of land on which the new schools and the parish hall now stand. The Prior of St Augustine's, Dom Norbert Lapworth, OSB, was the celebrant and also presided at the Absolution which followed, assisted by Dom Norbert Cowin and Dom Dunstan Pragnell, OSB,

as deacon and subdeacon respectively. The community of St. Augustine's sang the Mass, at which all the schoolchildren and a large congregation assisted. The Mother Superior and a number of the nuns from Holy Cross Convent, Ramsgate (founded by Miss Ellis), were also present. Exhorted by their zealous pastor, the Reverend Charles van Cauwenberghe, OSB, about two hundred of the congregation of St Ethelbert's had, on the previous Sunday, offered up Holy Communion for their benefactress; thus showing that their gratitude towards one to whom they owed so much had not diminished during the thirty years which had elapsed since her noble gift.

But the last word should go to Mother Marie Victorine Doutreloux, Superior General of the Daughters of the Cross, in a circular letter to her nuns, written at Liège the day after Frances' death:

> What a sweet and loving welcome will have been given her by Our dear Lord Whom she has so faithfully served! He who has promised an eternal reward for a cup of cold water given in His Name, what will he not have reserved for this noble, generous soul who considered herself the dispenser rather than the proprietor of the wealth God had given her! Her one desire was to give, and this desire carried her on until it reached—as far as she was concerned—a complete privation, closely touching sheer poverty. But what greatly enhanced the merit of her charity was the unassuming modesty that always accompanied these her acts. After lavishing her wealth on a church or a convent, Miss Ellis disappeared from sight, and so gladly escaped both praise and thanks.

You will no doubt remember, my very dear sisters, with what deep faith and piety she accompanied the singing in the little chapel at Hayle. Then there was her love of work: never did one see her idle, and this from principle, for as she said, God had imposed on all the duty to labour. What shall we say of her patience and resignation during the last years of her life when her infirmities and especially her total blindness occasioned her so much suffering? Yes indeed, my very dear Sisters, our good, dear Miss Ellis has done much for the Daughters of the Cross:—she has bestowed her riches on our dear English Province, but more than this she has been a continual source of edification for us on account of her many virtues, the remembrance of which will ever remain engraven in our memory.

A deep and sacred debt of gratitude now remains for us—that of hastening by our prayers and suffrages, her eternal possession of the Beatific Vision. May God grant her eternal rest and reward her a hundredfold for all she has done for us! May He help us to imitate the beautiful example of the virtues she has set us! May we employ the gifts He has given us, only and solely for His greater glory!

The grave of the Ellis Sisters at the Downes
By their fruits you shall know them (Matthew 7:16)

Notes

1. A reference to the new St Anthony's Hospital at Cheam.
2. The magazine of St Philomena's School at Carshalton.
3. The Feast of the birth of Mary, 8 September 1909.
4. Gardner had come with Frances from Waltham Place.
5. Frances paid the salaries of chaplains at Hayle and possibly other DoC houses. The annual rate was £100.
6. Archbishop Bourne visited Carshalton.
7. Queen Victoria.
8. Bishop Charles Graham, who had retired from the see of Plymouth the previous year, to spend his last days being cared for by the nuns at Hayle.
9. A fly is a light fast carriage, drawn by a single horse, in this case driven by Gardner the gardener.
10. 'Behold the high priest', the opening words of a motet usually sung in church on the arrival or installation of a bishop. The scroll had been worked by Sr Jeanne de la Croix.
11. Monsignor Hugh Jackman, chancellor of Westminster Archdiocese and close confidant of Cardinal Bourne.
12. Bourne was at Downside on Wednesday 1 May 1912 to bless new school buildings.
13. 'In the regions (of the infidels).' A formula used in a bishop's usually honorific title after the name of a defunct diocese conquered by Islam. Tiberias is a town on the west bank of the Sea of Galilee which was under Crusader control from 1099 to 1187.
14. The 'bear' presumably was a bear-shaped container, and 'Cap' perhaps the name of a cat or other pet in the convent at Carshalton, well known to both Frances and Iphigènie.
15. The schoolgirls at St Philomena's, Carshalton.
16. Iraq in those days was known as Mesopotamia.
17. See Chapter 3, p. 38.

18. The McKenzies were leading brewers in Co. Tyrone, and prominent members of the (Anglican) Church of Ireland. Alexander McKenzie, who built Donaghmore House, married Jane Lyle of the family that formed half of the Tate & Lyle sugar dynasty. Quite likely the house was built with sugar money.

7

CHURCHES FINANCED BY FRANCES ELLIS

Many churches owe their existence, in whole or in part, to the generosity of Miss Frances Ellis. They number forty, including thirty-five in Southwark, although, as we have seen, Canon St John asserted in 1909 that she had supported thirty-six. He may have got the number wrong—he made the statement in a pamphlet stating his case against Bishop Amigo after he had resigned as diocesan treasurer, a time when he was under great pressure and probably overwrought—and it is unclear whether he was speaking only about Southwark churches. In 1910 Southwark covered South London, Kent, Surrey and Sussex.[1] But the main demand for new churches was in South London, and that was the principal focus of the partnership between Miss Ellis and Canon St John.

As none of their correspondence has survived, it is impossible to say whether St John knew about her benefactions in the Plymouth Diocese; but he visited her there and it seems probable that she would have included news of her Cornish projects in her letters to him.

Of the forty churches Frances Ellis built, the first, and by far the most costly, was in the Anglican Diocese of Oxford.[2] Thirty-three were in Southwark, two in Arundel & Brighton (formerly part of Southwark), three in the Diocese of Plymouth and one in the Diocese of Brentwood (formerly part of Westminster).[3] All but two are still active churches. The Catholic churches are listed by their modern diocese and in the order of the first celebration of Mass. The tally does not include chapels in the various convents of the Daughters of the Cross of Liège which she supported.

Anglican Diocese of Oxford

St John the Evangelist, Littlewick Green, Berkshire (1893)
Architect: E. J. Shrewsbury

Littlewick Green lies off the A4 Bath Road three miles west of Maidenhead, and close to the former Ellis family home at Waltham Place. In 1893, Frances Ellis gave £15,000—a very large sum in those days—to build, furnish and endow this pretty Victorian Gothic church.

The area had always been heavily wooded, and historically its few inhabitants would have walked two miles to White Waltham church, next door to the Ellis' home at Waltham Place. In the early 19th century, the lack of provision for the locals' souls led to the construction of a wooden meeting house used by a variety of mostly non-conformist sects. In the later years of the century the Methodists took over. But new suburban building and a growing population in the area prompted the Church of England to erect a new parish.

The church, which seats 125, was designed by a Maidenhead architect, E. J. Shrewsbury, and built by R. Silver and Sons of nearby Tittle Row. In contrast to her later utilitarian brick churches in Southwark, St John's is built of finely dressed blue Pennant stone from Wales. The Arts and Crafts interior is also of high quality, with oak furniture, brass fittings and a beautifully tiled floor.

St John the Evangelist C of E Church, Littlewick Green

St John's was consecrated by the Bishop of Oxford, William Stubbs, on 27 December 1893, the Feast of St John the Evangelist. Stubbs was a High Churchman and an eminent historian, whose most noted work was *The Constitutional History of England*.

The church is cruciform in shape and has a small two-bell tower at the west end. Since its construction it has been further adorned with a fine east window by James

Silvester Sparrow. The four-lighted window tells the story of the Nativity.

Today St John's is one of the three churches of the parish of Burchetts Green, the others being St Mary the Virgin, Hurley Green and St James the Less, Stubbings.

CATHOLIC ARCHDIOCESE OF SOUTHWARK

St Mildred, Minster-in-Thanet, (1901)

Minster is near the western shore of Thanet, away from the sea. It was the site in pre-Reformation times of a famous community of nuns, dating back to the 7th century. St Eafe or Domneva (contraction of Domina Eafe), great-grand-daughter of that King Ethelbert of Kent who had welcomed St Augustine in 597, was granted the land as wergild for the murder of two of her brothers by King Egberht of Kent.[4] The Kentish Royal Legend recounts that she asked Egberht to give her as much land as her pet deer could run round. The deer duly covered a good part of Thanet, forcing the king to give her much more land than he had anticipated. She established a convent, whose third Abbess was St Mildred, one of the most popular saints of Anglo-Saxon England. The abbey had a long and complex history, which included being sacked by Vikings in the 9th century. Eventually it was abolished with all the other religious houses by King Henry VIII.

In the late 19th century, the Sisters of Mercy established a house in the village of Minster, though not on the site of the old convent. Abbot Bergh of St Augustine's was anxious to help them stay there and wanted to build a church. On 3 October 1900 he wrote to Bishop Bourne:

Seeing an opportunity of further advantage to our works here, I asked Mr Lee for help towards building Minster Chapel. He has given me £500 for the purpose. As this ought now to become an 'Oratorium Publicum' with entrance from the road, instead of being a mere nuns' chapel (with permission to the faithful to hear Mass and to assist at these services) I have formally to ask your Lordship's sanction for the building of a chapel and public oratory on our land at Minster. The sum to be expended is not very large and it will be a humble edifice. Still it will be a great benefit there, and considering there is no likelihood of a great increase of the village, it will permanently provide for its spiritual needs.

Bishop Bourne gave his assent to Abbot Bergh, and Miss Ellis had already provided the money through her agent Mr Lee. The site was next to the house occupied by the Sisters of Mercy. The foundation stone having been laid in late 1900, the little chapel was swiftly built, and Bishop Bourne consecrated it on 26 June 1901 with the most elaborate ritual. Over the door is a statue of Eafe and her deer. As with all the Catholic churches on Thanet it was the responsibility of the Abbot of Ramsgate, and one of his monks would have said Mass there for the parishioners and the Sisters of Mercy.[5] The Sisters left Minster in 1920 and were followed for a couple of years by the Sisters of the Poor Servants of the Mother of God.

An early priest in charge of St Mildred's was Fr Aidan MacDonald OSB (1845–1922), a distinguished classical scholar and one-time missionary in India and China. He was also a dedicated chaplain to the Catholic inmates of the Thanet Union and was well known and liked throughout Thanet.[6] Several thousand people attended his funeral in 1922. *The Tablet* reported:

> Further testimony to the respect in which he was held by the non-Catholic population was given last Sunday by the Protestant Vicar of Minster, who, in the course of a sermon to his people, alluded to the many virtues and the splendid character of Father Aidan Macdonald. But above all will he be missed by his brethren on account of his lively, cheerful disposition, his unfailing courtesy, and his wonderful kindliness and charity. [7]

The former Church of St Mildred, Minster-in-Thanet

In 1935 a relic of St Mildred was deposited in the church. It had been obtained by the Ramsgate monks from the St Lebuïnus church in Deventer, Netherlands. St Mildred's relics had originally been taken to Deventer by Egelsin, the last Saxon abbot of St Augustine's, Canterbury, presumably to prevent them falling into Norman hands. Their return to Thanet after 869 years would have delighted Frances Ellis, had she lived to see it.

The church continued to be served by monks from Ramsgate until the outbreak of the Second World War. Fr Augustine Keniry OSB, who served from 1939 to 1961, built a presbytery and was the first resident priest. The Benedictines were forced by lack of manpower to hand the church over to the Archdiocese in 1983.

In 1937, a community of Bavarian Benedictine nuns arrived at Minster and began to restore the medieval abbey ruins. St Mildred's Abbey flourished, and in 1993 the sisters built a fine modern chapel incorporating elements of the ancient building. The sisters welcomed lay worshippers to their services, but the little church in the village carried on until the 21st century.

Fr Kevin Fitzgerald, a diocesan priest, was offered the parish in 2006, but turned it down on the grounds that the church was in a poor state of repair, and the congregation very small. He suggested that if the sisters, whose own conventual Mass was at 8.30 on Sunday morning, would allow a second Mass to be celebrated for the public later in the morning, church, presbytery and large garden could be sold. This happened in 2009, and the church was in due course sold and converted to a private house. On the outside it retains its ecclesiastical character, including the fine statue of St Eafe with her deer.

St Ethelbert and St Gertrude, Ramsgate (1902)

Architect: Peter Paul Pugin

Through her friendship with the Benedictines at St Augustine's Abbey, Frances Ellis was aware that the splendid Pugin abbey church was too small for the growing number of Catholics in Ramsgate and was at the wrong end of town. Accordingly, she bought a house in Hereson Road, a mile east of the Abbey in the town proper. This she gave to the Diocese of Southwark, together with £3,100 for the building costs, and a further £4,000 as an endowment for a resident priest. Canon St John was her key collaborator, and he was one of the trustees of the church. The architect chosen was Pugin's youngest son, Peter Paul Pugin, also a specialist in Gothic.

Miss Ellis chose the dedication of the church to SS Ethelbert and Gertrude. St Ethelbert was the King of Kent who had welcomed Augustine to Canterbury, and whose own conversion to Christianity led to the mass baptism of the people of Kent. To St Gertrude of course she had a special devotion.

When it was opened by Bishop Bourne on 25 June 1901, the *East Kent Times and Advertiser* reported:

> The Church is in the early decorated style of Gothic architecture, and in dimensions is 80 feet long and 30 feet wide. There is a fine Gothic altar, with columns of Labrador granite, polished at Aberdeen. A stone statue weighing about six hundredweight represents St. Gertrude in an attitude of prayer, holding in one hand the Sacred Heart. A mouse running up a crosier represents the Temptation of the Devil. In the Lady Chapel there is a beautiful statue of the Virgin of Lourdes; to the right of the altar is a statue of the Sacred Heart. The confessional and seats are of Gothic

design from designs by Mr Pugin and furnished by Messrs Bolton Bros., of Cheltenham; the tabernacle of worked brass is by Hardman, of Birmingham. Externally, the church is executed in stock bricks and stone dressings. The charming traceried windows are lead glazed. The open timber roof is thickly traceried with Westmoreland green slating. There is a very fine west window. On the north side at the eastern end is a sacristy, while the south, or Hereson Road frontage, is the porch and the Lady Chapel. There is a gallery at the west end. The internal wood-work is pitch pine and there is a solid wood block floor covering concrete. It is intended that a chancel be added along with the erection of a graceful tower. Altogether, St Ethelbert's Church is a worthy addition to the public buildings of the district.[8]

In October of 1902, Bishop Bourne issued a pastoral letter dealing with building work in the Diocese. Of St Ethelberts he said:

> On August 17 the new church of SS. Ethelbert and Gertrude was opened on the East Cliff at Ramsgate, thus fulfilling the hopes, expressed in 1897, that a permanent memorial might soon be erected in that town of the Centenary of St. Augustine kept with such solemnity in that year. This church will render very great service to the development of religion in this important borough.

A presbytery was sited just to the east of the church, and during the First World War, Belgian refugees built a fine church hall. In 1928, St Ethelbert's Primary School was built on spare land next to the church given by Miss Ellis. The school has a good reputation, especially for religious instruction.

St Ethelbert's Church, Ramsgate

For the next 80 years, St Ethelbert's prospered as a parish. All its clergy were monks from St Augustine's until 1980, when a terrible tragedy occurred. Fr Edward Hull OSB, who was 88 years old, and his housekeeper Ethel Maude Lelean, aged 72, were murdered by a man who had called at the presbytery. Fr Hull had been a wartime RAF chaplain and headmaster of the abbey school. The killer was convicted of manslaughter due to diminished responsibility and sent to Broadmoor. The old presbytery was subsequently replaced with a modern building.

The Benedictines handed the parish back to the Archdiocese in 2010 as they prepared to leave Ramsgate after 160 years. The first diocesan parish priest was Fr Marcus Holden, who was also responsible for St Augustine's Abbey church. In 2012 Archbishop Peter Smith elevated the abbey church to the Shrine of St

Augustine, in succession to the original shrine at Canterbury, which had been destroyed in 1538.

In 2018 Fr Christopher Basden, who had been an inspirational parish priest at St Bede's Clapham Park for 25 years (see below), took over St Ethelbert's, while Fr Holden moved to St Bede's. It is hoped to restore some of the Puginesque splendour that was stripped out of the church after Vatican II.

Our Lady Help of Christians and St Joseph, Folkestone (1902)

Architect: Leonard Stokes

This fine Perpendicular Gothic church was built in 1889 to the design of the prolific Catholic architect Leonard Stokes. However, the church had continued to bear a debt, and Bishop Bourne, in his 1902 pastoral letter, noted:

> A benefactress, who desires to remain unknown, has contributed £500 towards the extinction of the debt on the church at Folkestone, and we trust that this generous example will encourage the faithful of that town to renewed and determined effort to help their pastor in his continued exertions to liquidate the remaining debt as speedily as possible.

Although the grant of £500 cannot be securely attributed to Miss Ellis, it fits with her involvement at the time with the Catholic Church in East Kent. It also brings the number of Southwark churches she assisted in whole or in part up to the thirty-six cited ten years later by Canon St John. In the 21st century Our Lady Help of Christians was given over to the former Anglicans of the Ordinariate of Our Lady of Walsingham—a destiny which might have pleased Frances Ellis, herself a convert from the Church of England.

St Gertrude, South Croydon (1903)
Architect: F. A. Walters

The first Ellis church to be built in the London area was a long time in gestation. Plans for a new mission in South Croydon were put forward in 1895 by Fr Joseph Wilhelm of Shoreham. Writing to Bishop Vaughan, he stated the case plainly:

> In 1894, the South Ward of Croydon... had 14,475 inhabitants ... Since then a great number of buildings, forming at least four new streets, have been erected. Others are in course of erection. These are small villas, houses of medium size and cottages. The principal property in the ward is Haling Park which, in the next generation, will pass into Catholic hands. The present holder is an old lady whose son has married a French lady, a Catholic with Catholic children.[9]

Fr Wilhelm had in mind a building plot on Warham Road, not far from the site of the present Whitgift School. This was valued at £900, to which he added £300 for a temporary chapel. But in 1898, Fr John McKenna, the parish priest at Our Lady of Reparation, Croydon, wrote to Canon St John to register his objection to the site, which he felt was too close to his own church. He wrote: 'I am not looking in any way to the interests of this church, but to the general prosperity of Catholicity in Croydon.'

St John agreed with him, and the plan was abandoned. In 1903 a different plot was purchased on the Purley Road a mile or so to the south. Frances Ellis paid the £3,000 cost of land and the construction of church and presbytery. The architect was the eminent Frederick Arthur Walters (1849–1931), who was responsible for designing 50 Catholic churches including those at Buckfast and Ealing Abbeys. St Gertrude's is in a simplified Romanesque style and lacks the characteristic Ellis round window on the liturgical west elevation.

St Gertrude's Church, South Croydon

Perhaps because of the speed with which the project had been completed, there was trouble finding the right priest for the job. It was first offered to Fr Germain Julien OFM, a French Franciscan based at Lewisham, who was reluctant to accept it without an express order from his superior. Fr McKenna objected that the prospective congregation was largely Irish. He wrote to Canon Moore at the Cathedral: 'We want an Irishman there with a kind heart and a fluent tongue.' His candidate, an Irish Franciscan, Fr O'Connor OFM, was a short-term rector from June 1903 to June 1904, when Fr Charles Turner took over.

Early documentation of the South Croydon mission is sparse. Although free of debt (thanks to Miss Ellis) it was clearly impoverished. The Southwark archives preserve letters from Fr Turner, that reflect both the hardship and his evident discontent. He had been moved from Ashford, Kent, and made it clear to Bishop Amigo that he felt he was in South Croydon on false pretences.

'I knew absolutely I need not have left Ashford. But two letters from yourself and one from the V.G. made it appear to me that I would be doing your will if I took Croydon. With the knowledge I have now I should certainly have stayed in Ashford.' There was insufficient money to live on, let alone improve the church. He lamented the lack of kneelers: 'It is hard to expect respectable people to kneel on the floor.' Fr Turner was also at odds with Fr McKenna at Croydon, who, he complained, benefitted disproportionately from additional chaplaincy income from local institutions.

Fr Turner was succeeded in 1907 by Fr Rudolph Bullesbach, who had come from Tooting where he had been notably successful in pioneering Catholic worship.

The 1908 visitation return shows that the was free of debt except possibly on the organ. The Stations of the Cross were erected in 1910. Fr Bullesbach was succeeded in 1914 by Fr John Torrance, who remained through World War I and was succeeded in October 1920, by Fr Edward Larkin. That year the was raised to the dignity of a parish. Fr Larkin built a new sanctuary at the cost of £1,500, and also a new chapel at Selsdon for £800.

By 1926, the parish was well established. In the returns for that year, Fr Terence Fichter stated that the number of Catholics in the district was about 600, while an average of 550 attended the Lenten Masses. Nevertheless, Fr Fichter's successor Fr William Pritchard (brother of Fr Erconwald Pritchard, first rector of St Francis de Sales Stockwell—see next church) lamented that a good number of his flock still attended Our Lady of Reparation rather than St Gertrude's.

The baptistry, gallery, confessional, sacristy and porch had been completed in October 1935 at a cost of £2,943 plus nearly £1,000 for furnishings. The finishing touch, a new high altar, was consecrated on 27 November 1936. Fr Pritchard's request that the church be consecrated that day as well was turned down by the Bishop, who suggested that they wait until the following summer and better weather, when they 'could hand over another church to the Lord.' In the event St Gertrude's was consecrated on 25 June 1937 by Bishop William Brown.

A bomb fell next to the church on 11th May 1941 and caused severe damage to the right or epistle side of the building. It destroyed the organ and the organ gallery, and for the rest of the war Mass was said in St Anne's convent. The damage was not fully repaired until 1951. The organ gallery was not replaced, and instead a new window was opened on that side of the nave, considerably improving the lighting in the church.

In the 21st century, St Gertrude's remains a lively, buoyant parish community with a particular emphasis on social action as well as prayer.

St Francis de Sales and St Gertrude, Larkhall Lane, Stockwell (1903)

Architect: F. W. Tasker

The first church Frances Ellis built in London proper was St Francis de Sales and St Gertrude, Larkhall Lane, Stockwell, designed by the well-known Irish ecclesiastical architect Francis William Tasker. Francis Bourne had been born in a house on Larkhall Lane and had a special devotion to St Francis de Sales. He was still Bishop of Southwark when building work began, but by the time it was opened he had been made Archbishop of Westminster. St Gertrude of course was Miss Ellis' favourite saint, and probably her confirmation name.

The site was about halfway between St Anne's Vauxhall (1900) and the great Redemptorist church of St Mary's at Clapham Common (1851). Stockwell had been a generally well-to-do suburb, but in 1890 the opening of Stockwell tube station as the then-southern terminus of the Northern Line led to development of factories and low-income housing and a change to a more socially diverse character. Many of the new inhabitants were Catholics from Ireland or the continent. A Catholic chapel was briefly opened in 1899 in Stockwell Lane but closed later the same year when the rector joined the Redemptorists at Clapham.

In early 1902 land was found at Larkhall Lane, and the church and presbytery (behind the church) built with money from Miss Ellis. As usual, no precise records survive to show how the process was organised, or by whom. It is built of London stock brick, on a Greek cross plan, with a large round window over the entrance.

St Francis de Sales and St Gertrude, Larkhall Lane

Its first rector, the recently ordained Fr Francis Erconwald Pritchard (always known as Fr Erconwald, or, by his fellow priests, 'Erky'), celebrated Mass there for the first time on 9 October 1903, his intention being for 'the most forgotten priest'. Other intentions he recorded later included 'For the Soul next leaving Purgatory', 'For the Grace of a Happy Death', 'For the Conversion of England' and 'For the most forgotten Soul'. Fr Erconwald remained until 1908, and subsequently enjoyed a long and fruitful ministry culminating as parish priest of Our Lady of Pity & St Simon Stock at Putney. As a canon of Southwark Cathedral, he was also the author of a regular 'Letter from Melchisedech', highly regarded within the Diocese in the years before the Second World War.[10]

The parish was sorely afflicted by both world wars. In the first war 29 men from the community were killed, the last on the day before the armistice. In the second war it was badly damaged by bombing intended for the factories to the north of the nearby Wandsworth Road. Houses next door to the church were destroyed by bombing in 1941, and never rebuilt, being replaced by a recreation area. Though the parish priest Fr Byrne confessed himself terrified by the bombing, he remained at his post and continued to offer Mass every day. The damage was initially made good by donations from the parishioners and later with a grant from the War Damage Commission.

St Francis de Sales and St Gertrude remained a mission until 1959, when it was raised to the status of a parish. In 1982 a substantial and much-used parish hall was built in the space between the back of the church and the presbytery. In 1992 a narthex was added at the front of the church, as well as an enclosed and soundproofed gallery-cum-meeting room at the rear of the nave. The interior was also substantially upgraded at this time, with better natural light and flat roofed side aisles separated from the nave by circular columns.

Subsequent developments included the addition of a marble altar from St Anselm's in Hindhead inscribed on the front *Unigenitus Dei Filius qui est in sinu Patris* (the only begotten Son of God, who is in the bosom of the Father).[11]

The parish evolved significantly during its first century, reflecting the economic and social changes in the country at large. London had always attracted large numbers of immigrants, Irish mainly in the 19th and early 20th centuries, later joined by people from Europe and the old British Empire. Then came the Spanish and Portuguese who settled in numbers around the South Lambeth Road, followed by Ghanaians, Nigerians and other West African nationalities. The church was also the home of the Southwark Latin American chaplaincy: Fr Tom Heneghan, inspirational parish priest through the nineties and into the new millennium, had been a missionary in Ecuador and remained deeply devoted to the people of South

America. By 2002, when, with the debt paid, Archbishop Michael Bowen consecrated the church, St Francis de Sales and St Gertrude boasted a truly diverse congregation, reflected in the liturgy and the many parish groups.

Finally, it may be noted that Francis Bourne, Bishop of Southwark from 1897 to 1903, and Peter Smith, Archbishop of Southwark from 2010 to 2020, were both born within the modern bounds of the parish of St Francis de Sales.

St Gertrude, South Bermondsey (1903)

Architect: F. W. Tasker

The next church that Frances Ellis built in London was St Gertrude's, in Debnam's Road just off Rotherhithe New Road, south Bermondsey, then as now a densely populated area. Tucked in close to the main railway lines running from London Bridge towards Kent, it is a plain brick building with a large circular window, which was the trademark of most of the subsequent 'Ellis boxes'. It is in the form of a Greek cross set in a square, with two chapels to one side. The attached presbytery was built at the same time. The architect was again Francis Tasker, and the builder William Romaine, the advisor to Canon St John castigated by the diocesan historian Fr Michael Clifton (see Chapter 4). It has been described as 'utilitarian sub-Romanesque'.

St Gertrude's was a poor church in a poor parish. The Diocese had owned the site in Debnam's Road for some years before the church was built. This may well have been one of the property speculations for which Canon St John was later criticised. Originally some humble cottages were let to tenants, but in 1896, after a demand from the local authority for extensive repairs, the Diocese decided to close the houses as the existing tenancies expired. The cottages were demolished, and church construction began in 1902. St Gertrude's was officially opened on 17 November 1903, six weeks after St Francis de Sales, Stockwell. The first rector was Fr Gifkins, and he must have had a difficult time. *The Tablet* reported:

> It is true that the church and presbytery are the gift of a benefactress, but all the furniture of church and house has to be provided. It is hardly necessary to point out that the parishioners of the new mission are blest with little of this world's goods, and therefore the Rector, the Rev. M. G. Gifkins, will be very grateful for any help towards this and the many other expenses entailed by the formation of a new parish. Mass is said on Sundays at 9 a.m. and 11 a.m. and evening service at 7 p.m. Confessions are heard (in English, French, and German) on Saturdays from 6 till 9.[12]

St Gertrude's Church, South Bermondsey

The first episcopal visitation by Bishop Amigo was on Sunday 26th February 1905. He thanked the (anonymous) benefactress of the church and praised the congregational singing.

In 1906 Fr Gifkins was honoured at Rotherhithe Town Hall on the silver jubilee of his ordination and for his devoted work in Bermondsey and throughout South London, especially on behalf of Catholic education.

That same year, Fr Arthur Mostyn, a priest at St Andrew's Thornton Heath (also supported by Frances Ellis), was asked by Bishop Amigo to take over St Gertrude's. Fr Mostyn was shocked by the state of the place, and wrote to the Bishop:

> There is not a stick of furniture in the house and the walls are soaking wet. I haven't any money and I really can't see how I am to furnish a house without it... If your Lordship cannot let me have some money, I feel I shall have to decline the mission.

It seems the money was found, and Fr Mostyn moved in. In 1908 he was able to report that the church was in good order, though unpainted. There was room for 200, worship was 'well organised' but attendance was only 'fair'. Offertory income was a little over £100 for the year, with an additional £73 raised from concerts staged in support of decoration. There was the bare minimum of one chalice, two ciboria and one monstrance. He opened the church only for Mass and confession, an indication that the area was a rough one subject to burglary and vandalism. During the previous year, one lasting a week had been given. But there were sixteen altar servers, one confraternity (the Children of Mary) and the organ was in good repair. Fr Mostyn lamented that there was no school to visit.

In the 21st century, St Gertrude's continues to minister to a large and diverse congregation. Where a hundred years earlier the majority would have been Irish, today it is African. The church remains, as it always has been, plain on the outside and austere inside, the interior nevertheless expressing a quiet and prayerful dignity.

Holy Cross, Sangley Road, Catford (1904)
Architect: F. W. Tasker

In 1903 Frances Ellis purchased a site at Sangley Road, Catford, in southeast London, intended to relieve the pressure on Lewisham, where the parish kept outgrowing the buildings available to it (in fact the current church of St Saviour and St John the Baptist and St John the Evangelist, Lewisham was built several years after Holy Cross). The foundation stone was quickly laid, and Bishop Amigo celebrated the inaugural Mass at Holy Cross on 14th September 1904, the Feast of the Triumph of the Cross. The presbytery next door to the church was actually finished first.

Holy Cross is the last Ellis Box positively known to have been designed by F. W. Tasker, who died the year it was completed (though see St Thomas Apostle, Nunhead and other possible Tasker churches). Architecturally it is very similar to his churches at South Bermondsey and Larkhall Lane, being built of London stock brick on a Greek cross plan, with a round window. Initially there was only one chapel, dedicated to Our Lady. The official opening on the Feast of the Exaltation of the Holy Cross was an elaborate affair:

> It is a plain, unpretentious structure built on the plans of the late Mr. Tasker, and is the gift of a lady whose name is withheld from the public. For the

present it is to be served from Lewisham, but it is intended by-and-by to support a resident priest. The want has been felt for a long time in a neighbourhood which is rapidly being covered with miles upon miles of new houses, and experience shows that wherever a new church is built a congregation is found to fill it. In Catford alone ten miles of streets have been added in ten years, and every day the houses continue to be multiplied. The new church is dedicated to St. Cross, and on the Feast of the Exaltation of the Holy Cross it was accordingly solemnly opened. The Bishop of Southwark was present and preached. He referred to the generous donor to whom their gratitude was due for a free gift which left to the people the charge only of supplying the furniture and maintaining the services. A presbytery was being built, and schools were needed to make the mission complete. Sir John Knill, Bart., and Lady Knill attended in state, and a large congregation after Mass was presented to the Bishop by Father Tatum at an informal reception. The celebrant was the Rector, the Rev. G. B. Tatum, M.A., and he was assisted by Father Wallis as deacon, Father Reville as subdeacon, and Father Pritchard master of ceremonies. The Bishop was attended by Canon O'Halloran as assistant priest, Canon St. John and Father Armstrong as deacons at the throne, and Father L. Fichter as ceremoniarius. A priests' choir, with Father Minnett at the organ, supplied the music, which was Gregorian. They were Fathers Wilderspin, Sheehan, Sprankling, Shepperd, Hayes, Brown, McKenna and Julien.[13]

Holy Cross, Catford, with the presbytery on the left

The new mission church was bare, apart from the altar, and everything had to be found by the parishioners. Miss Lacon presented a relic of the True Cross as well as a sacristy bell. Mr Whiting gave the pulpit and font, which he had carved himself of Farleigh Down stone. Miss Stephanie Horspool made and presented the first altar frontal. Miss Tucker gave altar linen, and Mr Hodgson some candlesticks. Vestments came from the Sacred Heart convent in Brighton, while another convent in Balham presented a chalice and ciborium. The altar crucifix and sanctuary lamp were donated anonymously. The statue of the sacred heart of Jesus was presented by Mr and Mrs Harrington in memory of their son Eric.

For a few months Holy Cross was served from Lewisham, until a resident rector, Fr Edward Escarguel, was appointed in January 1905. He was one of the first diocesan priests trained at Wonersh, having been ordained in 1895. Fr Escarguel remained for a quarter of a century and worked hard to establish the Catford mission and build the Holy Cross community.

The first two baptisms, of Elizabeth Weeks and Agnes Williams, took place on 19 March 1905. Since then, nearly 5,000 have been baptised. Bishop Peter Amigo confirmed Martin O'Dowd on 10 May 1908, the first of nearly 2,500 confirmations. The first wedding took place in 1905, since when there have been more than 1,500.

Major developments in the early years included the construction of the sanctuary, sacristy and organ in 1924.

An influential figure was Fr Joseph Fagan, the sixth parish priest, who served 33 years from 1956 until 1989. From the start he was determined to involve the people in running the parish and planning for the future. A gregarious man, he was popular with fellow priests as much as with the laity. Among many other achievements he built the primary school, on land behind the church and which was opened in 1975. Rated 'Outstanding' by Ofsted, it is the only Catholic school in the parish, and is permanently over-subscribed.

Holy Cross was consecrated in 1960, and there have been many architectural changes and improvements. It has always been a centre of mission and evangelisation in a vibrant part of London, with a constantly shifting population. In 1996, the growth of the Ghanaian community within the parish (and across London) led to the appointment of Fr James Kwabena Enin as its chaplain, based in the Holy Cross presbytery.

Music has always been central to worship at Holy Cross. Gabriele Finaldi, director of the National Gallery, is a long-term parishioner, and is a cantor and organist. From its earliest days, when there were at best 200 Mass attenders,

Holy Cross has grown to encompass 600 families, with typical Sunday Mass attendance of 750 parishioners.

St Gregory, Garratt Lane, Earlsfield, London (1904, destroyed in World War II)

Architect: F. W. Tasker (?)

The St Gregory's we see today replaced the church built by Miss Ellis in 1904. That was destroyed by enemy action in WW2. The original was a typical Ellis Box, plain, of London stock brick and in Romanesque style. It may have been built to the designs of F. W. Tasker, but this is speculation. It was named for St Gregory the Great, the 1300th anniversary of whose death fell in 1904.

From the 1890's, there had been a growing need for a church in Earlsfield, whose people had to travel to St Thomas Becket in Wandsworth. The population was poor, and constantly shifting, and difficult to keep tabs on.

Bishop Bourne, as he then was, announced in 1903 that a site had been secured on Dunts Hill, and the church and presbytery were raised by local builders and boys from the Southwark Rescue Society (the chief of Canon St John's charitable enterprises) in the summer of 1904. It was plain inside as well as out, and there were complaints about the cold.

The first parish priest was Fr Henry Aust-Lawrence, who served two years. He celebrated the first Mass on Sunday 20 November 1904. In his homily he asked for a spirit of unity which would be vital if the mission were to succeed. That Sunday afternoon, sixty children arrived to be enrolled in catechism classes, and it was clear that the mission was truly launched

But it was a poor parish, which depended on donations from the people themselves. They began to give furniture and plates, vases for the altar and kneelers. A neighbouring priest gave two sets of vestments. Surviving correspondence between Fr Henry and the Diocese provides evidence of the poverty of the parish, and of the priest himself. Weekly takings averaged only 22 shillings (£1.10p). In one letter Fr Henry complains that Canon St John, the treasurer, had promised him £50 but sent only £25.

The best known of Fr Henry's successors in the early days of St Gregory's was the newly ordained Fr Benedict Williamson, who served from 1909–1915. Williamson was a holy and remarkably talented man, who as a history of the parish records, was 'architect, monk, refounder of a religious Order, preacher and retreat-giver, spiritual adviser, newspaper correspondent, friend and benefactor to countless people.' Fr Benedict's prodigious energy was directed at many causes, not least the bringing of souls to God: through the course of his life, he was instrumental in countless conversions and many vocations to the priesthood and religious life. Although he did not design St Gregory's, he was architect of 20 other English churches (including seven of Miss Ellis'), a number of presbyteries and Tyburn Convent.

Williamson believed strongly in display. He did not think the Catholic church should be shy. He led public processions round Earlsfield 'fully vested, with acolytes and a holy water bearer', he blessed houses and shops at Rogationtide, he held open air meetings to explain Catholic teachings.

At St Gregory's he transformed the interior into what the Tablet called, simply, 'Rome'. His model was San Gregorio on the Caelian Hill, the church attached to an ancient Camaldolese monastery whose roots go back to Pope Gregory the Great in the 6th century; it was the very church from which St Augustine and his forty monks set out for England in 597. In 1910—with further financial assistance from Miss Ellis—Fr Benedict installed a new marble altar and stone columns, a baldachin over the altar, and new communion rails inspired by San Clemente, another Roman church. Archbishop Bourne remarked approvingly: 'Fr Benedict has turned a barn into a very good church.'

Fr Benedict had for many years been eager to revive the men's side of the Bridgettine Order which before the Reformation had featured twin houses of men and women under an Abbess. In modern times there were Bridgettine nuns but no monks. In 1915 he resigned from Earlsfield to begin such a community but gave up after a year and became an army chaplain. He served eighteen months on the Western front, was popular with the soldiers, was wounded and gassed. After the war, Bishop Amigo was prepared to send him back to Earlsfield, but only as a diocesan priest, not as the abbot of an unofficial monastic community.

As Williamson's damaged lungs were unequal to the rigours of the English winters, he retired to Rome and spent the rest of his life there, working as a hospital chaplain and preacher. He admired Benito Mussolini during the early years of his rule, contributing to a laudatory book about *il Duce*.[14] It is not clear whether his views changed as the fascist government became more oppressive and warlike. He died aged 80 in 1948 and was sadly aware of the destruction of St Gregory's in the summer of 1944.

Incendiary bombs fell on the church the night of 18 February 1944, and rendered it unusable, but the contents of the sacristy were saved, and the hall prepared for use as an emergency church. Four months later a flying bomb completely destroyed the church, the hall and the presbytery. The parish priest Fr Hayes and the housekeeper were both seriously injured but there were no fatalities. The neighbouring Congregational Church provided a temporary place of worship, and the Anglicans generously found accommodation for the clergy.

Reconstruction commenced with a new presbytery in 1952, while the new church itself was opened in 1956 and blessed by Archbishop Cowderoy on 30 September 1957. The new, larger St Gregory's bears no resemblance to its predecessor. The parish has continued to thrive.

St James the Great, Elm Grove, Peckham Rye (1905)

Architect: F. W. Tasker (?)

With money from Miss Ellis, the Diocese bought land and two Regency houses in the Holly Grove area of Peckham Rye, where there was a growing Catholic population. In 1899 a guidebook assessed Elm Grove thus: '... trees, shady, but has seen its best days. Lower middle class, occasional servants. Peckham Liberal Club here.' [15]

Construction began in 1904 and was completed the following year. The church is a typical Ellis design, plain, Romanesque, in London stock brick and with a round window on the liturgical west front. The architect's name is not recorded, but it looks very much the work of Francis Tasker, who died in 1904.[16] The two Regency houses became and remain to this day the presbytery. As in all Ellis churches, there was to be a monthly Mass, in perpetuity, for Holy Souls in Purgatory.

St James the Great, Peckham

The mission's first priest was Fr William Alton, who came from Chatham, where he had been a naval chaplain. The date of the first Mass is not recorded, but Fr Alton conducted the first baptism, of baby John Arrowsmith, on 27 August 1905. Attendance increased steadily during the first years, and in 1909 Alton was granted permission to add a second Sunday Mass. The Stations of the Cross were blessed and installed in 1906. Fr Alton retired after six years, it is said with a substantial naval pension. He left to St James a silver chalice given to him by his Chatham parishioners; it is still in use.

Fr Alton was succeeded in 1911 by Fr Reginald Pitts, who added the south aisle and the gabled entrance porch with Gothic window (not architecturally in keeping with the rest of the church, but attractive nonetheless). Bishop Amigo visited in 1912 and congratulated Fr Pitts on his instruction of the children of the parish. During his seven years, the church gained a monstrance, brass candelabra and a sanctuary carpet, and became altogether more welcoming. In 1915 the parishioners paid for a fine statue of St Anthony.

Fr Leo Fichter took over in 1918, and technically became the first parish priest when St James was declared a parish in 1920. This was despite a relatively small income and suggests that Miss Ellis' initial generosity ensured that the mission had not been saddled with much debt. Fr Fichter blazed a trail in Elm Grove by installing electric light in the church and presbytery. His successor, Fr Edward Larkin (1927–1933), added wooden panelling, and, with £1,500 left by Fr Fichter, installed a new altar. He also obtained from France a cast version of Leonardo's Last Supper which was used for many years as the altar frontal.

The Knights of St Columba bought a surplus army hut in 1928, and Fr Larkin allowed them to erect it in the presbytery garden to be used as a parish hall. The overall cost, including expanding and fireproofing the original hut, came to £400, which was met by the Knights themselves. In 1938 the Knights sold the hall to the parish for £225.

Following Fr Larkin's departure in 1933, two successive parish priests suffered emotional difficulties. One celebrated Mass so slowly that half the parishioners deserted Peckham Rye for Nunhead and other churches. This may have been related to his 'scruples'—an unhealthy obsession with some aspect of Catholic doctrine to the exclusion of all else. It was a poignant and painful situation. Eventually Bishop Amigo was forced to order him to resign. In his letter, Amigo wrote: 'Perhaps this trial will make you see that scruples do not please God, and that they prevent your usefulness in the priesthood. Do not lose heart, but pray very earnestly that with God's help you may yet be spared to work fruitfully for souls for many years.'

The next priest was of a nervous disposition, as became apparent when he fell out with the Dean of the Camberwell conference. Personal antipathy was compounded by a suggestion from the Dean that the priest should apply himself to the inhabitants of the new London County Council flats on Dog Kennel Hill. It was suggested that the Catholics there were being neglected, and their children were deserting the Catholic schools. The parish priest of St James vehemently disputed the Dean's account, and it is impossible after eighty years to tell who was in the right. The priest incurred Amigo's displeasure when he refused to be present for the Dean's statutory visitation, merely leaving the account books out for him to inspect. Eventually, in 1939, the dispute was sidestepped by the drastic measure of transferring St James from Camberwell to the Bermondsey deanery.

Fr Thomas Smith arrived in 1940.[17] He saw the parish through the Second World War and on to 1960. The war was hard on Peckham, lying on the track of bombers and V-weapons heading for central London. Numbers attending Mass fell as children were evacuated, civilian adults sought safer havens and many men and women joined the armed forces. But Fr Smith was staunch. Once, when the alarm sounded during Sunday morning Mass, he advised the congregation to shelter under the pews while he granted them a general absolution. In fact, the church survived the war more or less unscathed, although some debris from a disintegrating German plane fell through the roof of the church hall.

After the war, Fr Smith petitioned successfully for St James to be returned to the Camberwell deanery. He wrote to the Vicar General Mgr Cyril Cowderoy: 'My principal reason for wanting the change back is that many things arise in relations between this parish and Dulwich, Camberwell and Brixton, and could be so easily settled by meeting at Camberwell.' Cowderoy annotated the letter: 'Approved—notify Deans.'

The parish recovered quickly after the war. In 1945 there were only 267 at Sunday Mass, increasing to 500 in 1950 and 2,000 in 1961. The makeup of the parish also began to change. There had always been a strong Irish contingent, with further waves of immigration from Ireland in the 1950's and 1960's. And from about 1950 Caribbean immigrants also began to join the parish. Many were from St Lucia, and Fr Charles Walker became their chaplain. Since then, they have been joined by many other nationalities, notably Vietnamese and people from a number of African countries.

The huge increase in numbers attending Mass meant that even with up to seven Masses on a Sunday, the church was just too small to cope. One solution, in 1963, was to add a new north aisle which allowed a further 50 seats. In 1968 a choir loft and organ were installed in the northwest corner. Three years later a new sanctuary and other temporary structures were added. 'Temporary' because at the time the church stood in the path of a projected motorway.[18] The longer-term plan was to knock down the old church and use the garden to build a much larger one. The road scheme faded away, but despite that in 2009 a new plan for St James's was agreed with the council. However, the projected cost rose to £2.5 million, and a new parish priest, Fr Jack Dillon, who had been a missionary in Kenya, decided to abandon the plan as impractical.

Instead, he re-oriented the interior of the church by 180 degrees, so that the altar now stands beneath the rose window, at what was formerly the liturgical west end of the church. This solution seems to have worked better than the re-orientations at churches like Nunhead and West Norwood, where the altar was turned 90 degrees. Fr Dillon did not like the idea of an altar in the middle of the long wall because for the priest it was like "watching tennis", turning his head this way and that to see the congregation as he preached.

The parish has always been rich in societies. From the early days there were the Knights of St Columba and the Legion of Mary. By the 21st century there were the Society of Saint Vincent de Paul, the Archconfraternity of St Stephen, the Guild of the Blessed Sacrament and the Pioneers of the Sacred Heart.

In addition, the parish has become a focus of advocacy and advice for social issues. It works with local schools to document positive images of young people's activities within the community to counter negative stereotypes portrayed in the media. It helps run an advice service for people in the private rented sector. The parish also lobbies the local council to treat council tenants with greater consideration.

For most of its history there have been Catholic primary and secondary schools within reasonable traveling distance. St Thomas Apostle secondary school for boys opened at Nunhead in 1965 on the site of the former Marist convent that had been destroyed by wartime bombing. It retains a strong Catholic ethos and is rated 'outstanding' in all categories by Ofsted.

But it was not until 1987 that St James got its own primary school, also called St James the Great, 400 yards away just off the Peckham Road. This school had originally belonged to St Alban's in Herring Street but moved when the church and old school were demolished to make way for Burgess Park. It retained the name St Alban's when it moved for a number of years before becoming St James. The school is consistently rated 'good' by Ofsted, but 'outstanding' for Personal Development, Behaviour and Welfare

St Alban, Herring Street, South Walworth (1904)
Architect: Benedict Williamson (?)

Miss Ellis paid for St Alban's in Herring St in 1904, as a chapel of ease for English Martyrs, Walworth. No trace survives of either church or street. The once densely populated area south of Walworth, north of Camberwell and west of Peckham was pulled down after 1970, and turned, against much local opposition, into the 153-hectare (378-acre) Burgess Park, one of the largest in south London.

In the early 20th century, this was a crowded neighbourhood, with mixed residential and light industrial buildings. Unlike today, most of the inhabitants lived in small terraced houses, often cheek by jowl with noisy and noisome factories and workshops. Herring St was a small L-shaped turning off Neate St; the latter actually still exists within Burgess Park, though today it is a road without buildings. St Alban's was situated just at the dog-leg corner of Herring St, with the entrance facing due east. Liturgically, the church was oriented back to front. Across the way, and stretching down to Neate St, was a tannery, a particularly malodorous neighbour for a church and school.

The church was opened in September 1904, a week after the opening of Holy Cross Catford. *The Tablet* reported:

> It was solemnly opened on Wednesday last in presence of the Bishop. His lordship was attended by Canon St John and Fathers Newton, Armstrong and Fichter. The celebrant at the High Mass was Father Doubleday, who fitly shared in the inauguration of a work which has sprung from the fruit of his early labours in Walworth. Fathers Lutz and McCarthy assisted him, and Father Williams, rector of the parent mission, was master of ceremonies. The Vicar-General, Father Brown, preached. The church, like that at Catford, is the free gift of a lady whose name is withheld from publication, and is a welcome and much needed addition to a densely populated area of the poorer London. To make the mission complete a presbytery and schools are needed, and meanwhile the church will be served from the mother church of the English Martyrs.[19]

A surviving photograph from 1979 shows the (liturgical) north side of a modest brick building with only two lights in the clerestory. The church board displaying the times of Mass is in the middle of the north side, facing down Herring St towards Neate St. There is no record of the architect nor indeed much archival evidence about the mission. Stylistically the chapel, almost as tall as it is long, seems closer to Benedict Williamson than it does to Tasker.[20] Next to it was St Alban's school, which has also since disappeared. There is a record that the children of St Alban's would have their lunch at the neighbouring and much larger St George's C of E school—a notable early testament to ecumenical generosity.

Running parallel with Neate St was the Surrey Canal which connected to the Surrey Docks at Rotherhithe and enabled heavy goods to be transported to and from Camberwell. The banks of the canal were lined with warehouses. This is one of the reasons there was so much industry—and therefore employment—in the area. Unfortunately, the canal also gave the Luftwaffe an easy guide and aiming point when attacking South London by night. The area was hit hard during World War II. St Alban's suffered blast damage but was relatively easily repaired. The house next door was completely destroyed, while the school escaped serious damage. Late in the war, during 1944 and 1945, a number of V-weapons fell in the area.

The church was patched up after the war and continued to serve the neighbourhood until it was pulled down in 1987. Much of the congregation also disappeared along with their former dwellings. Those who remained were thereafter catered for by English Martyrs Walworth and Sacred Heart Camberwell. The school moved to Peckham, where it thrives still as St James's the Great RC Primary School, attached to the parish of St James the Great.

St Matthew, West Norwood, London SE27 (1905)

Architect: F. W. Tasker (?)

Following an unspecified donation from Frances Ellis, St Matthews' foundation stone was laid on 26th September 1904 and the church completed early the following year.[21] The first Mass was celebrated on 30 March 1905. A number of authorities state that the building is probably the work of Francis Tasker, who died in 1904. There is a similarity to other known Tasker churches, in particular the pairs of clerestory windows, each separated by a thick concrete mullion, on the side elevations. As usual it is of London stock brick with a slate roof.

In 1937 the church was lengthened by two bays added at the east end. In the Second World War it suffered bomb damage to the west end. After the war the architect D. Plaskett Marshall completely redesigned the west front in plum-coloured brick with red brick dressings. It is gabled, with a large central archway and recessed orders of brickwork, enclosing two smaller round-arched windows. Between the windows is a fine statue of St Matthew by Joseph Cribb (1892–1967), formerly an assistant to Eric Gill, who had worked with the master on the stations of the cross at Westminster Cathedral.

The congregation grew rapidly after the war, with rising prosperity and the arrival of many Catholic immigrants, especially from the Caribbean and Ireland. In 1972, it was decided to increase the capacity of the worship space by moving the altar from the east end of the church to the aisle in the middle of the south wall. Some of the square piers were removed to provide sufficient space for the new sanctuary. The architect was W. Stone. This re-orientation also took place in other Ellis churches in south London.

St Matthew's Church, West Norwood

Twelve years later the architect Derek Phillips designed a new narthex on the north side of the building with one of the two entrances facing the new altar. The access was now from the generous car park, an improvement on the old entrance which was directly off the pavement of the very busy High St, and adjacent to a bus stop. At the same time long horizontal windows were introduced into the south aisles, and over the years these have benefitted from the addition of stained glass.

A matching set of marble altar, font and lectern were installed between 1986 and 1992. Four stained glass windows of the Evangelists in striking reds and blues were also installed in 1992. Near the altar is a carved statue of St Patrick, and in the Blessed Sacrament chapel are statues of St Matthew and the Risen Christ carved in wood by the Mussner G. Vincenzo studio in northern Italy.

St Thomas Apostle, Evelina Road, Nunhead, London SE15 (1905)

Architect: F. W. Tasker (?)

Nunhead is an inner suburb of southeast London, adjoining Peckham and east Dulwich. Historically it formed part of the extensive Anglican parish of Camberwell and remained largely rural until the middle of the 19th century. The 52-acre Nunhead Cemetery was laid out in 1841, and in 1865 the railway was extended from Brixton to Crystal Palace via Nunhead. Development then began in earnest, and by the late 19th century Nunhead was a large mostly working-class community.

In 1903 Frances Ellis bought a smithy in Hollydale Road, near the corner of Evelina Road, as well as the former blacksmith's cottage next door. The latter served as the first presbytery. Together the cost of the site and the construction totalled £3,000. The church was close to the railway line and Nunhead Station.

St Thomas Apostle, a typical Ellis Box in London stock brick very similar to St Francis de Sales, Larkhall Lane, was completed in November 1905. That was a year after the death of F. W. Tasker, but it may be that he had already drawn up the plans for Miss Ellis when she bought the site in 1903. The first Mass was celebrated by Fr Peter Ryan, the priest in charge of the mission, on Sunday 5 November, and Bishop Amigo officially opened the church on the 10th. However, Amigo thought the church was too small and the presbytery inadequate.

Accordingly, a small piece of land was added, and the presbytery extended.

St Thomas Apostle, Nunhead

St Thomas Apostle began and remained for many years extremely poor, described by *The Tablet* in 1927 as the poorest parish in South London. Weekly offerings were accordingly low. At one stage Fr Ryan appealed to Bishop Amigo for £30 to pay tradesmen's bills.

Fr Stephen O'Beirne was an early parish priest who complained that there was no school. He asked to be transferred to a parish with a curate, so that, according to Bishop Amigo, he 'could have some conversation'.

Fr George Leidig took over the parish during and after the First World War. Although he had been born and bred in Deptford, his German surname excited suspicion and discrimination during the war. Some local tradesmen refused to serve him, but parishioners came to his rescue, cooking him meals which he, clearly rather a saintly man, often shared with beggars who knocked on his door. Fr

Leidig died in 1923 and was replaced by Fr Cornelius O'Donoghue. He improved the finances by introducing seat rents for the better off and was able to build the church hall. He was also responsible for the fine Stations of the Cross which were installed in the mid 1920's at the substantial cost of £170. Made by Burns Oates & Washburne, they are thought to have been designed by the noted craftsman Anton Dupré.

The presbytery was rebuilt in 1934–7 but destroyed by a bomb in September 1940. The blast also blew out all the windows in the church. Although the damage was made good during the war, the reality was that by the middle of the century the church was simply too small for what had become a large and devout population. Typically, there were six Masses every Sunday, and on Good Friday the liturgy was relayed via loudspeakers to the hall and to the crowds standing outside.

Fr Hugh Lagan, who took over the mission in 1958, started planning the expansion of the church. He wanted to rebuild completely but could only get planning permission for an extension. At this period there was considerable uncertainty about the possibility of a major new road being built through the church site. Luckily that never happened. The eventual compromise, completed in 1974, was to turn the nave of the old church into the sanctuary, knock down the north wall and build a new nave with a low ceiling. Essentially the church had been re-oriented at right angles. The old Ellis building is completely recognisable from the outside.

Clear at last of debt, the church was consecrated by Archbishop Bowen on 26th November 1989. Relics of the Apostle Thomas and St Philip Howard were deposited in the altar.

Today, lively as ever, St Thomas Apostle Nunhead is in the care of the Missionaries of St Paul, a Nigerian order of priests which is helping to re-evangelise Britain and Europe.

Our Lady of Grace, Charlton (1906)
Architect: Eugéne-Jacques Gervais

Close to the Woolwich Arsenal, many factories and the River Thames, Woolwich in the late 19th century was prime mission territory for the resurgent Catholic church. However various efforts to establish a foothold failed. In 1903 a group of French Sisters, Oblates of the Assumption who had been expelled from Bordeaux, bought a Regency villa called Highcombe on the ridge line above Charlton and Woolwich. This had been previously the residence of Sir William Barlow, architect of St Pancras station, and before him of Sir William Congreve, father of military rocketry. Today the house is the presbytery.

These nuns were a particularly independent operation. The Superior Mère Franck and her sister were Jewish converts to Catholicism. Founded in 1872, Mère Frank's congregation amalgamated with the Oblates of the Assumption in 1883, but some resumed their independence as Augustines de Notre-Dame de Consolation in 1912 and returned to France leaving the Charlton house to continuing Oblates.

They had arrived at Charlton in 1903 with their own chaplain, Fr Benedict Caron. Tenacious and resourceful, and encouraged by Bishop Bourne, they immediately established a chapel in the bow-fronted ground floor room at Highcombe. The first Mass was celebrated by Fr Caron on 19 July 1903, with the community joined by five lay Catholics.

Within a few weeks the numbers had swelled to 100 or more, and it was clear that a church was needed. Mère Franck also established a Sunday school at Highcombe.

An architect active in Bordeaux, Eugène-Jacques Gervais, was commissioned to produce the exuberant neo-Romanesque design on a plot next to Highcombe. Bishop Amigo laid the foundation stone on 27 August 1905, in the presence of the Assumptionist Superior General, Fr Emmanuel Baily, AA. It was opened the following September by Fr Darbois, Superior of the Assumptionist in New York. Bishop Amigo wanted the church dedicated to St Alphege, an Archbishop of Canterbury who had been martyred by Vikings at Greenwich in 1010. But Mère Franck had discovered the existence of a nearby pre-Reformation shrine to Our Lady of Grace, and her will prevailed over the bishop's.

Our Lady of Grace, Charlton

The Foundation stone is inscribed:

> O Blessed Virgin Mary fountain of Pardon
> Mother of Grace, hope of the world,
> Hear your children, brothers and sisters,
> called Augustinians of the Assumption.
> Banished from their homeland, but near to you, no longer exiles,
> Eagerly desiring a new harvest.
> Mary, mother of Grace
> They laid the first stone of this building dedicated to you AD 1905
> During the reign of His Holiness Pope Pius X
> During the Episcopacy of the Most Illustrious Peter Amigo, Bishop of Southwark.

The church, built by Jones and Son of Erith, cost £5,000. It seems that Frances Ellis' support was not for the church itself but for the convent and the school that the nuns built nearby. The records are scanty, and largely in the form of a reckoning given by one of the nuns, Sr Gelase Uginet, at the time the sisters returned to France in 1912. In her letter, Sr Gelase states that the church was paid for by a £3,000 mortgage from the Bishop (presumably Amigo rather than the Archbishop of Bordeaux), a £1,000 loan from the Assumptionist fathers and £1,000 from Mère Franck herself.

At this point the Assumptionist Fathers took over the running of Our Lady of Grace. They also purchased Highcombe as the presbytery. The sisters moved a few hundred yards to 34 Charlton Road, where they started the Assumptionist Convent School. In 1926 the church hall was built on part of Highcombe's front garden.

In 1929 the sisters opened a convent at 84 Victoria Road, formerly the Westcombe Park Working Mens' club. Part of the building was used as a hostel for young ladies from France who wished to learn English. However, in 1937, with war looming, the Royal Artillery compulsorily purchased the property in Victoria Road for £18,000 to be used as an anti-aircraft headquarters. The nuns moved to two other nearby houses, and a year later bought a house a couple of hundred yards from the church where they started a primary school. This was blessed and opened by Bishop Amigo in 1938.

Both school and church suffered damage from bombs and rockets during World War II. By God's grace, no one was killed. In the late fifties the war damage to the church was repaired and a lady chapel, baptistry and new entrance was added along the western side of the building. The church was consecrated by Archbishop Cowderoy on 13 September 1960.

Education has always been central to the mission of Our Lady of Grace. In 1956, the Assumptionists sold four acres of land behind the church to the Diocese, who built St Austin's, a new secondary school. St Austin's was closed in 1991 and the pupils were transferred to St Joseph's in Lee. Most of the land on which it stood was sold off for housing, with the exception of the playing field. More recently Our Lady of Grace primary school was moved to a modern building on the site. Our Lady of Grace is heavily over-subscribed. In 2017 Ofsted rated it 'Outstanding' in all areas.

Our Lady of Grace remains a powerful witness in Charlton, with a strong and vibrant community. Inevitably in the 120 years since its foundation, there have been many changes. The Assumptionist sisters left in 1972, returning to their mother house across the river in Bethnal Green. They were followed in 1989 by the Assumptionist priests, who handed the parish over to the Archdiocese. Fr Michael Leach was the first diocesan priest.

In 2012, the Archdiocese gave the parish to the Spiritans, also known as the Holy Ghost Fathers. Fittingly for an order originally founded to bring the word of God to Africa, most of the Spiritan fathers who have served at Our Lady of Grace are themselves Nigerians or Ghanaians, fervently re-evangelising England, Mary's dowry.

St William of York, Forest Hill (1906)

Architect: unknown (Clement Jackson?)

From 1895 the area formed part of the Brockley and Sydenham missions, but rapid housing development and a growing Catholic population prompted the Diocese to plan a new mission in Forest Hill. In 1903, Frances Ellis gave £4,000, with which, in 1905, the Diocese purchased a house on Brockley Park, Forest Hill for £2,200. This house became and remains the presbytery. The balance of the money was put towards the purchase of land adjoining the house, and for the construction of the church, which was completed in 1906. The total cost of land, church and fittings was £3,431, leaving a debt of some £1,631. The section of land beyond the church was purchased, according to a note made in 1939, in order to prevent the church being crowded by further building. In the long run, this was a doubly wise investment, as it allowed the construction of a primary school in 1971.

At least two mortgages totalling £1,300 were raised on the church, house and land, most of this money being used to build Corpus Christi church at Tonbridge, Kent. It is unusual to find so much financial detail in parish archives, and it is worth recounting to illustrate how the Diocese, and in particular the then-treasurer, Canon

Edward St John, strove to pay for the ever-expanding needs of the faithful in Southwark.

St William of York, Forest Hill

The original church was a simple Italianate building in stock brick with a Tuscan gable over the west entrance and a round-headed window. The architect is unknown, but may have been Clement Jackson, who also designed the not dissimilar Ellis church at Streatham Hill. In keeping with Frances' wishes, it was dedicated to an old English saint, William of York (c. 1100–1155). A relic of St William survived the Reformation, due to the devotion of Sir Richard Weston, who took it and other relics from St Georges Chapel, Windsor, and concealed them in his house at Sutton Place. The Westons remained a notable recusant family, and their descendants held on to Sutton Place until 1919. St William's relic was given to Fr James Hayes, the first rector, when he arrived in 1905, and is in a reliquary beneath the altar. The stations of the cross were erected in March 1907.

Fr Hayes had moved across directly from the adjacent Brockley mission. This was subsequently assigned to the Augustinians of the Assumption (Assumptionists). He wrote to the Bishop from Brockley on 7th October 1905, stating his willingness to take on Forest Hill. He knew 102 Catholics in the northern part of the mission district and felt sure there were as many in the southern half, which had been carved out of Sydenham. He wrote: 'I believe there is a great future before the new mission.'

Fr Hayes also sounded out Amigo on the establishment of a much-needed secondary school in Forest Hill to serve the wider district, including Brockley, Lewisham, Catford and East Dulwich. He also suggested that the spare land next to the church could be used for a small convent and primary school, and that one of several orders of nuns could be persuaded to take on the task of teaching in it.

In December 1905 Hayes wrote again to Amigo to tell him that he had celebrated Mass in the new church for 97 people, while a further 72 had attended an evening service—despite no advertisement having been published. The offertories amounted to £1 12s. 6d. (£1.62½p).

Money was always short in the early years, as it usually was with the Southwark missions. Fr Hayes wrote to Fr Emile du Plerny at the Cathedral explaining his problems. Before leaving Brockley, he had been forced to pay a £70 bill for correcting the drains at the school: 'The Assumptionists ... are getting the benefit but I had to pay.' Fr du Plerny's reply has not survived.[22]

Fr Hayes had a dispute with the Augustinians in his old parish over the location of the Sacred Heart primary school. He wrote to the Bishop to complain that although the school was within his mission boundary, the Assumptionists at Brockley were getting all the benefit. He made it plain in forthright letters to the Bishop and other diocesan authorities that he regarded the Assumptionists as opportunists, or, as he put it, 'blacklegs'.

The first visitation return, from February 1908, records a debt of £57 17s. 6d. to Canon St John for furnishing the church, and a bank overdraft of £465 6s.11d. Offerings in the previous year totalled £125 10s. 2d.

There were already sixteen altar servers, and three societies: Blessed Sacrament Guild, Living Rosary and Sanctuary Guild. There was at that time no school—the nearest was the one in the Brockley district which had cost him such pains—but Fr Hayes prepared children for the sacraments himself. Catechism, he said was 'fairly well organised' and attended by up to 35 children. He asked the Bishop to mention, on his next visit, attendance at daily and evening Mass (both 'very bad') and the upcoming bazaar which was being held to repay the £58 debt to Canon St John (namely the Diocese).

Fr Hayes got his wish as to teaching sisters, when St Francesca Cabrini (the first American citizen to be canonised) brought her Missionary Sisters of the Sacred Heart of Jesus to Honor Oak. She herself came to Mass at St William of York during her British sojourn in 1910.

With the congregations growing, and the work at the convent and school, the Bishop decided to send a slightly reluctant Fr Hayes an assistant priest, Fr Clement Constable, in early 1915. The reluctance of course was to do with money, but he nevertheless accepted the decision.

The mission was elevated to the dignity of a parish in 1921. Important extensions to the church were added in 1930, all the work of the architect Wilfred Mangan. Two aisles were built, as well as a baptistry, sacristy and Lady Chapel. They were skilfully executed in dark red brick which complements rather than clashes with the stock brick of the original building.

Fr Gillett arrived in 1936 and by 1939 he had reduced the debt from £1,200 to £500. In June 1939 Amigo paid a visit to Honor Oak convent and to St William at the climax of a triduum to celebrate the beatification of Blessed Frances X Cabrini.

The church survived the Second World War unscathed, though bombs 'rained' on the Sacred Heart convent at Honor Oak. Further architectural changes followed the end of the war, but the most important development was the opening of the St William of York primary school in 1971 on the spare land next to the church.

In 1986 the church was extended and re-orientated by architects Williams & Winkley. This work entailed radical change to the fabric. A new chancel was built to the north, replacing the former north aisle. The former sanctuary area was divided into two floors with meeting rooms, while the former sacristies were converted into a lobby and toilets; they were also extended upwards. The former sanctuary and sacristies became a new Parish Centre, with access from the church. The ground floor meeting room is connected to the church by folding doors which allow it to be used as overflow worship space.

Fr Patrick Aikens 1986–2007 was a long serving and active priest who did much to further the parish's mission. He wrote the fine parish prayer of dedication which concludes:

> Lord, we mean all that we have said,
> but we realise that we are weak.
> So we pray that you will help us, Father, through
> the life of your Son within us,
> and under the guidance of the Holy Spirit,
> to be faithful, loyal and active members of your family.

Today St William of York remains a very busy parish, with numerous societies and groups, as well as its well-regarded primary school.

St Andrew, 45 Brook Road, Thornton Heath (1905)

Architect: unknown

At the beginning of the 20th century, about 6,000 Catholics were living in Thornton Heath, attracted by the railway. There was no church closer than Our Lady of Reparation, Croydon. In 1903, Fr John McKenna, the rector at Croydon, established a mission at Beulah Road (now Brook Road) in a former Masonic Hall which had also been used as a dance hall. Frances Ellis gave an unstated sum of money to buy the hall and convert it for

Catholic worship. It was opened in 1905 and began to serve the Catholics in the area. The church was able to accommodate 280 people, many more than the typical Ellis Box. The dedication to St Andrew is relatively rare among English churches. It is probably due to Bishop Amigo's wish around this time for Miss Ellis to dedicate her churches to apostles rather than early English saints. The mission's first rector was Fr Mostyn, soon to move to the Ellis church of St Gertrude's at South Bermondsey. In the minutes of the diocesan finance committee for September 1908, note was made of a request from Fr Mostyn to be allowed to borrow money from a parishioner at 3½% interest in order to build a presbytery. Canon St John, still the treasurer and secretary, was to ascertain whether the building was held in the name of the Diocesan trustees. If so, Fr Mostyn could borrow a maximum £550.

Records of the next 50 years are scant. In the late 1960's, the rector Fr Furey began to build a replacement on the site of the old church. This modern functional structure opened for worship in 1971 and was consecrated by Archbishop Bowen in 1980. A fine stained-glass window by Joseph Nuttgens was installed in the Blessed Sacrament chapel.

St Helen, Robsart Street, North Brixton (1905)
Architect: F. W. Tasker

St Helen's, architecturally similar to St Francis de Sales only a mile away, was a rare failure among the Ellis churches. Not that it was an immediate failure: it remained a mission for nearly fifty years, and doubtless was loved by its congregation. But its unhelpful location, and lack of a school, eventually undermined its ability to thrive.

The design of St Helen's strongly suggests that the architect was Francis Tasker, though no records of its construction survive. The first rector was Fr James Kavanaugh, who worked hard to establish the new mission and was popular with his parishioners. He came from a well-known Catholic family active in Clapham and had previously been attached to a number of other parishes in Southwark. Sadly, he died aged only 53 in December 1908.

The former Church of St Helen, Robsart St, Brixton

In December 1930, the Cardinal Archbishop of Westminster, Francis Bourne, opened a bazaar being held for the building fund by St Helen's parish priest, Fr Peall. This was another of his regular—some might have said somewhat irregular—visits to South London, especially those parts with which he was personally connected. According to *The Tablet*:

> His Eminence had three reasons for being with the people of Stockwell that day. Firstly, he was always anxious to help on any good work such as

the providing of a new, or the extension or renovation of an existing church, or the erection of a Catholic school. The raising of funds, the maintaining of interest, and the repayment of capital were sources of constant anxiety to the clergy... His second reason for attending was that Stockwell was one of the parishes which he had planned during his occupancy of the Southwark See, along with several others which he did not remain to see fully established before his translation to Westminster. Like many another church in South London, it had been made possible through the extreme generosity of Miss Ellis, who died only a few months ago. Thirdly, he was always pleased to revisit Clapham, the district where his earliest years were spent, a locality which he had seen grow and change. As in many other districts, such growth and development had brought about corresponding development for the Catholic Church, so that the parent church— old St. Mary's, Clapham, which they all loved— gradually became inadequate to meet the demands made by such growth, and mission after mission had to be added, of which theirs at Stockwell was one.[23]

There is little information in the archives concerning the early decades of St Helen's. But a visitation note from Mgr William Brown, dated April 1932, puts the problem succinctly:

> The church is certainly too small. It could be enlarged if several of the cottages in Halstead adjoining were acquired. Fr Peall will make discreet enquiries. The boundary (with) St Helen's Camberwell is Brixton Road. The distance from the church to the boundary is very short. Fr Peall

suggests that the question be considered of giving Stockwell a portion of territory on the other side of Brixton Road. The want of a school makes things very difficult…

There came an unexpected crisis in 1936, when the rector, Fr Bartholomew O'Donovan, was arrested while on his regular annual holiday in Germany. There the priest fell into conversation with a young man in the street who turned out to be the son of a Nazi official who had him arrested. He pleaded guilty to soliciting a minor, was sentenced to two months' imprisonment but was released because he had already spent that time on remand. The matter reached the British newspapers, and he resigned his position at Robsart Street.[24] Given the amount of scandal and comic gossip in the popular press, Southwark was anxious to be rid of him. In hiding back in London, O'Donovan wrote to Bishop Amigo to see if he could find him a job in another English or Irish diocese. Amigo replied: 'There is no likelihood of your being accepted by any Bishop in England or Ireland after the publicity given to you by the papers.'[25] He eventually returned to his home village of Leap, Co. Cork, where he lived precariously though remaining in holy orders. He died aged 70 in 1954.

Fr O'Donovan was replaced at St Helen's by Fr A. G. Kavanagh. He immediately complained to the Bishop that Miss Katherine Collins, Fr O'Donovan's 18-year-old niece, was living in the presbytery at 87 Stockwell Park Road. The outcome is not recorded.

St Helen's soldiered on and was extended with a Lady Chapel by J. O'Hanlon Hughes shortly before the outbreak of World War II. However, after the war the Diocese purchased the war-damaged Brixton Independent Church (built 1870), and reopened it in 1953 as Our Lady of the Rosary, Brixton Road. This large church could easily absorb the congregation of St Helen's, and thus Robsart St was closed and deconsecrated.

After its deconsecration, St Helen's became at first an annexe to Corpus Christi primary school, before being turned into flats. It is still recognisably an Ellis church, with the characteristic large round window above the lean-to entrance, and an arched doorway.

St Joseph (formerly St Egbert), Kingston Road, New Malden (1905)

Architects (1923): Osmund Bentley and Adrian Gilbert Scott

In the late 19th century Catholics from this rapidly developing suburb of southwest London had to walk nearly three miles to St Agatha's church in Kingston. Fr Caspar Lutz, parish priest at Kingston, was keen to launch a mission in New Malden, and in 1902 he received Bishop Bourne's agreement in principle. Lack of money forced a delay but in April 1905, Frances Ellis gave £1,800 to purchase a substantial house called Inglenook at the corner of Kingston Road and Montem Road.

The house was rapidly adapted to provide a chapel of ease (or Mass centre, as it would now be described) on the ground floor, as well as a sacristy. Fr Lutz celebrated the first Mass at 9 am on 15 October 1905, with a Catechism Class in the afternoon, and the Rosary, sermon and Benediction in the evening.

As was her practice Frances Ellis chose an early English saint for the dedication, in this case St Egbert, a largely forgotten Northumbrian monk. Egbert or Ecgberht was born in 639, and in his youth travelled to

Ireland, where he studied at the monastery of Rath Melsigi in Carlow. There, after surviving the plague, he vowed to remain a perpetual pilgrim. He played an influential part at the Synod of Birr (697), where the laws protecting women and others in time of war were, remarkably, accepted by both the Irish and the Anglo-Saxons. He inspired many other monks from Ireland and Northumbria to cross the sea to Germany and proselytise the Frisians. He helped convince the Irish to adopt the Roman method of dating Easter: fittingly he died at Iona on Easter Day, 729, aged 90.

As St Egbert's was served from Kingston, and there was no need for a presbytery, the upper floor of Inglenook was initially rented to private tenants. In 1908 these were replaced by three nuns from the Congregation of the Nativity of Our Lord.[26] Later they acquired their own house across the street. The date of their departure from New Malden is not recorded, but the site of their house is now the public library.

In 1907, Fr Lutz was succeeded at Kingston by Fr Eugene O'Sullivan, a most energetic and tenacious priest. After only two years he petitioned the Bishop to allow him to give up Kingston so as to dedicate himself entirely to St Egbert's. His first act as rector of the mission was to process the Blessed Sacrament around New Malden, the start of a parochial devotion to the Sacrament which has flourished into the 21st century.

The congregation grew steadily, and by the outbreak of hostilities in 1914 there were up to 150 Sunday Mass-goers. The room at Inglenook could not contain such numbers and so Fr O'Sullivan began to press for the Diocese to build a proper church. Bishop Amigo agreed, but the plans were deferred until after the war. Permission to demolish Inglenook and erect a Gothic church in red brick was granted in 1921. At a cost of £3,607, the south aisle and Lady Chapel were complete by 1923, allowing 125 to be seated at Mass (Frances Ellis was not involved). But at this point, Fr O'Sullivan dismissed the architect, Osmund Bentley, seemingly because the priest did not like his plan for a tall, pitched roof. Bentley's replacement was Adrian Gilbert Scott, who completed the church with a lower roof and different windows, presenting an altogether more modest and less starkly gothic structure.

Both architects had good pedigrees. Osmund Bentley was the son of Francis Bentley, architect of Westminster Cathedral. Adrian Gilbert Scott was the grandson of Sir Gilbert Scott, son of Gilbert Scott, and brother of Giles Gilbert Scott, all distinguished architects. Giles had designed Liverpool's Anglican Cathedral and would later design the red telephone box. Both of the men who worked on St Joseph's were able and imaginative architects in their own right, but they met their match in Fr O'Sullivan.

The Nave, North Aisle (Sacristy side), the Transepts, the St Pius X Chapel, the Sacred Heart Chapel, and the Organ Gallery were all completed by 1928, at a cumulative cost of £9,552. A new presbytery was built in 1929, and two years later, the sanctuary, upper aisles and Parish Hall were erected. The total cost of more than £13,000 was met from a variety of sources (not including Miss Ellis), but remarkably more than half had been raised by the parishioners themselves.

Neither Fr Lutz nor Fr O'Sullivan had been keen on the dedication to St Egbert, and both had petitioned the Bishop to change it. In the early years, Fr Lutz had wanted it dedicated to Our Most Holy Redeemer, which he thought would be more acceptable to the Nonconformists who, he claimed, 'infested' New Malden. Amigo was reluctant to change the name while the mission was still based in the house purchased by Miss Ellis. But once the new building was up in 1923, he allowed it to be rededicated to St Joseph.

Fr O'Sullivan died in November 1948 after more than forty years in charge of St Joseph's. At the time of his death there were as many as 700 Sunday Mass-goers. The mission was elevated to a parish on 19 March 1949. The new parish priest, Fr Hugh Hunt, completed the interior of the church, installing many statues. By 1951 he had cleared all the parish debts, and so Bishop Cyril Cowderoy, who had succeeded Amigo in 1949, was able to consecrate St Joseph's on 26 November 1951. He was back on 20 May 1954 to consecrate a shrine to Our Lady facing Kingston Road which would 'remind the world that England is Our Lady's Dowry'.

Today St Joseph's remains a lively and vibrant parish with more than a thousand Sunday mass-goers and more than 70 parish groups.

St Wilfrid, Lorrimore Road, Kennington Park (F. E. bought land 1905, built 1914)

Architect: F. A. Walters

The area west of the Walworth Road was developed in the middle and later part of the 19th century, and, as ever in central London, attracted a large and largely Irish Catholic population. A mission was established in a temporary chapel and served from St George's Cathedral. In 1905 Frances Ellis bought a plot of land with an abandoned stable in Lorrimore Road. The cost was not recorded. The stable was converted into a chapel, and the first Mass was celebrated there on 3 November 1905. The first priest to take charge of the mission was Fr George Palmer.

As time went on, Fr Palmer hoped and prayed for what he called 'a more worthy building'. He urged his parishioners to join in the devotion of Seven Sundays to St Joseph, and in 1914 a wealthy lawyer and his wife, Mr and Mrs Henry Smail, gave £5,000 to build a church on the site. The architect F. A. Walters designed a red brick church with stone dressings in late Gothic.[27] It was opened on 11 June 1915.

On the west front there is a window with six traceried lights, and to the left of the west front a four-storey tower surmounted by battlements and a 'Hertfordshire spike'. Although displaying a certain modesty, it is a more elaborate building than the typical Ellis Box.

St Bede, Thornton Road, Clapham Park (1906)

Architect: Clement Jackson (?)

Frances Ellis gave Hyde House and its one-acre garden to the Diocese in 1903. There is a strong tradition in the Archdiocese that this had been her own home, a tradition for which, however, there is no documentary evidence. She and her sister Rose had been living at Waltham Place near Maidenhead until 1897, and by 1901 she was living in Cornwall: in the intervening four years circumstantial evidence places her in Thanet where she possessed another large house. Of course, she certainly owned Hyde House, and she may well have used it as a London base. It was one of several large stucco mansions built at Clapham Park by Thomas Cubitt in the mid-19th century, and today, as the presbytery, is one of just two remaining. It is listed Grade 2 by English Heritage.

Her friend Bishop Francis Bourne, then still at Southwark, intended the house to be used as a prep school for the diocesan seminary at Wonersh, of which he had been the first rector. It was also to be a chapel of ease for St Mary's Clapham Common. Bourne thought that he would live in the house, which would enable him more effectively to oversee the senior and junior seminaries while also running the Diocese. This notion gives a foretaste of what was shortly to develop into an almost obsessive desire to retain influence over Southwark and Wonersh once Bourne had been translated to Westminster (see Chapter 4).

A room on the ground floor of Hyde House was converted into a chapel dedicated to St John Berchmans (1599–1621), a young Belgian Jesuit scholastic, and on 8th September 1903, Bishop Bourne celebrated the first Mass there. That was almost his last official engagement as Bishop of Southwark, because on 11 September he was appointed Archbishop of Westminster. Fr Peter Amigo replaced him at Southwark the following year: their tortured relationship was to be a feature of Catholicism in London for the next three decades, and St Bede's, to which both men were deeply attached, was to play its part in the drama. In fact, before his consecration as Bishop, Amigo made his personal retreat in the house.

Hyde House was initially used as a prep school for boys who intended subsequently to progress to Wonersh. Their numbers were briefly augmented by some of the younger seminarians. This somewhat unsatisfactory arrangement continued until 1907, when all returned to the seminary. There followed an ultimately fruitless period of discussion about the possibility of using Hyde House as a secondary school for the predominantly middle-class boys of the parish, as many parents were worried that Clapham College, run by the Xavierian Brothers, was too "mixed"— a euphemism for working class.[28]

In 1905 Fr Michael Hanlon decided that the house-chapel was inadequate to the needs of the growing mission and set about building a church next door to the house.

The foundation stone was laid by Amigo on 4 November 1905, and the church opened on 27 April the following year. Built of London stock brick in a plain Italianate early-Christian style, it was designed to seat 250 people. The architect is unknown, but may have been Clement Jackson, also responsible for St Simon & St Jude, Streatham and, perhaps, St William of York, Forest Hill. The builder was E. B. Tucker of Lavender Hill. The stations of the cross were installed on 30 October 1906. The cost of building the church was £2,107; according to Cardinal Bourne, Miss Ellis paid for the construction. But she may not have covered other costs, such as furnishing, as the debt was not paid off until 1970, when the church was finally consecrated.

The dedication to the great scholar and historian St Bede (672–735) would certainly have been acceptable to Frances, who favoured early English saints, and to Bourne and Amigo, both of whom were greatly concerned with fostering scholarship at Wonersh.

The close connection with Wonersh—Bourne's obsession and the source of Amigo's clergy—was maintained after the last of the students left Hyde House. There was a rapid turnover of clergy in the early years, shuttling between Clapham Park and the seminary, until the arrival of Fr Thomas Hooley in August 1909. Hooley was then aged 32 and had taught at Wonersh since being ordained there in 1899; he had also been 'Regent' of the junior seminarians. The two men were firm friends. Bourne had desired Hooley to become rector of Wonersh, against the wishes of Amigo, but failed to get his way.

St Bede's Church, Clapham Park, with Hyde House to right

There arose a strange situation. Francis Bourne had been born in Larkhall Rise, on the borders of Clapham and Stockwell, was baptised and later ordained priest at St Mary's Clapham. This part of south London was very much his patch. He had also chosen Fr Hooley as his confessor and crossed the Thames every month to make his confession at St Bede's, followed by lunch. Also, during his 33 years at Westminster, Cardinal Bourne occasionally stayed at Hyde House on private retreat. It is not clear whether he sought Bishop Amigo's permission: the correct procedure for one bishop entering another's territory is to ask first. Bourne claimed that he did, though there is no record of it (see below). As these visits were private, and even slightly eccentric, perhaps Amigo simply turned a blind eye.

Fr Hooley and Cardinal Bourne at St Bede's, 1932

In May 1912, at the height of the Bourne-Amigo controversy, the Archbishop's adherents in South London—of which there seem to have been a large number—staged a celebration of his belated elevation to Cardinal at St Bede's. *The Tablet* reported that the High Mass was celebrated by Canon St John, who was then in a sort of clerical limbo before being appointed chaplain to Liverpool prison the following year.

But it was a different case in 1932 when Bourne (again accompanied by Canon St John, now living at Westminster after his twelve-year exile in Liverpool) presided at official ceremonies at St Bede's that would normally be reserved for Amigo as the local bishop. These were to mark the expansion of St Bede's, where the chancel and Lady Chapel had been added at a cost of some £6,000. Bourne's address on that occasion included a helpful summary and assessment of Miss Ellis' benefactions and their place in the Divine scheme:

Cardinal Bourne assisted at High Mass and preached on Whit Monday at St Bede's, Clapham Park, the occasion being the opening of an extension to the building.

His Eminence congratulated the rector and congregation on the completion of so spacious an extension, and expressed his particular pleasure at being allowed to share their joy. He took the deepest possible interest in all the Catholic developments in the Clapham district, a locality with which he personally had many associations. He had known Clapham all his life— most people knew that there he was born, and there, also, he was ordained, in the old St. Mary's church, where he had likewise shared in the joys of many events of the parochial history. When he became Bishop of Southwark a scheme was drawn up for providing churches in several parts of South and South-West London, already largely developing, and where it was anticipated many Catholics would be found. Though the scheme was comprehensive, realisation appeared impossible through lack of funds. Then one of the greatest benefactresses the Church in England had had for many years—the late Miss Ellis—placed a considerable sum at his disposal, with the wish that the buildings would be simple in character. Of that group of many churches, St. Bede's was the last.

There were three objects, said the Cardinal, in setting up a centre in that locality. Firstly, there was the need to relieve the pressure on the old Redemptorist mission; secondly, it was originally intended to start a preparatory school, chiefly for those who might be discovered to possess vocations; and, thirdly, as it was felt that the Bishop ought to have some place of retirement or retreat to which he could occasionally withdraw from the strain of work at St. George's Cathedral, the purchased house and garden at Clapham Park was chosen for the purpose. He, as Bishop, had only possessed it a few months when, quite unexpectedly, he was called to occupy his present position; but his immediate successor at Southwark kindly suggested that he should continue to utilize the premises just the same as though he had remained Bishop of Southwark. Though this was scarcely possible, he had taken advantage of the Bishop's generosity to the extent of becoming a frequent visitor to St Bede's presbytery; and hardly a month passed without his spending at least a few hours' relaxation from the anxieties of his office with their rector, Father Hooley, whom he had known personally for upwards of forty years, and whose parochial work there he had watched closely for the past twenty-three years, so that he was fully acquainted with the details of St. Bede's development, almost as fully as with that of parishes in his own Archdiocese. The scheme for which Miss Ellis had found funds had been justified beyond expectations, as in almost every instance extensions to the original small church first erected had had to be made to keep pace with the growth of population. The development of any Catholic mission was an example of that plan of Divine Providence, frequently too easily forgotten by priests as well as the laity, that though Almighty God was working quietly at the back of all undertakings for the spread of the Church, He expected us individually to share in that work. The rebuilding of the Faith in this land—with the exception of a few isolated cases where everything was provided at the commencement— was one of progress based on

> small beginnings and long sacrifices by priests and their people, which taught the lesson of dependence on God, together with co-operating in all the opportunities He presented to us. Their work at St. Bede's was not yet finished, as they had a debt to remove before handing over their now more spacious church for Consecration.[29]

Fr Hooley was to remain as rector of St Bede's for 43 years, through two world wars, huge social change and the fruitful growth of the local Catholic population. His first project was to start an infant school in what had been the stables adjoining Hyde House. The La Retraite sisters took on the task of teaching 42 children. That early initiative flourishes still as St Bede Infant & Nursery School. In addition, the parish is closely bound to St Bernadette Junior School and La Retraite Girls' School.

The Second World War hit St Bede's hard, as it did many London parishes. The worst disaster took place on 16th October 1940, when a German bomb destroyed St Joseph's Home for disabled Catholic boys directly across King's Avenue from the church. Eight people were killed: four of the children; Mr and Mrs Murphy, who ran the home; Helen O'Flaherty, a nursemaid; and Fr Richard Barry, a young priest much involved in the care of Southwark's children. Other parishioners were killed on active service. A curate, Fr Quinlan, served first as a firewatcher before becoming a chaplain to the commandos during the bloody fighting in Belgium and Holland in 1944–5.

In 1958 an open loggia was added at the main entrance, a new stone altar replaced the original wooden table, and stained glass was installed in the circular east window.

Fr Hooley died in 1952, but the parish has continued to thrive, with relatively few rectors over the succeeding decades. Fr Ronald Salmon, who was at St Bede's from 1968 to 1981 completely reconstructed the old servant's quarters and kitchen of Hyde House and made it into an active social club. Mgr Leo White, originally a Capuchin friar born in Malta, was a dedicated missionary in Kenya. There he was responsible for creating the Diocese of Garissa and bringing many Kenyan young men and women to realise their religious vocations. This distinguished and devoted priest spent his later years at St Bede's, before passing away in 2018, aged 92.

Fr Christopher Basden was parish priest for 25 years, from 1993 to 2018. He worked hard to build up the congregation and to restore devotion to the sacraments after the upheavals that followed Vatican II. He also made the house available to a large number of overseas priests in London for study or pastoral purposes. In 2018, he swapped parishes with Fr Marcus Holden from Ramsgate, who has continued with the work. There is a strong emphasis on liturgical music, with several choirs. The parish is multi-ethnic, and very young. There are 500 regular Mass attenders, with a focus on catechesis and study. Among normal parishes, St Bede's is also the home of the largest Latin Mass congregation in the country. The parish has many clubs and fraternities.

Since its foundation in 1906, St Bede's has had many vocations to the priesthood and religious life. Between the wars, the Beck family produced two priests and a nun: Fr Andrew Beck went on to be Archbishop of Liverpool. In more recent years, Fr Philip de Freitas was ordained here in 1998 and Fr Tom Lynch, a former altar server, said his first Mass here in 2014.

Hyde House remains the presbytery and is also the base for a number of priests from overseas. Among them at the time of writing is Fr Romany Fathy Samaan Shenouda, originally from the Coptic Catholic Eparchy of Sohag in Upper Egypt. Fr Romany says Mass in Arabic for Arab and Coptic Christians in London. St Bede's also has a link with the missionary centre for formation in Warsaw, which since 1995 has sent thirteen priests to St Bede's to learn English and to prepare for the missions.

The Handmaids of Mary came to the parish in 1998 (following the La Retraite Sisters who had been in the neighbourhood since 1880 and had many vocations from St Bede's parish). In 2015 some of the clergy went to the Mother House of the Handmaids of Mary for the first profession of Sister Carol Cardenas whose whole family was one of the first supporters of the parish's Latin American Mass. She was educated at the La Retraite high school.

St Simon and St Jude, Hillside Road, Streatham Hill (1906)

Architect: Clement Jackson

In 1904, Frances Ellis was asked for the money to provide a church for what was initially known as the Tulse Hill mission. Its location is on the high ground roughly halfway between Tulse Hill and Streatham proper. The land was purchased from the London, Brighton and South Coast Railway Company, and the architect Clement Jackson was commissioned to provide designs. As soon became clear, too little attention had been paid to the suitability of the land to support a large building.

Building began in 1905 and Mass was first celebrated on 27 July 1906. The priest in charge was Fr Rory Fletcher, who before ordination had been a surgeon at the Charing

Cross Hospital. The relics placed underneath the altar are of the English Martyr St Philip Howard, and St Francis Xavier, the great Jesuit missionary to India, Japan and China.

St Simon & St Jude, Streatham Hill

The dedication to the Apostles St Simon (the Zealot) and St Jude was unusual for an Ellis church. She preferred early English saints. Bishop Amigo had asked Frances to build twelve churches dedicated to the twelve apostles, but only four churches resulted, dedicated to six Apostles in total. (St Thomas Apostle Nunhead, St James the Great Peckham Rye, St Philip & St James Herne Hill, and St Simon & St Jude).

The church, as usual with Ellis churches, is constructed of London stock brick and is Italianate in style. But with its stucco rendering, Palladian pediment, and prominent Diocletian window, it strikes a very different note from the typical Ellis Box. Initially, the nave was short, and without aisles. Jackson's plans, which are preserved in the presbytery next door, show much greater ambition, intending a much larger church in what has been described as an 'Edwardian Arts and Crafts version of free Classical style'.

Unfortunately, the site stood on what had been a cattle pond fed by a stream which still runs under the church. It also lay on a slope and had inadequate footings. This caused immediate problems with subsidence, and swiftly stymied any idea of significantly extending the church. Only six years after its opening, major remedial work was undertaken.

The exquisitely carved Stations of the Cross are by Ferdinand Stüflesser the younger and were donated by Father Nugent in thanksgiving for his silver jubilee of ordination, shortly before his death in 1948. Two silver-and-gold-plated altar candles were made at the end of World War I by Caustins of Camberwell. Another pair of brass candlesticks for use in the proclamation of the Gospel were given by Fr Adrian McKenna-Whyte.

A large parish hall was built in the garden behind the church in 1935. The church was extended in 1937 by the addition of a chancel to house the sanctuary.

By 1985 the church was again suffering from subsidence and an urgent programme of underpinning and repair was undertaken. At the same time the sanctuary was raised by one metre and a new altar of Ancaster stone backed by an oak dossal and damask hanging was installed. Cheshire sandstone was used for the Tabernacle pillar and the pulpit base. Gilding was applied to the great crucifix and the two Polish hand-carved angels. An Ahlborn electric organ was installed at the side of the sanctuary. A programme to fill the windows with medieval-style stained glass was undertaken by the artist Andrew Taylor of Devizes.

In 2018 the parish began another major restoration and renovation programme, still ongoing at the time of publication. One particular embellishment was the installation of a Divine Mercy stained-glass panel in the central section of the Diocletian window over the liturgical west front, which is particularly striking when backlit at night.

The parish remains a very active one, with parishioners drawn from 28 countries speaking 24 languages. The motto of the parish is 'Love without Limits'.

St Mary Magdalen, East Hill, Wandsworth (1906)
Architect: Lawrence Butler

In 1902, at the request of Bishop Bourne, a group of Salesians from nearby Battersea established the East Wandsworth mission in a Georgian house on the site of the current presbytery. The funds to purchase the house were provided by Frances Ellis. Three years later, the Diocese commissioned the architect Lawrence Butler to design a church: the resulting building was not an Ellis Box.

The church sits next to the historic 'Mount Nod' Huguenot cemetery, which had opened in 1687 and closed to new burials in 1854. The irony of a Catholic church appearing next to the cemetery did not escape the Huguenot Society, which erected an elaborate memorial there in 1911. On it is inscribed:

> Here rest many Huguenots who on the Revocation of the Edict of Nantes in 1685 left their native land for conscience' sake and found in Wandsworth freedom to worship God after their own manner. They established important industries and added to the credit and prosperity of the town of their adoption.

Interior of St Mary Magdalen, East Hill, Wandsworth

Opened for worship on St Crispin's Day, 25 October 1906, St Mary Magdalen is a mild exercise in late Victorian Gothic executed in red brick with stone facings under a slate roof.[30] In liturgical terms the church is back to front: the 'east end' faces west, and the 'north' faces south. However, any confusion disappears on entering the church, which was spectacularly decorated by the Salesian priest-artist Fr George Fayers SDB, who had studied with Sir Edward Burne-Jones.

The graceful influence of Fr Fayers' artistic mentor is strong throughout. The ceilings are adorned with painted panels depicting saints and various sacred symbols. There is a rood screen at the sanctuary arch, the lower part of which seems to have been removed in the 1970's. On the rood beam is a frieze of angels playing instruments. The rood figure above is a painted Tau cross. Behind the high altar is a timber painted reredos, with five panels of saints framing the larger central panel, with arabesques above and below.

The rather more sombre central panel of the reredos was painted in 1960 by a Yugoslav artist, Ivan Tomlanovich: it depicts Mary Magdalen at the foot of the Cross, against a pre-gentrification backdrop of the industrial banks of the Thames, including Battersea Power Station.

Further enhancements, including the Byzantine-style hanging lamps, were designed and installed by the parish priest Canon Martin Edwards.

In the 21st century, St Mary Magdalene has become a principal church of the Latin Mass Society. Every Sunday, four Masses are celebrated: two said Masses, one Sung Latin Mass and one Family Mass.

St Boniface, Mitcham Road, Tooting (1907)

Architect: Benedict Williamson

Around the turn of the century, Tooting was expanding rapidly, as were many outer London neighbourhoods. Catholics were served by priests from Holy Ghost, Balham, including Fr Rudolph Bullesbach. In 1899, Fr Bullesbach was also appointed chaplain to Fountain Hospital.[31] Mass was celebrated at first in the chapel of St Joseph's College, Upper Tooting Park, until the college moved to Denmark Hill. Then the mission moved to Holly Lodge, on the Mitcham Road, and finally to a large nearby house known as Hereford Lodge. In 1899 Hereford Lodge was purchased for use both as a school and as a chapel. There was great difficulty raising the £2,073, which was finally obtained on a mortgage agreed in August 1899.

By 1903, when the first Catholic schools were opened nearby, Tooting's Catholic population was estimated at 2,000, making provision of a mission church a priority for the Diocese. Fr George Williams, who had succeeded Fr Bullesbach, convinced Bishop Amigo of the need to act. In 1906, Frances Ellis gave the money for both the land and the church itself. The exact sums have not been recorded but are unlikely to have been less than £4,000. Another benefactress, Mary Allanson, settled the debts on the schools and the presbytery and paid for the completion and decoration of the church. The architect was Benedict Williamson, whose last commission this was before he entered the Beda College in Rome to study for the priesthood.

Williamson initially took as his inspiration the Roman monastery church of Santi Vincenzo e Anastasio alle Tre Fontane, believed by many to be the site of St Paul's martyrdom. But time and financial constraints forced him to compromise.

Instead, he designed a recognisable Ellis Box, taller than the Tasker versions, Romanesque in style, in stock brick. The nave had five bays and two side aisles, also making it larger than most of Miss Ellis' churches. There was no time to complete the sanctuary, which instead was fitted into the easternmost bay. The west front, on Mitcham Road, was plain, but with a large rose window instead of the plain round windows in other Ellis churches.

The foundation stone was laid on 17 November 1906. *The Tablet*, in a thoughtful essay, put this single new foundation in its broader context:

> Gothic and Roman, great and small, urban, suburban and rural, in all directions churches are springing up like mushroom growths on every side. It is an era of church-building. Whether art and architecture will approve the results time and another generation will tell. With the most conspicuous example in the Westminster

Cathedral, a reaction seems to be in full tide from the imitation Gothic of the Victorian period to the imitation Roman of the present prevailing fashion. But the fact of overwhelming importance is that space is being found for the increasing thousands of souls who make up the household of the faith. And yet the mere multiplication of churches may produce a disproportioned impression, for, indeed, with all their multiplying numbers, they are as the poor loaves and fishes compared with the hundreds of thousands which they are set to feed. Of this the church at Tooting, the foundation of which was laid on Saturday afternoon, is a striking illustration. From the bridges trams and trains leave St. George's, the mother church, Vauxhall, Brixton, Battersea, Wandsworth, Clapham, and Balham, to right and left and behind, with the million or two, more or less, who swarm there, only to begin the line of interminable shops stretching along the main road, with the long dreary streets of terraces and small villas at right angles to it—square miles of houses with scores of thousands of people, veritable wildernesses of bricks and mortar, some already showing the premature decay of their modernity; and there on the outer verge is set the new church, to minister to a faithful few among the estranged thousands and the tens of thousands of those to whom religion of any kind or sort is little more than a name. Nearly a mile along the Mitcham-road from Tooting Broadway the new foundation has been laid of a church which is to replace the school chapel previously built. The ceremony took place on Saturday afternoon. Drenching rain fell all the morning, but in the afternoon the sun burst through the clouds for a time and all was well. The Bishop of Southwark officiated, and among the clergy assisting the

Bishop and present were Canon St. John, Fathers Bourdelot, Dooley, Turner, Newton, O'Halloran, W. Fichter, Cosmo Brown, Westlake, Kelly, Taunton, and the rector, Father George Williams.

Father Williams was associated with the Bishop when the latter was rector of Walworth, and it is with the knowledge of the energy and zeal which manifested themselves in that densely populated and poor mission that he has set Father Williams the onerous task of developing the new and promising mission at Tooting. In the course of a short address the Bishop dwelt on the gratitude which the people owed to God for the gift of the church which a pious benefactor had made to them. Through many difficulties their outlook had been almost hopeless. In answer to their prayers to St. Boniface, to whom the church was dedicated, they had found a friend, and he exhorted them to continue their fervent prayers to the great English Saint. He reminded them that while the church, such portion of it as was to be at present erected, was given to them by a friend, the subsequent completion of the building and the furnishing of the church would devolve on the people of Tooting and their friends.

At present only five bays of the nave, with a temporary sanctuary, will be proceeded with, giving accommodation for 400 worshippers, and it is expected that the opening will take place in March. The design is on the lines of some of the basilicas of Rome of the fourth and fifth centuries, the completed plan consisting of nave and aisles with transept and apse, and is the work of Mr Benedict Williamson, who, it is interesting to learn, almost immediately leaves for Rome to enter the priesthood. The people of Tooting are to be congratulated on the possession of a beautiful church, an experienced and energetic rector, and the rest, for a full and worthy success, depends on their own whole-hearted co-operation.[32]

St Boniface, Tooting

The church, still unfinished, was opened for worship on 18 April 1907. Frances Ellis had asked for the church to be dedicated to St Boniface (675–754), the great apostle of Germany who had been born in Devon.

To use a modern expression, St Boniface hit the ground running. The first visitation (i.e. inspection) took place in February 1909. The two priests, Fr Williams and his curate, reported excellent attendance at the three Sunday Masses. The church held 350 people, many more than in other Ellis boxes. Offertories for the first year were £154, while the fees earned from attending Holy Family convent, care homes and the Fountain Hospital brought in another £183. Fr Williams reported the girls were well prepared for catechism, the boys less so. Catechism was well attended, he said, because regulars got a treat (unspecified).

The 1912 visitation recorded 500 at Sunday Mass, with annual offertories up to £208. 'Accommodation severely taxed at Children's Mass and sometimes at 12.' The Guild of the Blessed Sacrament had 60 members, the Apostleship of Prayer 160, the Children of Mary 30, while no figure was given for the Society of St Vincent de Paul, although it was the only society that had a dedicated monthly collection.

Schooling had problems typical of the time, including anti-Catholic prejudice on the part of the local authority. Amigo commented:

> If the Surrey Council authorities insist on refusing to pay for children at school, we must find some way of helping children to get a Catholic education. The Confraternity of Christian Doctrine ought to be started for this purpose.[33]

To the question 'Have secret societies, spiritualism or socialism obtained any footing among your people?', the priest replied: 'I think not.'

From 1927, further expansion and elaboration of the church exterior began under the direction of Fr Benedict Williamson, by then living in Rome, and his partner J. H. Beart Foss. The result was an exuberant transformation of Williamson's original classical simplicity. As Denis Evinson put it in *Catholic Churches of London*:

> Whatever Williamson had intended to build in 1906—probably a simple version of his prototype's nave gable, with a low atrium before it which masked the lean-to aisle roofs—his ideas by 1927 had crystallised into something considerably more complex. In the commentary that accompanies his illustration, Williamson claims that the west front 'has not been built in any of the recognised styles of architecture; rather is it an endeavour directed towards the production of a new style'.
>
> In this west front, Williamson incorporates a north-west campanile, the belfry stage ornamented with alternating bands of purple brick and Portland stone; and terminated by a copper-covered spire; the rose window of the nave is framed beneath a boldly moulded arch and supported by massive columns; the great central doorway, with its lofty arch supported on engaged columns, is flanked by arcading on either side, with smaller entrances to the aisles. By 1927 Williamson had long been interested in ancient Egyptian architecture, and his preoccupation here with Egyptian capitals together with his over-generous use of Portland stone result in a confection far removed from the restrained Early Christian revival work characteristic of the turn of the century.

The repose of the interior is in pleasing contrast. Above the west narthex and first bay is the gallery, its organ case designed in 1950 by C.S. Kerr Bate. Seven bays of nave and aisles are followed by the apsidal chancel and flanking chapels one bay deep. There are round-headed windows to the aisles and clerestory, and circular piers with cushion capitals bearing bold relief symbolism on their faces. The nave is surmounted by a kingpost roof. From the west entrance the overall impression is one of familiar and competent Early Christian revival work. A major attraction are the aisle walls, panelled to a height of seven feet, and between this and the springing of the lean-to roofs a large continuous iconographical scheme in mosaic of the Stations of the Cross, with stylised figures and generous surrounds in subdued colours, all tastefully designed and executed c. 1930 by L. Oppenheimer. The original high altar, with gradine and tabernacle, is still in situ and there is a new forward altar and ambo in memory of Canon Thomas Clifton.[34]

St Boniface has continued to prosper and by 2020 at least 45 nationalities were represented in the parish.

St Vincent de Paul, Altenburg Gardens, Clapham Common (1907)

Architects: Kelly & Dickie

St Vincent de Paul is the fourth of the Ellis churches to be carved out of the original parochial territory of St Mary's Clapham Common (the first three being St Francis de Sales Larkhall Lane, St Helen's Robsart St and St Bede's Clapham Park). The area to the north of the Common had previously abounded in market gardens growing fruit, vegetables and flowers for the metropolis. But with the arrival of the railways these gave way to new housing. The Shaftesbury Park Estate north of Lavender Hill had a disproportionate number of Catholic residents. Catholics who lived round the western end of the Common had to walk either to St Mary's or to the Salesians at Battersea. The Bishops of Southwark had been pressed for some years to build a new church but were constrained by lack of money.

Then in 1903, at the urging of Canon St John, Miss Ellis gave a substantial sum to buy a large house in Altenburg Gardens, just off the North Side of the Common, together with an adjoining patch of apple orchard. On 10th September, Fr George Grady, previously rector of Northfleet on the Thames Estuary, was appointed first rector of the new mission. He immediately knocked two rooms together, converting them into a chapel, and began appealing for funds to build the church. Frances Ellis had given sufficient money to cover the repairs and alterations needed for the house chapel, but not for the new church. In total she provided £3,915 12s. 5d. to the mission.

Fr Grady took up residence on 2 October 1903, offered Mass in the house chapel on 3 October, and the following day, Rosary Sunday, celebrated the first public Mass. The response was immediate and overwhelming, so that Fr Grady scheduled two Sunday morning Masses at 8.30 and 11, with devotions at 6.30 pm. Nevertheless, the small house chapel was inadequate to the needs of the 300 or so parishioners who regularly crowded in for Mass.

Fr Grady placed a large poster in the orchard next door which proclaimed:

> CATHOLIC CHURCH St Vincent de Sales—
> Subscriptions and Donations gratefully received.

For three years the orchard served as the venue for the annual parish garden party, and during this time Grady managed to secure several hundred pounds in donations. Then early in 1906, Bishop Amigo gave his permission, and loaned £2,000 of diocesan funds, while further public appeals raised another £711.

Fr George Grady

The architects Kelly & Dickie prepared plans, and senior partner Mr Kelly entered a sketch of the Italianate building, with a campanile, to the Royal Academy summer show. The original plans also included an aisle on the right-hand side of the nave, but neither aisle nor campanile were ever built.

The builder was F. J. Bradford of Leicester, a devout Catholic, who personally supervised the project to ensure it was completed to the highest standard. The foundation stone was laid on 28 July 1906 and the church was opened on the Feast of St Joseph, 19 March 1907. The minutes of the Southwark diocesan finance committee for 20 March noted that 'the cost seems to be £3042'. The nave was 66 ft. long and 34 ft. wide, with a generous apsidal sanctuary. The Lady Chapel was to the right of the sanctuary, and the organ gallery took up the two eastern bays. The organ itself came from an unnamed Cambridge college. The church was furnished with electric light—something of a sensation in those days—as well as gas-fired heating.

Fr Grady celebrated the first Mass in the Lady Chapel at 7 am. Bishop Amigo was unable to attend the pontifical high Mass at 11, but Mgr Brindle, Bishop of Nottingham, stood in for him. The sermon was preached by Mgr Croke Robinson on the theme 'My yoke is easy and my burden light'. The music was provided by a choir of juniors from Manresa House, the Jesuit novitiate at Roehampton.

Architecturally St Vincent de Paul was, and remains, a triumph, fitting gracefully into the handsome terraces of Altenburg Gardens. From that point of view, it was probably a mercy that there was never enough money to raise the proposed campanile.

St Vincent de Paul, Altenburg Gardens, Clapham

Fr Grady was clearly a man of taste who was determined that the new church would adorn the neighbourhood on the outside and give fitting glory to God on the inside. He was also fortunate in the generosity of his parishioners. The nave was in a plain renaissance style, with a semi-circular roof and five bays carried on Corinthian columns. The sanctuary was raised two feet above the floor of the nave, approached by four marble steps given by a parishioner. The altar, the gift of the Spaul family, was raised a further three steps above the sanctuary, giving excellent sight lines from anywhere in the church. The altarpiece, the gift of Mrs Chitty, was an oil painting on the unusual subject of St John giving Holy Communion to Our Lady.[35] The subject wrote Fr Grady, was of 'supremely greater excellence than the artistic merit of the work.'

Grady continued, with the help of parishioners, to decorate the church. This was sometimes in defiance of the diocesan financial controllers. They asked him to explain unauthorised debts, and grumbled about expenditure on ecclesiastical fittings from the great designers Hardman & Co. But the record suggests that his superiors also recognised his energy and zeal for souls, and that Altenburg Gardens was a true adornment to the Diocese of Southwark.

The church was consecrated in 1935—its debt having been paid off in less than thirty years, which was swift by diocesan standards. It was also richly redecorated, especially in the apse and Lady Chapel. New communion rails and Stations of the Cross were installed and a text was painted around the apse:

DEUS PROVIDEBIT SIBI VICTIMAM HOLOCAUSTI
God will Provide for Himself a Victim for the Sacrifice

In 1965, it was re-ordered by Fr Bernard Smith in accord with the liturgical changes in the wake of Vatican II, the altar being brought forward, and a baptistry added in the southwest corner, where the original architect Mr Kelly had intended.

A further re-ordering took place in 2008, with a new altar and other fittings provided in Caen stone. The rich colour scheme was replaced with a uniform cream paint, and only the capitals in the sanctuary were repainted in gold. The capitals of the columns in the nave had previously been painted silver but they too emerged in the uniform cream.

The congregation has changed over the years. It was mainly Irish initially, but by 2023 the largest group was French, people working in London and living in and around Clapham Junction.

The dedication to St Vincent de Paul is at odds with Miss Ellis' wish for her churches to be named for old English saints. It appears that in early 1903, some French nuns, the Sisters of Charity of St Vincent de Paul, took a house in Altenburg Gardens. There they ran a small school and were helpful to Fr Grady in various ways. The nuns moved to Walworth, which they thought more fruitful for their mission, in March 1906, even before the laying of the church's foundation stone. It is possible to speculate that Mother Superior prevailed on Fr Grady to favour St Vincent de Paul. If so, he left no evidence. But he would have agreed that St Vincent de Paul is an excellent saint and a stirring example to all Catholics of how to live in this world.

St Philip and St James, Poplar Walk, Herne Hill (1906)

Architect: F. W. Tasker?

Herne Hill lies southeast of Brixton, west of Dulwich and north of Tulse Hill. The arrival of the London, Chatham & Dover Railway in 1862 led to the development of housing, both middle and working class and a huge increase in population. By 1900 there was a pressing need for a Catholic church. In 1905, at the request of Canon St John, Miss Ellis paid for the construction of the church, with a presbytery next door. The church is similar to many other Ellis boxes, being of London stock brick laid in English bond, with a large round window over the west end. It may have been built to an earlier design by F. W. Tasker, who had died in 1904.

The dedication to SS Philip and James was at the request of Bishop Amigo, who during this period also asked for apostolic dedications at St Simon & St Jude Streatham Hill, St Thomas Apostle Nunhead, St James the Great Peckham Rye and St Andrew Thornton Heath. Frances Ellis, of course, favoured early English saints, but she would not have opposed the Bishop's specific wishes.

St Philip and St James, Herne Hill

Bishop Amigo approached the Augustinian Canons (Canons Regular of the Lateran), who twenty years earlier had established a priory and a parish church at Stroud

Green in North London. Although Stroud Green was in Westminster, the Augustinians were an autonomous religious congregation and it was permissible for them to assist another diocese, assuming they had the manpower.

Two Augustinians, Fr Smith and Fr White, scouted the neighbourhood in early December 1905. They reported back to Amigo that they would be glad to take on Herne Hill, even though they had been unable to find the site of the church. At the same time, they confirmed that the order would be ready to adopt the parish of Dover, which would make for 'easier intercourse' with their communities across the Channel. Dover was probably what they really wanted, and in the end, as far as South London went, the Augustinians instead took on Eltham, where in due course they established a new priory.[36] Fr James Lonergan, who had been rector of the mission at Eltham, was switched to Herne Hill.

Amigo wrote to Fr Lonergan in March 1906, informing him that the Canons Regular would take over Eltham on 1 May. This was a particularly appropriate date as 3rd May was the Feast day of both St Philip Apostle and St James the Less.[37] He also promised £100 to buy furniture while 'the rest of the money will keep you in the first year which is generally the hardest.' Amigo felt confident that the mission would be self-supporting after the first year and promised to attend a solemn opening on 1 May.

A week after the opening Fr Lonergan wrote to Fr du Plerny at the Cathedral to ask for a map with the boundaries of the mission and a list of the 400 Catholics who were supposed to live in the mission area. Fr du Plerny's note to himself answers the second question with the curt phrase 'shoe leather', implying that Fr Lonergan should be walking the streets of Herne Hill and knocking on doors rather than bothering the Diocese with such petty requests.

The first parish visitation, dated 13th March, 1908, reveals a not entirely satisfactory situation. Fr Lonergan complains that the house and sacristy are damp. Total receipts for the previous year had been barely £60. The church could accommodate 170 people. It was open only for Mass. There were ten altar servers, but at this early stage no confraternities. There was an organ 'lent by a friend'. Fr Lonergan himself prepared the children for First Holy Communion. He also served the workhouse at Constance Road.[38]

Fr Lonergan stayed at Herne Hill for 30 years, and thus can truly be said to have established the parish. It remained poor, however: in 1934 he turned down the offer of a curate from Bishop Amigo on the grounds of poverty. 'It is only by observing the strictest economy that I am able to make ends meet.'

Fr Lonergan retired in 1936 and was replaced by Fr Henry Dodd who served throughout World War II and stayed until 1951. After him were two more long-stayers: Fr Laurence Ryan (1951–73) and Fr Peter Clements (1973–87). Through 2023, there have been only nine priests over 118 years.

Numbers of parishioners grew steadily throughout the 20th century, and in the 1960's plans were hatched to demolish the church and replace it with a new and larger one at Denmark Hill. In 1977 these plans were abandoned, the Denmark Hill site was sold and the profits put towards a major re-ordering of St Philip's. As at other Ellis churches (see St Thomas Apostle Nunhead), the altar was moved from the east end of the church to the centre of the long southern wall. Movable seating was wrapped around the altar, increasing the capacity in the nave to more than 200. At the same time the parish hall which had been placed between the north wall and the presbytery was demolished. The north wall was pierced so that additional movable seating could be placed there. But to allow the space to be used as an occasional hall, there are demountable screens to separate it from the nave.

Striking modern glass was procured from the Buckfast Abbey workshop of Dom Charles Norris, most notably in the round window over the west entrance. The glass in the seven lights of the southern clerestory represent the Seven Sacraments. In 1982, an organ by Hill, Norman and Beard was placed on a high platform at the west end.

Our Lady of Loreto and St Winefride, Kew (1906)
Architect: Canon A. J. C. Scoles

In 1898, Canon Bagshawe, the parish priest of St Elizabeth's Richmond, was finding it difficult to cover a parish that stretched along the south bank of the Thames from Kew to Richmond. Bishop Bourne gave him permission to approach a religious congregation for assistance. The Marist Fathers, who were based near Leicester Square, agreed to help, and sent him Fr Thomas. He bought a large house at 14 Kew Gardens Road and set about turning it into a mission. Another Marist, Fr Michael Cummins, was appointed the mission's first rector, and he found a plot of land immediately behind No.14 which would be suitable for a new church. This land he purchased for £1,200, before looking around for the money to build on it.

Meanwhile, yet another Marist, Fr McCamphill, parish priest at Paignton in Devon, had approached Frances Ellis for money to build a new church there. She listened sympathetically, but pointed out that Paignton already had two churches, and she would prefer to support another church in South London. Fr McCamphill sportingly directed her to Fr Cummins, and it was to him that Miss Ellis gave £3,000 for the design and construction.

The architect was Canon Alexander Joseph Cory Scoles, son of the notable Gothic Revival architect Joseph John Scoles, best known for his design of the magnificent Jesuit church of the Immaculate Conception at Farm Street, Mayfair. Fr Alexander trained as an architect under his father and became a priest of the Diocese of Clifton. His brother Ignatius, also an architect, was a Jesuit. Between them, the three Scoles designed many of the best Gothic Revival churches in Britain.

Canon Scoles' first design for Kew was, unsurprisingly, very much a Gothic church. He sent the plans to Frances Ellis at Hayle for her approval. She demurred, and so Scoles came up with the elegant Italianate classical design we see today.

Our Lady of Loreto and St Winefride, Kew

Then came the question of the church's dedication. Fr Cummins, as a good Marist, suggested Our Lady of Loreto. But Miss Ellis wanted an English saint, as with the other churches she had supported. In the case of Kew, she proposed St Winefride, who happened also to be her sister Rose's confirmation saint. This led to a polite tussle, ended by the obvious but unwieldy compromise of Our Lady of Loreto and St Winefride. Frances may, however, be said to have got her way in the long run: parishioners have always referred to the church as St Winefride's.

Fr McCamphill was transferred from Paignton to Kew as curate, and he preached the sermon at the ceremony for the laying of the foundation stone on 21 November 1905, the Feast of the Presentation of Our Lady. Building began immediately, and was completed by summer 1906, though without the two wide aisles specified in Scoles' plan. Sadly, Fr McCamphill died two months before the church itself was officially opened on 17 July 1906. The inaugural Mass was celebrated by Fr Moran, the Marist provincial, in the presence of Bishop Amigo. Canon Scoles, the architect, and Fr Cummins, parish priest, also officiated.

The parish has flourished ever since, though the Marists were forced by lack of manpower to turn it over to the Diocese in 1987. The long-delayed side aisles were installed in 1968, along with new chapels, confessionals and a baptistry. A further re-ordering was carried out in 1977, with the old altar being replaced by a table, while some marble from the original altar was reused in the tabernacle. A generous legacy from a parishioner, Mrs Moya Rinkenback, cleared the remaining debt, allowing Archbishop Michael Bowen to consecrate the church on 27 April 1979.

St Winefride's is arguably the most elegant of Miss Ellis' churches and is a decided adornment to the Kew street scene. It has always been a busy and active parish, with many societies and parish groups. Its Chapter of the St Vincent de Paul Society is thought to be the oldest in the country. Music has also been of a high standard. The organ is one of the finest in Britain, and notably was played only by lady organists until the 1970's.

St Matthias, Worcester Park (1906)
Architect: Benedict Williamson

The genesis of this parish was intertwined with Frances Ellis' other great commitment, to the Daughters of the Cross. They had established their novitiate at Carshalton in 1893, and in 1904 Frances purchased an old coaching inn at nearby Cheam to serve as a hospital—St Anthony's (see Chapter 5). A separate hospital chapel was built in 1905, and Fr Bernard Kelly became the first chaplain.

The following year Miss Ellis paid for a small permanent chapel on Brinkley Road in Worcester Park, which was also intended to serve neighbouring Ewell. The architect was Benedict Williamson, about to begin his studies for the priesthood. Building began in early June, and the first Mass was celebrated by Fr Kelly on Rosary Sunday 7 October 1906. The chapel, built of brick, seated only 65. It was not one of Williamson's more elaborate efforts.

The chapel was dedicated to St Matthias, chosen by lot to replace Judas (who had betrayed Jesus and taken his own life) among the ranks of the Twelve Apostles, as related in Acts 1:15–26. Matthias had been with Jesus since His baptism in the Jordan. Bishop Amigo tried to insist, not always successfully, that the new Ellis churches be dedicated to Apostles, rather than to her favoured old English saints.

Typically, there were 50 people attending the main Sunday Mass and a mere seven for the evening service, despite the fact that the mission area included Ewell, more than two miles away. Fr Kelly got Bishop Amigo's permission to reserve the Blessed Sacrament at St Anthony's rather than at St Matthias, because the area was still largely undeveloped, and safety could not be guaranteed. Fr Kelly continued living at Cheam, as did his immediate successors. As St Matthias' own parish history says, it was a small and struggling parish and priests tended not to stay long.

The outlook changed in 1914, when Miss Ellis paid for the construction of the expanded St Anthony's Hospital at Cheam. This hospital, run and staffed by the Daughters of the Cross, was immediately successful, and, together with the fast pace of housebuilding across southwest London, led to a growth in St Matthias's congregation. For many years men outnumbered women at the church, due to the large numbers of Irish labourers building houses in the area as well as to the southern extension of the Northern Line to Morden.

In 1921, Bishop Amigo suggested to Fr Sparling, then in charge of the mission, that he rent a house to use as a presbytery and thus ensure that St Matthias had a resident rector. But Fr Sparling gave up and returned to St Anthony's. Finally in 1930, another rector, Fr Crawford, who had been at North Cheam, took a house in Brinkley Road close to St Matthias. As the eighth rector in 25 years, he was then able to devote his full attention to the mission.

In 1930, Fr Crawford enlarged St Matthias by adding a side aisle, as well as a choir loft. Later he built a large sacristy which also served as a modest parish hall. Fr Crawford also purchased the land for the future St Cecilia's church in North Cheam, as well as a site for a junior school.

The congregation continued to grow, and in 1937 the Diocese purchased land on Cheam Common Road, where the new rector Fr Smoker built a presbytery and a hall. But lack of money, and the intervention of World War II, meant that the new church had to wait nearly thirty years.

Fr Smoker also built a new temporary church of St Clement at Ewell and when that was made a separate mission in 1940, the Bishop elevated Worcester Park to the status of a parish and Fr Smoker became the first parish priest. He stayed only another year however, as after the destruction of St George's in April 1941, he swapped places with the Cathedral administrator, Fr Farrell.

Post-war, the focus of activity was building up two excellent Catholic schools: St Cecilia's primary in North Cheam, and Richard Challoner secondary school for boys in New Malden.

In 1961, the Diocese decided to split the Worcester Park parish in two, with half going to North Cheam. It also renewed the effort to build the new church on Cheam Common Road, which finally received planning permission in 1962. The fine new Italianate church was ready in late 1965, with Bishop Cowderoy officially opening it with a Mass on the Feast of St Matthias, 24 February 1966. Fr Beausang, the energetic new parish priest, was to remain at St Matthias until 1998, and was able to be present at the parish's centenary celebrations in 2006.

The old Ellis chapel in Brinkley Road was sold to a developer and demolished in 1967.

Holy Innocents, Orpington (1908, replaced 1980)

Architect: Benedict Williamson

The dedication to Holy Innocents—the babies of Bethlehem slaughtered by King Herod—reflects Southwark's struggle to care for thousands of Catholic orphans and otherwise abandoned and destitute children whose existence shamed London in the late 19th and early 20th century. Two orphanages at Orpington, St Joseph's and St Anne's, were at the heart of the church's response, and their shared chapel, Holy Innocents, grew in due course to become the parish church.

The current extremely modernist church was built in 1980, replacing a tall brick chapel designed by the prolific architect and future priest Benedict Williamson and financed by Frances Ellis in 1907. The origins of the parish date back to 1887, when Bishop Butt acquired 60 acres in Orpington under the aegis of the Southwark Rescue Society. At that time the area of the modern parish was divided between Bromley, St Mary Cray and Sevenoaks. In 1891, the Society built St Joseph's orphanage, which for the first few years of its existence housed boys and girls. The boys were the responsibility of the Presentation Brothers, and the girls of the Sisters of Mercy.[39]

A separate girls' orphanage, St Anne's, was started in 1898 and completed in 1900. The Sisters of Mercy began with 230 girls, and a very tight budget of 2 shillings and sixpence (12.5p) per girl per week. It should be noted that late 20th century allegations of abuse against the Sisters of Mercy in some of their Irish institutions centred heavily on malnourishment of inmates. Many years later, a nun recalled that there was local opposition to the arrival of 'papists', but that in due course their presence was accepted, and some non-Catholic neighbours even became benefactors.

There was enough land to instruct children in basic agricultural skills. This tied in with the Diocese's programme of sending orphans to Canada, where they were cared for initially by the Catholic Canadian Emigration Society before placing them with Irish-Canadian farming families. This programme was overseen in Southwark by the diocesan treasurer Canon Edward St John. Indeed in 1906, the year that Holy Innocents was being planned, St John spent two months in Canada assuring himself that the programme was working (see Chapter 4). It is possible that Miss Ellis contributed to the running costs of the Southwark Rescue Society, but there are no surviving records to support the theory.

When the orphanages were first established there were few Catholics in and around Orpington. Some began to attend Mass at St Joseph's, usually celebrated by the resident chaplain, Fr Linnett. But with more than 400 children and dozens of brothers, nuns and lay Catholics, a separate chapel was needed. Canon St John asked Miss Ellis for the money, and she commissioned Benedict Williamson to design the new chapel.

The chapel was sited on unused land between the two orphanages and was completed in 1908. The tall brick building with its bell tower would not have looked out of place in Italy. Old Girls of St Anne's donated the church bell, and Old Boys of St Joseph's the tabernacle and six large candlesticks. Local lay Catholics attended the chapel for Mass but had to go to St Mary Cray for baptism, confirmation or marriage. The boys and male staff sat on the Epistle (right) side and the girls and Sisters on the Gospel (left) side, so the locals sat in the side aisle. The St Joseph's boys had an enthusiastic brass band which accompanied the singing but also, a parishioner remembered many years later, made it difficult for some to say their prayers. The band was also the subject of complaints from non-Catholic neighbours that it started practising at 7 o'clock every morning except Sunday, continuing for an hour.

In 1937 Fr Lawrence Bovington became priest-in-charge at Orpington, and was assigned an assistant, the fondly-remembered Fr Louis Fitzmaurice. With two priests it was possible to have an extra Mass as well as Benediction on Sunday. For the first time there was a proper choir. Fr Bovington established a Mass centre in the ballroom of the Daylight Inn at Petts Wood—the first step towards the creation of a new parish. During the war, the children were evacuated, as the area was on the Germans' flightpath towards London, and many bombs fell in the vicinity.

Although the children returned in 1945, the orphanages both closed some years later and the buildings were turned into a primary school and a secondary school.

Post-war housing development across all the neighbouring suburbs led to a substantial increase in the number of Catholics, and the need for new churches. In 1964, after long planning, Holy Innocents, with the generous help of many parishioners, gave birth to St Michael and All Angels Farnborough.

In 1971 Holy Innocents formally became the parish church of Orpington. Some years later the church and the two orphanage/school buildings were found to be suffering from subsidence and had to be demolished. The new, very modern, church was built about 100 metres from the old chapel, and most of the remaining land sold for housing. Holy Innocents Primary School was rebuilt nearby and continues to flourish. The new church was dedicated by Archbishop Bowen on 20 September 1981.

St Osmund, Castelnau, Barnes (established 1907, rebuilt 1955)

Architects: A. J. Hodsdon Archard & Partners

The present church was erected in 1955, replacing a chapel of ease established in 1907 in a house at 77 Castelnau, the lease of which had been purchased from the Church Commissioners with a grant from Frances Ellis. The price has not been recorded but would have exceeded £3,000.

The ground floor drawing room was used as the chapel, the first mass being celebrated in 1908. St Osmund's—the dedication chosen by Bishop Amigo—was served first by Salesians from Battersea, but in 1910 the first resident priest, Fr Michael Lawrenson, occupied the upper floor over the chapel. In the early twenties, Miss Catherine Leake became the first-floor tenant, while her nephew Fr Oscar Leake was responsible for the chapel.

In 1924 the Diocese purchased the freeholds of 77 and 79 Castelnau from the Church Commissioners. No.79 became the presbytery, while Fr Peake extended the chapel at number 77 into the garden. None of this was satisfactory, and accordingly Bishop Amigo commissioned plans for a new church from A. J. Hodsdon Archard & Partners. The plans were delivered in 1939, but their implementation was delayed by the war and subsequent shortages. The church was finally built in 1955 and opened a year later.

St Bartholomew, Hepworth Road, Norbury (1908)
Architect: Benedict Williamson

St Bartholomew's was built by Frances Ellis on land she had purchased from the Southern Railway on the borders of Streatham and Norbury. The site was a short distance west of the London-Brighton road (now the A23) and was also close to Norbury Station. The district of Norbury in those days was just beginning to develop. There were houses along the main road and nearby, but much of the land west of the church site and stretching towards Streatham Vale was still given over to market gardens. Just to the south, and across the railway line, was the National Westminster Bank's sports ground, opened in 1900. At the time, the nearest Catholic church was English Martyrs in Streatham, built in 1893 about a mile to the north.

The architect of St Bartholomew's was the indefatigable Benedict Williamson, then a student at the Beda in Rome and a year away from his priestly ordination. He designed a tall 'Ellis Box' of London stock brick, consisting of the sanctuary, two side chapels and a short nave. The interior was unadorned brick. There was room to seat perhaps 130 people. A small presbytery was built at the same time.

The first Mass was celebrated at St Bartholomew's on 20 September 1908, and Bishop Amigo preached there on 11 October. It appears initially to have been regarded as a chapel of ease to English Martyrs. Fr Peter Bovenizer was designated priest-in-charge. He came over from Streatham once a week to say Mass for very small congregations, sometimes as few as a dozen. Weekly offerings were slender, as little as a shilling (5p)—which before World War I would just have purchased six pints of beer. At one point Fr Bovenizer was threatened with arrest for failure to pay rates and had to be rescued by a parishioner.

St Bartholomew's Church, Norbury

From these modest beginnings, the church began to grow rapidly. It was designated a mission in August 1918, and on 7 November (four days before the armistice), Fr William Taunton took up residence as rector. He increased the number of Masses to three on Sunday and one each weekday. An organ was installed. Once the congregation adjusted to peace, it began to thrive. A choir was established as well as Chapters of the Catholic Women's League and other sodalities. The finances eased and, on 4 July 1920, St Bartholomew's was canonically elevated to a parish.

Unusually for a Catholic church, the parish established a popular tennis club on eleven acres of land which Fr Taunton and three parishioners purchased for £1,000 from the Streatham cemetery. Any surplus income was directed to the parish, and this seems to have been the beginning of St Bartholomew's prosperity. Membership was largely confined to Catholics for the first decade or so, but the restrictions on non-Catholics were eased in the thirties, and the club largely passed out of the hands of the parish. It seems to have ceased to function during the Second World War.

Meanwhile the church itself was enlarged in 1929 by the completion of the nave (with rose window) and the addition of a narthex and baptistry. The extensions blended perfectly with the original building, lending weight to the belief that they were prepared by Fr Benedict Williamson and/or his architectural partner J. H. Beart Foss.

In 1935 the parish of St Bartholomew's celebrated its first priestly vocation with the ordination of Fr Albert Coleburt. The second ordination followed in 1942, when Fr William Butler entered the Society of Jesus.

Fr Cyril Walmsley, parish priest from 1938 to 1944, began to build a parish hall at Pollards Hill, Mitcham, which he also intended to use as a Mass centre.

From 1963–93 Fr James Carolin was parish priest, and during his time the church was extended in two phases, under the direction of Anthony Stalley of Broadbent, Hastings, Reid & Todd. In 1964 the bare brick walls of the church interior were plastered and a new reinforced concrete gallery with narthex below built at the west end, along with confessionals. Then in 1967 a retro-chapel was built behind the sanctuary, as well as a new sacristy and an extension to the presbytery.

In the early 1970's the church and congregation, led by Fr Carolin were at the centre of resistance to the plan by the Ministry of Transport to thrust a motorway from Brighton (the northern section of what became the M23) right into the heart of London. The plan was dropped in

1974, and, with no doubt many prayers of thanksgiving and a sigh of relief, the parish resumed its upward trajectory.

Fr Carolin built a repository at the west end, octagonal in form to correspond with the adjoining baptistery. A new organ was purchased from F. H. Browne of Canterbury, and subsequently twice enlarged by them. The venerable Birmingham firm of Hardman & Son supplied mosaics above the west doors and side altars, as well as new stained glass. The church was then consecrated on 6 May 1975.

In 1997–98 a major internal re-ordering was undertaken by Tim Gough of Austin Winkley Associates, involving the removal of the arcading and wall which separated the retro-chapel from the sanctuary and the introduction of new liturgical furnishings and artworks.

In the 21st century St Bartholomew's remains a thriving parish in a multicultural Norbury much altered from its early days. A Hindu temple is a neighbour around the corner in Colmer Road. The parish priest Father Deodat Msahala was born in Tanzania. In 2019 Tomasz Margol, a former parishioner, though born in Poland, was ordained priest and assigned to St Bart's as curate. He is the latest of more than a dozen men of the parish who have become priests.

St Elphege, Stafford Road, Wallington (1908)

Architects: Benedict Williamson & J. H. Beart Foss

A mission was established at Wallington from Sutton in 1908. Frances Ellis provided the funds for a chapel of ease and the plans were drafted by the prolific architect (and later priest) Benedict Williamson. The church was similar to a number of his others in and around London, and could be described as a tall Romanesque barn, with three arched windows over the west door facing Stafford Road. An almost identical church is St David's, Abbey Wood, opened a year after St Elphege. *The Tablet* reported:

> The new church was opened on Tuesday last by the Bishop of Southwark. It was designed by Mr Benedict Williamson, assisted by Mr Foss, and built according to their plans by Messrs. Muirland of Walworth. The building is of Kentish brick with Kentish rag facings. The presbytery is built on to the church. The church will accommodate about 160 people, and the measurements are 60 by 25 feet.
>
> At the High Mass, sung by Father Warwick of Sutton, the Bishop spoke of the advantage possessed by the people in having a church of their own. A distance of two and a half miles had separated them from the neighbouring missions of Sutton and Croydon, rendering it difficult for the people to attend to Mass and their duties regularly. The Bishop urged the congregation to make good use of the blessings the new church would bring to them. The Mass (Turner) was sung by the Croydon choir. At the luncheon following the service, Canon Cafferata spoke of the excellent and solid work done by the builders. He had seen nearly every brick laid, and could guarantee the soundness of construction which characterised the whole building. Great praise was due to the architects and builders, who together had given the Diocese a building of which it might indeed be proud.[40]

Churches Financed by Frances Ellis

The former Church of St Elphege, Wallington

St Elphege, (or Alphege or Ælfheah as it is also spelled), was born in 953 near Bath. He became a monk, certainly at Bath Abbey and possibly for a time at Glastonbury. He was a protégé of St Dunstan. As Bishop of Winchester, Elphege played an important part in the negotiations that ended Viking raids in Wessex and led to the conversion of the Norwegian king Olaf Tryggvason. He became Archbishop of Canterbury but was captured by another Viking army at the siege of Canterbury in 1011. He was taken to Greenwich and held hostage for eleven months, but he refused to allow ransom to be paid for him. Eventually, according to the Anglo-Saxon Chronicle:

> The raiding army became much stirred up against the Bishop, because he did not want to offer them any money, and forbade that anything might be granted in return for him. Also they were very drunk, because there was wine brought from the south. Then they seized the Bishop, led him to their hustings[41] on the Saturday in the octave of Easter, and pelted him there with bones and the skulls of cattle; and one of them struck him on the head with the butt of an axe, so that with the blow he sank down and his holy blood fell on the earth, and sent forth his holy soul to God's kingdom.

Wallington was made a separate parish in 1920. The church was extended in 1935 with a new Lady Chapel and side aisle to designs by Beart Foss and enlarged again in 1954 by the addition of a transept designed by Conor P. Fahy.

In 1966 the congregation had outgrown the capacity of the original Ellis church and a competition was held for a new design. This was won by Austin Winkley, with an initial two stage brief: the first stage would be the new church, while in the second phase the old church would be converted into the parish hall and linked to the new building. The link was never built, and after a period as the Ellis Hall, the old building was converted into three flats and sold off.

Our Lady of the Assumption, Links Road, Tooting (1908, land only, present church 1988)

Architects: Sanders & Michelmore

Frances Ellis bought the land in 1908 at a time of intensive housebuilding in the area. The church was intended to serve the needs of an anticipated population of working-class Catholic commuters. The site is half a mile from Tooting railway station which had been expanded and rebuilt in the previous decade, but there were insufficient funds to build a church.

Initially a scout hall stood here, and Mass was regularly offered by priests from St Boniface, Tooting. During World War Two the scout hall was replaced by a public air raid shelter. Finally in 1963 Canon Thomas Clifton of St Boniface built a wooden church on the site, and the mission was properly established. The wooden church was badly damaged in the 1987 hurricane, and the foundation stone of the present church was laid in the Marian year of 1988.

At this time the remains of the medieval Merton Priory, a mile and a half from Links Road, were being excavated during the construction of a new supermarket. Fragments of stone from the Priory were used at Our Lady of the Assumption, in particular in constructing the cross which is embedded in the altar front. The church, which was consecrated in 1997, contains relics of St Thomas of Canterbury and St John Southworth.

St Benet, Abbey Grove, Abbey Wood, London SE2 (1909)

Architect: Benedict Williamson

St Benet's mission was founded from St Patrick's Plumstead in 1907. With Frances Ellis' financial backing, Benedict Williamson designed the church, which was opened on 1 August 1909. It is a standard Williamson design for Miss Ellis, a Romanesque barn with three arched windows over the liturgical west end, built of London stock brick with stone facings and a slate roof. It is situated among terraced houses on Abbey Grove, a street that backs on to the railway line from central London to north Kent. The presbytery, also paid for by Frances Ellis, is next door. As a chapel of ease for Plumstead, it accommodated about 100 worshippers.

Benet is the traditional old English variant of Benedict and was chosen in this instance by Frances Ellis in keeping with her preference for old English saints. At Abbey Wood the patron saint was the Northumbrian St Benedict Biscop (623–690), founder of the double monastery of Wearmouth-Jarrow, whose greatest son was St Bede the Venerable (672–735).

Early records for St Benet's are scant, the first surviving visitation form dating from 1913, recording a visit by Bishop Amigo. It notes that the annual income was tiny, about £26, and that there was no school, a vital consideration for all Catholic churches in those days. About a dozen children attended Saturday catechism classes taught by nuns.

The chapel was served by priests from Plumstead. Sunday Mass was at 9 am, while on holy days it was at 7.30 am. There were 'occasional' weekday Masses at 7.30 am. The 1913 visitation noted that about half the

Catholics in the area made their Easter duties, but that there were few if any regular communicants. Confession was available before Sunday Mass. The chapel was not licensed for weddings. Altogether the early years of St Benet's did not present a dynamic picture.

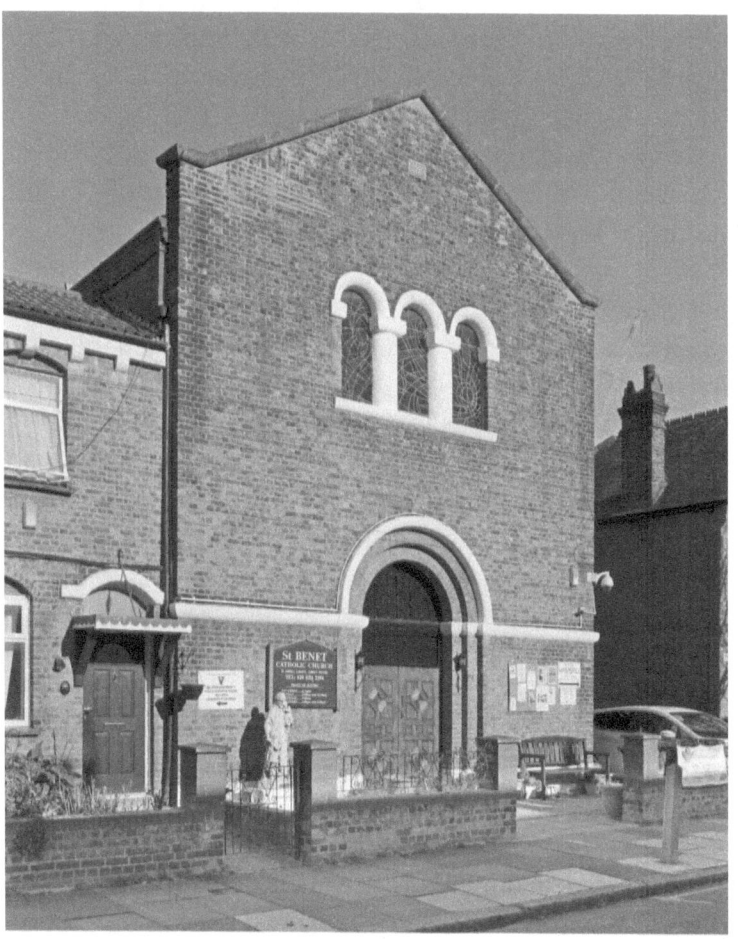

St Benet's Church, Abbey Wood

At some stage after World War I the mission got its first resident priest, but his name is not recorded. Nor is it possible to trace the development of the mission prior to World War II because there are no records in the archives between 1913 and 1944. However, in 1939 St Benet's was separated from Plumstead, and elevated to a parish, with Fr Peter Crommelin as its first parish priest. In late 1943 he moved to Ewell and was replaced by Fr Patrick Frawley, who had been curate at Tooting.

In March of 1944, the 80-year-old Archbishop Amigo left behind a detailed analysis of St Benet's.[42] In his visitation report to the new rector, Fr Frawley, he admits that he had doubted St Benet's capacity to become a parish but is impressed by the efforts of the people. He was glad too that there was a choir able to sing a full high Mass on Sunday. He asked the people to pray for the Pope, now that the Germans were in Rome, and for the soul of Miss Ellis. Amigo exhorted Fr Frawley to do something about cracks in the brickwork, but lack of funds prevented any work being done until 1962, when a general renovation took place, including the installation of a panelled ceiling to the nave.

Post-war development led to increased numbers of parishioners. Between 1955 and 1959 the London County Council built 3,000 new houses on recently drained marshland the other side of the railway line, known as the Abbey Wood Estate. In the mid-sixties, the LCC's successor authority the Greater London Council began building Thamesmead, an ambitious new development between the Abbey Wood Estate and the river, also on drained marshland. As in the Abbey Wood Estate, the initial inhabitants of Thamesmead were cockneys, white working-class families being moved out of London's overcrowded and bomb-damaged slums.

From 1957, Fr Michael Collins was the dynamic parish priest who started the area's first Catholic primary school, St Thomas Becket, and began to plan for the expansion of the parish. In 1964 St David's church, an extremely modern structure, was opened on Finchale Road. Its parish boundary lay north of the railway line while St Benet's catered for the area south of the line.

By 2023 the largest ethnic group in Thamesmead and Abbey Wood were of African heritage, among whom there were many Catholics. Both St Benet's and St David's were in the care of African priests of the Vincentian Order (the Congregation of the Mission, or CM).

St Swithun, Bromley Common (1910)

Architect: Benedict Williamson

St Swithun's was intended as a chapel of ease—an overflow church—for the parish of St Joseph's Bromley, which was being overwhelmed by rapid suburban development. Thus, at the time of its construction—one of the last collaborations between Frances Ellis and Canon St John—it did not have the status of a mission. The Catholic population was expanding due to the increasing affordability of the suburban railways, which attracted more commuters to the green fringes of London. Paradoxically, St Swithun's was built and opened while St Joseph's was still operating from a temporary building.

The architect was, once again, Fr Benedict Williamson, by then parish priest at St Gregory's, Earlsfield (p. 183 above). As St Swithun's was initially run from Bromley, there is little surviving early documentation. However, the parish priest at St Joseph's, Fr Walter Cooksey, wrote an informative letter to Bishop Amigo on 6 June 1910.

St Swithun's Church, Bromley Common

My Lord

After an unexpected delay, caused by the non-delivery of goods long-ordered, I was able yesterday to open the new church at Bickley, about 100 people assisting at the first Mass, and an equal number at Benediction in the evening.

It will be impossible for some weeks to say definitely how many people will make use of the new Church, as some were drawn from other districts by curiosity, while many Catholics known to me in Bickley and Bromley Common, did not attend. The new Church is fully and efficiently fitted and furnished and is ready for use in every way.

With this new Church open, and Keston as a going concern, it has become needful for me to ask your Lordship for permanent assistance. I have been able so far, by the help of friends and by engaging a priest from Eltham, to fulfil the obligations and I can continue to do so for a few weeks longer.

It is no news to your Lordship that I should like to have the help of my old and good friend Mr Evans when he is ordained and I can manage alright until the July ordinations. The enormous growth of Bromley renders permanent help all the more necessary as the entire district is becoming densely populated, and there is every prospect of a vast increase with the advent of third class season tickets which the Railways have now under consideration.

Your Lordship will be glad to hear that with the advent of Fr Thompson all friction with regard to Keston has ceased, and that he is doing all in his power to induce his outlying parishioners (at

West Wickham) to take advantage of the available Mass there.

I am, My Lord,

Your obedient servant in Xt

Walter Cooksey

In the fifties, Bishop Cyril Cowderoy designated St Swithun's a mission, and in 1977 Archbishop Michael Bowen elevated it into a properly constituted parish. Its debt paid off, Bowen consecrated the church on 28 May 1985. Relics of St Urbicius and St Oliver Plunkett were deposited under the altar.

However, the shortage of priests meant that in 2013, when Fr Bob Mercer retired as parish priest, St Swithun's was once again served by the priests at St Joseph's. In 2017 Bishop Pat Lynch decided that it would join with St Joseph's to form a single parish.

Of all the Ellis churches, St Swithun's is one of the least altered. It is a simple rectangular neo-Romanesque building constructed of London stock brick. The interior was re-ordered in 1972 to conform to the post-Vatican II liturgical changes, a choir loft was added at the west end, and wood panelling installed throughout.

Christ Church, Eltham (1912)

Architects: Canon A. J. C. Scoles & G. Raymond

There had been a mission in Eltham High St since 1870, and a small church, St Mary's, had been built in 1890. In 1906, the Canons Regular of the Lateran took over the missions at Eltham and Mottingham with the intention of building a new church as well as establishing a priory.[43]

In 1910 the Canons bought Eagle House as their headquarters and renamed it Christchurch Priory. There was enough land attached to the priory to build a badly-needed parish church. One of Miss Ellis' favourite architects, Canon A. J. C. Scoles, together with his nephew and partner Geoffrey Raymond, designed a church in Perpendicular Gothic Revival style, striking, but already old-fashioned at this date. *The Tablet* reported:

> The co-operation of various Religious Orders makes it possible from time to time to add to the number of churches, which are steadily increasing, in Southwark, and the Canons Regular of the Lateran, who have charge of the ancient Catholic district of Eltham, are providing the Diocese with a new church for the locality. In the presence of many members of the Order, including the Very Rev. Father Smith, C.R.L. (Visitor of the Province), Prior Gilbert Higgins, Prior O'Leary, Prior McElroy (Bodmin), and Prior McAdam (Swanage), as well as members of the Community for other localities, and a number of secular clergy of Southwark, the foundation-stone of the new church was laid on Thursday by the Right Rev. Abbot White, C.R.L. The Perpendicular style has been adopted by the Very Rev. Canon Scoles and Mr Raymond, the architects, and the cost of the structure when completed will, it is estimated, exceed £4,000 At the conclusion of the ceremony, an address was delivered by the Very Rev. Prior Higgins, who pointed out that the new edifice, when completed, would draw people to the truth of Christ. It had been argued that many of the churches in the land were not used to any considerable extent, that they were unhappily very often empty. How could it be otherwise? he asked. They did not possess the supernatural magnet for the drawing together of souls: 'For more than nineteen hundred years the Catholic Church had taught that in the Blessed Sacrament was to be found the true magnet of souls.'[44]

Frances Ellis is said to have been the principal benefactress of Christ Church, though there is scant surviving evidence. Eltham is included in a handwritten list of Ellis churches kept in the Southwark archives. There is also an entry in the diocesan finance committee minutes for May 1907:

> The church has been completed and paid for. The cost of the land remained a debt. Canon St John was to try and get Miss Ellis to pay for it.[45]

Incidentally this note is a rare surviving record of the process by which the Diocese, through St John, involved Frances in expansion projects. A principal reason for the lack of evidence is the unexplained gaps in the minute book of the Council of Temporal Administration. The minutes begin in 1893 when Bishop Butt established the Council, but astonishingly, between 1897 and 1907 only one meeting is recorded, for January 1900.[46]

What can be said with certainty is that Christ Church would have been the last church Frances Ellis built for Southwark. Her collaborator Canon Edward St John, who had fallen out so spectacularly with Bishop Amigo and the Southwark Chapter, moved to Liverpool, where his friend and patron Cardinal Bourne had secured for him the chaplaincy of Walton Jail. Thereafter Miss Ellis confined her philanthropy to the Daughters of the Cross of Liège.

It is worth noting the continuing dedication of the parish and Archdiocese to Catholic education in Eltham. Both St Mary's RC Primary and St Thomas More Catholic Comprehensive School are rated 'Outstanding' by the regulator Ofsted. The St Thomas More website adds:

Christ Church, Eltham

All pupils admitted to the school come from fully practising Catholic families who attend Mass every Sunday. There is a very strong Catholic ethos built around the mission statement 'To encourage each individual to grow and develop through love and the teachings of Christ'.

A century on, that statement continues to reflect Frances Ellis' gift to the people of Southwark.

Arundel & Brighton Diocese

St Erconwald, Esher Avenue, Walton-on-Thames (1906)

Architect: Frank Reckitt

A modest chapel of ease was built here in 1905 and opened in 1906. At this date Walton-on-Thames was in Southwark Diocese.[47] As part of her agreement with Canon St John, Frances Ellis paid the £1,000 cost. As was common practice at the time, the Diocese of Southwark immediately raised a £1,000 mortgage on the building, leaving the mission to find £40 a year in interest.

The chapel was designed by Frank Reckitt, a promising young architect who had just gone into independent practice. Built of brick, and quite plain, it was not a standard Ellis Box, rather a simple shed-like structure with a pitched tiled roof. Inside, from surviving photos, it was well furnished. According to the parish website, Mr A.M. Burke paid for the altar, Dr Scannell provided a chalice and Mr Hasslacher donated the benches. There was seating for perhaps 75.

The mission was served from Our Lady Immaculate, Surbiton, a priest cycling over on Saturday evening and usually staying with a local family in Walton. Bishop Amigo later required the mission to raise £100 a year to cover the mortgage and the cost of supplying a diocesan priest to celebrate Mass. Some years later the duty was taken over by the Josephites of St George's College at Addlestone, and they continued until 1929. In that year Fr Stephen O'Beirne was appointed by the Diocese as rector of the mission.

From the outset there was an intention among the local Catholics to build a larger parish church. Fr O'Beirne and his successor Fr Fred Copsey were determined to realise the ambition. In 1931 Fr O'Beirne bought a plot of land next to the chapel, and Fr Copsey began the building in 1937. War interrupted the work, and the new church was finally ready for occupation in 1947.

The original chapel of ease, which stands immediately next to the new St Erconwald's, was stripped of its furnishings and converted into the parish hall. In more recent years St Erconwald's has joined with the churches at Hersham and East Molesey into a triple parish.

St Hugh of Lincoln, Victoria Road, Knaphill, Surrey (1908)

Architect: unknown

Miss Ellis provided the money to build the first Catholic church and presbytery in Knaphill, though the amount and the architect are unknown. The area had strong military connections, being close to Aldershot and numerous British army installations. The first priest in charge of the mission was Fr Henry Drage, who was transferred to Walworth after four years. He was replaced in 1912 by Fr Stanley Mason, who remained for a decade, including the period of the First World War which had a particular impact on this area. Fr Mason moved to St Edward's Sutton Place in 1922, and it seems the church was then closed.

St Hugh's reopened in 1946 after a substantial growth in the local Catholic population. At first it was served from Woking, before being elevated to a parish and receiving its own resident priest. The old church was too small, so additional services were held at Brookwood Hospital, the Inkerman Barracks and the British Legion hall until a church hall was built in the 1960s: this was used for services until a new permanent and very modern church was erected in 1971.

Brentwood Diocese

Our Lady of the Rosary and St Patrick, Walthamstow (1908)

Architect: Fr Benedict Williamson

The only Ellis church north of the Thames was designed by Benedict Williamson for a site on Blackhorse Road, Walthamstow. It is dedicated to Our Lady of the Rosary and St Patrick. When constructed in 1908, Walthamstow was part of Westminster Archdiocese, but in 1917 it, along with the rest of London east of the River Lea and all of Essex, was separated into the new Diocese of Brentwood.

In 1905, Fr William O'Grady became parish priest of the newly built Church of Our Lady & St George in Shernall Street, Walthamstow. It was quickly apparent that the church was unable to accommodate the 3,000 souls who wanted to attend Mass every Sunday, many of them forced to walk long distances to get there. He was able to buy a site for what he intended as a chapel of ease for St George's near the western boundary of the parish.

The seller of the land was HM Customs Annuity and Benevolent Fund. Although it was probably coincidence, Canon St John's father had been head of the Customs, so there may have been a useful connection. It is more likely that Fr O'Grady's search for land and money had come to the notice of his Archbishop, who had put him in touch with his friend St John. In any case, Frances Ellis contributed £1,000 for the purchase of the land, and a further unrecorded sum for the building of the church itself.

Once again, Fr Benedict Williamson was architect, together with his partner J. H. Beart Foss. He seems to have undertaken the commission while completing his studies for the priesthood in Rome and before his first appointment as parish priest of Earlsfield.

Williamson designed Our Lady and St Patrick in a simplified Romanesque style in, as usual, London stock brick. As with most of the Ellis boxes, there is a round window at the west end. It is modelled on a Roman basilica: a rectangle with gabled roof, lean-to aisles on each side, and an apse.

Our Lady of the Rosary and St Patrick, Walthamstow

As a chapel of ease, the church was served for a couple of years by priests from St George's, Shernall Street. It received its own resident priest in July 1910 and was then recognised as a mission. In 1914 the Stations of the Cross were installed, but World War I and the poverty of the congregation delayed further improvements. Our Lady and St Patrick was canonically elevated as a parish in 1919.

A second wave of expansion and decoration took place in 1930, and it is thought that Fr Benedict Williamson was again the architect. This programme added the Lady Chapel, sanctuary and sacristy to what had previously been a bare building.[48] Further improvements followed in 1936 when a high altar, pulpit and altar rails in marble were designed and installed by F. G. White & Co. of Hampton Court.

During World War II industrial Walthamstow was a regular target of German bombs and rockets, and Our Lady of the Rosary and St Patrick suffered considerable damage from bombing. The worst incident was in December 1944, when a V2 rocket landed 150 yards away at Longfield Avenue. In addition to killing 10 people and destroying many houses it wrecked part of the parish hall.

In 1958, a tympanum with an Italian mosaic of Our Lady with the Child Jesus and St Patrick was placed over the entrance. If there were any doubt as to the character of the congregation at that time, St Patrick is depicted proffering a shamrock to the Blessed Babe. The 21st century congregation is a diverse one, with many parishioners of Polish and African extraction.

In 1965, a gallery and organ loft with raked seating was added, while further re-ordering took place in 1982. Free of debt at last, the church was consecrated in 1985.

Plymouth Diocese

Our Most Holy Redeemer, Keyham, Plymouth (1902)
Architect: Canon A. J. C. Scoles

The large church at Keyham was designed to serve the Plymouth naval base and naval dockyards. The land was acquired for £1,000 from Lord St Levan by Bishop Graham and the Catholic naval chaplain. Lord St Levan's agent Edward St Aubyn—himself an architect—gave more land valued at £624, and the Admiralty, which demanded a seating capacity of 500, donated a further £500 as well as an annual sum to cover maintenance.

In late 1900, Frances Ellis, at this stage still nominally an Anglican and living in Ramsgate, gave £5,000 towards the building of Holy Redeemer—a particularly generous sum which must have covered all or most of the cost. The offer was made by her agent James Lee. Initially, in August 1900, he told the Bishop that Miss Ellis wished to present an endowment of £3,000 to the Diocese. It is not clear whether the earlier offer was superseded or complemented by the larger, second sum. She was already planning to move to Cornwall—she, with Mr and Mrs Lee, are recorded as living in Penzance in March 1901—and the offer of an endowment was probably meant as an introduction to her intended Diocese. It may be that Bishop Graham, having been made aware of this new benefactress, asked her to consider instead supporting the expensive construction of this large new church for which at that point he had only the land and the architectural plans.

It is characteristic of Francis Ellis' approach that Lee asked the Bishop not to mention her name in his pastoral letter announcing the building of Most Holy Redeemer.

She had asked him to stress that she was 'merely assisting in the efforts of the people to build the church'.

The church was designed by the well-known Gothic revival architect Canon A. J. C. Scoles, the first of his five collaborations with Miss Ellis. It was significantly larger than most of the churches she subsidised. The foundation stone was laid by Bishop Graham on 10 April 1901, and the church was open for worship in early July 1902. A presbytery for two priests was built alongside it, and, four years later, a school was opened on spare land next to the church. Apparently, this was in the teeth of anti-Catholic municipal opposition, always strong in the West Country.

Most Holy Redeemer is built of unevenly coursed limestone, and consists of a wide nave with five bays, aside isles and a square chancel with two side chapels. There is no tower.

The church was bombed in April 1941, losing its roof and suffering widespread internal damage. Mass was celebrated in the school until the church was restored and reopened in 1950. The lost organ was replaced by one given by the monks of Buckfast Abbey, who also built and installed it. The church was consecrated in 1957. Further extensive re-ordering took place in 1988. More recently it became part of Holy Trinity parish.

Most Holy Trinity, Newquay, Cornwall (1903)

Architect: Canon A. J. C. Scoles

For many years Catholics in and around Newquay could only hear Mass in the private chapel of The Tower, ancestral home of the staunchly Catholic Molesworth family. In 1903 Lady Molesworth, an American, gave land for the building of a new church. Someone—probably Bishop Graham of Plymouth, with whom she had developed a warm friendship—approached Frances Ellis, who by then was living 25 miles away at Hayle. She donated £500, less than she usually gave for new churches, but it is likely that local Newquay Catholics, including Lady Molesworth, would also have contributed.

Most Holy Trinity, Newquay

Most Holy Trinity, though not a large church, is not an 'Ellis Box', again suggesting that plans were well in hand before Frances became involved. Once again, the architect was Canon Alexander Joseph Cory Scoles, one of a remarkable trio of Catholic architects: his brother Fr Ignatius Scoles SJ and their father J. J. Scoles had designed many of the finest Gothic Revival churches in England. A. J. C. Scoles was a canon of the Clifton Diocese, and, at the time he designed Most Holy Trinity, was parish priest of Holy Ghost, Basingstoke.

At Newquay, Scoles designed a simple but handsome gothic church built of buff sandstone with granite dressings. The church has been much altered and extended since 1903 and is now the centre of a very active Catholic community centred on Newquay, with satellite churches at Perranporth and St Agnes.

Sacred Heart and St Ia, St Ives, Cornwall (1908)

Architects: Canon A. J. C. Scoles & G. Raymond

The Catholic and Anglican parish churches at St Ives share a dedication to St Ia, though the Catholic church has the additional dedication to the Sacred Heart. This is unsurprising as St Ia is the first saint connected with the area and gave her name to the town itself (St Ives is an Elizabethan corruption). She was one of a group of Irish or Welsh missionaries who came to west Penwith in the 5th century. She built an oratory at St Ives; when she was martyred with several other missionaries on the orders of Theodoric, a local chieftain, her relics were deposited in her oratory. When the original parish church was rebuilt in 1434, her relics were translated to the new building, known today as St Ia and St Andrew, its tall tower dominating the centre of the town.

Cornwall held on to its Catholic faith well into the 16th century, as witnessed by the Western Rising or Prayer Book Rebellion (1549). This was in response to the new protestant Prayer Book in English, a language most 16th century Cornishmen neither spoke nor read. The rebellion was bloodily suppressed in a series of battles in which the Cornish in particular often fought to the death. The Crown's hard-won military victory was followed by a reign of terror, culminating in the murder of John Payne, the Catholic mayor of St Ives: Sir Anthony Kingston,

Provost Marshal of the Crown forces, invited him to lunch at the George & Dragon, where he was seized and summarily hanged. Writing some years after the Rising, the Cornish antiquarian scholar Richard Carew observed drily that Kingston 'hath left his name more memorable than commendable'.

Over the succeeding three centuries, Cornwall lost its Catholic character, although the Civil War showed that Cornishmen remained strongly royalist and tended to oppose the Puritan strain in the Church of England. Beginning in the 1740's, John Wesley and his brother Charles preached widely in Cornwall, and by the early 19th century Methodism was the dominant strand of Cornish Christianity, particularly among the rural poor. Catholics reappeared in numbers in the 19th century, especially Irish miners working in the tin mines. In 1843, Fr William Young of the Oblates of Mary Immaculate, sometimes referred to as the 'Apostle of Cornwall', built the Church of The Immaculate Conception of Our Lady in Penzance.

In 1901, when she was living temporarily at Penzance, Frances Ellis purchased a shop and warehouse at Street-an-Pol in St Ives and invited the Canons Regular at Bodmin to use it as a church.[49] The first Mass was celebrated on 16 February 1902, and, with numbers growing over the next five years, it was clear that a purpose-built church was needed. Frances bought a corner site at the top of Skidden Hill facing Tregenna Hill, and again commissioned Canon A. J. C. Scoles and his partner Geoffrey Raymond to design it.

At St Ives, she did not insist on a plain Italianate 'Ellis Box' as she would have done in London but accepted the 13th-century French Gothic design proposed by Scoles and Raymond. This suited the site, and was in keeping with the vernacular architecture, and especially the ecclesiastical style of West Penwith. The total cost of the site and church was reported as 'very near £ 4,000'.

Sacred Heart and St Ia, St Ives

The foundation stone of the new church was blessed and laid by Bishop Graham on 5 March 1908. The *Western Morning News* reported a large and mostly respectful crowd for what it described as a semi-private ceremony.

> But the behaviour of a section, chiefly young fishermen and young women, was certainly not in accord with the sacredness of the ceremony. As the Bishop, wearing above his rochet the amice, alb, girdle, stole, cope, and mitre, and carrying his pastoral staff, preceded by cross and candle-bearers, walked in procession with the priests, a good deal of derisive laughter was indulged in. This

behaviour was even more evident when the Bishop was conducting the ceremony, in the course of which the mitre was occasionally removed.

Whatever the opinion of the fishermen and their girlfriends, the construction of the church proceeded at a rapid pace over the summer, thanks to the builder Mr J. R. Sandry, of St Ives. Bishop Graham, attended by many priests, dedicated the church on 21 September 1908, having blessed the high altar the previous day. Frances Ellis was also in attendance; this was probably only the third or fourth of 'her' churches whose opening she witnessed. *The Tablet* reported:

> The walls are built of Trelyon Downs stone with dressings of Cornish granite.[50] The church consists of nave, sanctuary, one aisle and sacristy. Below the aisle and part of the nave is a large room for parochial and social purposes. The nave is 54ft. long by 22ft. wide, and 30ft. high from floor to apex of the ceiling, which is of plaster divided by wooden ribs into panels; the aisle is of the same length as the nave and eight feet wide. At the end of the aisle is the lady altar, set anglewise across the corner on account of the small space available, an arrangement which allows it to be well seen from the nave. By the side of this altar is the principal door to the sacristy. The sanctuary is divided from the nave by a lofty arch, and is 16ft. wide by 14ft. deep. The ceiling is groined in pitch pine. The stonework of the interior is Bath, and the walls are finished with terra-cotta coloured stucco. The style of the high altar is early decorated, or 15th century architecture.[51]

The next day, Sunday, in thanksgiving for the building of the new church, a solemn votive Mass of the Most Holy

Trinity was sung in the presence of the Blessed Sacrament. In the evening the Bishop preached and confirmed six candidates, two adults and four children. There was still a debt of about £1,000 on the church.

In 1913 a single bell was given to Sacred Heart and St Ia. It was replaced in 1954 by electronic bells. In 1949 a bronze plaque commemorating the martyrdom of John Payne, by Fr Charles Norris of Buckfast Abbey, was installed on the south wall facing the street. Sacred Heart and St Ia was consecrated on 8 May 1946. It is now, along with the church at Hayle, part of the parish of Penzance.

Notes

1. In 1965, the Diocese of Arundel & Brighton was carved out of Southwark, alongside Portsmouth which had been separated from Southwark in 1882. A careful search of the records of all three dioceses, together with individual parish websites, has failed to produce any other possible Ellis churches.
2. Eight years before she became a Catholic.
3. The first three in East Kent, the remaining thirty-three in or around south London. Two of the latter are now in the newer Diocese of Arundel & Brighton.
4. Wergild is, in ancient Germanic law, the amount of compensation paid by a person committing an offence to the injured party or, in case of death, to his family. In certain instances, part of the wergild was paid to the king and to the lord—these having lost, respectively, a subject and a vassal.
5. The Abbot of Ramsgate was the *parochus* for the whole of the Isle of Thanet, and thus responsible for all parishes. Under Canon Law, he was the parish priest for each parish or mission, to which he assigned priests in charge. These were all monks of Ramsgate Abbey, and thus they were doubly under his discipline as abbot and parish priest.

6. The Union system replaced the old parish workhouses between 1834 and 1929.
7. *The Tablet*, 7 January 1922, p. 28.
8. *East Kent Times and Advertiser*, 25 June 1901
9. The lady in question, after she was widowed, sold Haling Park in 1931, and in 1936 it was demolished.
10. Personal information about Fr Pritchard from the late Fr Michael Clifton, and from the author's wife Fiona Cadwallader, Fr Pritchard's great-great niece.
11. Jn 1:18.
12. *The Tablet*, 26 September 1903, p. 514. See also *The Tablet*, 21 November 1903, p. 835.
13. *The Tablet*, 17th September 1904, p. 472.
14. A. Turati, B. Mussolini, B. Williamson. *A Revolution and its Leader*. (London, Alexander-Ouseley, 1930).
15. At that date, the Liberal Party was the party of the working man. The Labour Party was founded a year later, in 1900, and displaced the Liberals after the First World War.
16. A number of 'Ellis boxes' postdate Tasker's death. Four churches are definitely his: South Bermondsey, Larkhall Lane, Robsart St and Catford. St James Peckham Rye very probably is a fifth. It may be that his simple and easily adapted master plan was used by the builders of subsequent churches.
17. Fr Smith, a Spanish speaker, was also at this time chaplain to the 12,000 wartime refugees from Gibraltar.
18. The same motorway threatened the Ellis church of St Thomas Apostle, Nunhead.
19. *The Tablet*, 24 September 1904, p. 490.
20. Williamson later designed Orpington, Tooting, Norbury, Worcester Park, Abbey Wood, Bromley Common, Wallington and Walthamstow for Miss Ellis. Once ordained, he was appointed rector of the Earlsfield mission where he carried out extensive improvements.
21. The donation was probably around £3,000. Unfortunately, the Diocese kept no records of Miss Ellis' largesse, and unless noted elsewhere, it is necessary to rely on estimates.

22. Fr du Plerny, a Frenchman, was associated with the Empress Eugènie, widow of Napoleon III, and the founder of Farnborough Abbey. After a dispute between the family of the Earls of Mexborough and the Diocese over the running of St Raphael's church, Surbiton, Fr du Plerny was installed as parish priest there between 1897 and 1908. He also had administrative duties at the Cathedral.
23. *The Tablet*, 20 December 1930, p. 848.
24. These events took place not many years after the tragicomedy of the Anglican rector of Stiffkey had absorbed the British public, and newspapers were keen to find more prurient stories of the clergy.
25. Although not strictly relevant to the subject of this book, Fr O'Donovan's case is interesting in light of modern concerns about safeguarding within the church. He was an intelligent and highly educated loner who had taken an erratic path towards the priesthood. Following ordination in 1917 aged 33, he suffered health problems which led to him being addicted to morphine. Having kicked the habit, he nonetheless had a poor reputation among fellow clergy who regarded him as lazy and unreliable. It is clear that colleagues, including Bishop Amigo, were aware of his sexual predilections. Amigo wrote to him in March 1939: 'Have nothing whatever to do with boys or young men in private. You had trouble enough in Germany and you ran greater risks in Stockwell than you ever imagined... You are too weak and you must pray all the more earnestly.'
26. Founded at Valence, SE France, by Jeanne de Franssu in 1813. They had two English houses, at Eastbourne and Sittingbourne.
27. Presumably Miss Ellis was not consulted about the architectural style.
28. Joanna Bogle, *One Corner of London: A History of St Bede's Church*. (Leominster: Gracewing 2003). pp 8–11.
29. *The Tablet*, 21 May 1932, p. 672.
30. The 491st anniversary of the battle of Agincourt. Presumably the date was not chosen as a gratuitous insult to the neighbouring Huguenots.
31. A 400-bed fever hospital erected by the Metropolitan Asylum Board in the 1890's. St George's Hospital now occupies the site.

32. *The Tablet*, 24 November 1906, p. 822.
33. Southwark Archives, Amigo visitation notes, 1 March 1912.
34. D. Evinson, *Catholic Churches of London* (Sheffield: Sheffield Academic Press 1998) p. 254.
35. In Jn 19:26–27, Jesus from the cross gave His mother into the care of St John. There is an ancient tradition that she lived the latter part of her life on earth in St John's house at Ephesus.
36. See Christ Church, Eltham, below.
37. St James the Less was so called to distinguish him from St James the Great, brother of St John. 'Less' because he was either shorter or younger than St James the Great. St James the Less, who went on to lead the early church in Jerusalem, is identified with James 'the brother of Jesus', probably his cousin. He was martyred in AD 62 or 69.
38. Now St Francis Road. Built in 1896, the workhouse was taken over by London County Council in 1930 and turned into part of Dulwich Hospital.
39. The Presentation Brothers are a community of lay men who take vows of poverty, chastity and obedience. The Sisters of Mercy combine works of mercy and education with contemplation, a similar charism to the Daughters of the Cross.
40. *The Tablet*, 19 December 1908, p. 983.
41. Council.
42. In 1938, in recognition of the golden jubilee of his priesthood, Pope Pius XI had conferred on Amigo the personal title of Archbishop. The Ecclesiastical Province of Southwark was erected by Pope Paul VI in May 1965, thus raising the Diocese to Archdiocesan status.
43. See St Philip & St James, Herne Hill.
44. *The Tablet*, 9 November 1912, p. 737.
45. This refers to St Mary's, built in 1890. The note is in Canon St John's own hand.
46. For a detailed discussion of this topic please see Chapter 4.
47. It became part of the new Diocese of Arundel & Brighton on 28 May 1965.

48. In 1932, a new neighbour arrived next door to OLRP with the construction of the Walthamstow Baptist Church. The two churches have always enjoyed cordial relations.
49. In 2021 the site of the old chapel was a popular café.
50. Trelyon Downs lie just south of St Ives.
51. *The Tablet*, 3 October 1908, p. 555.

GLOSSARY

Mission: A mission (or quasi-parish, as it is now sometimes called) is the first step in the establishment of a new parish. The priest in charge is known as the rector. Very often, the mission starts life without a church building. This was the case with some of the Ellis churches: St Vincent de Paul, Altenburg Gardens and Our Lady of Grace, Charlton are good examples, where worship began in a dedicated room in a house, and the church itself was built a few years later. When a mission has been started, the intention is that it should in course of time be elevated to the status of a parish. Canon Law rules that to achieve this status, the parish needs to have a church, a settled and reasonably sized congregation, and to be free of debt. Some of the Ellis churches in poorer areas took many years to pay off all debts. That also allows the bishop to formally consecrate the church: for example, St Francis de Sales in Larkhall Lane, Stockwell, opened for worship in 1903, but was only consecrated, by Archbishop Michael Bowen, in 2002.

Chapel of ease: A church building other than the parish church, situated within the bounds of a parish for the attendance of those who cannot reach the parish church conveniently. St Bede's, Clapham Park and St Osmund's, Kew both started as chapels of ease to nearby large parishes. Both were subsequently elevated to parish status. A chapel of ease differs from a mission only in its original purpose, and in practice it is difficult to differentiate them.

Church orientation: Traditionally a church is oriented east-west, with the sanctuary, containing the altar, at the east end, and the entrance door at the west end. In practice this is often not possible, and so architects refer to the altar being at the 'liturgical east end', even when it is facing a different direction. An example of east being west and west being east is found at St Mary Magdalen, East Hill, Wandsworth.

Rose Window: A generic term often loosely applied to a circular window in a church, but in this book, it is used for those found in Gothic or Gothic-style cathedrals and churches. Rose windows are divided into segments by stone mullions and tracery, usually containing stained glass. Miss Ellis often asked that her plain brick churches had a round window at the west end, as at St Gertrude, South Bermondsey. A few Ellis churches now have rose windows, for instance, St Boniface, Tooting, where the new window was installed in 1927.

BIBLIOGRAPHY

Bellenger, A., & Fletcher, S., *Princes of the Church: A History of the English Cardinals.* Stroud: Sutton Publishing, 2001.

Bogle, J., *One Corner of London: A History of St Bede's Church, Clapham Park.* Leominster: Gracewing, 2003.

Clifton, M., *History of the Archdiocese of Southwark.* London: The Saint Austin Press, 2000.

Clifton, M., *Amigo: Friend of the Poor.* Leominster: Gracewing, 2006.

Evinson, D., *Catholic Churches of London.* Sheffield: Sheffield Academic Press, 1998.

Gasquet, F., *A Short History of the Catholic Church in England.* London: Catholic Truth Society, 1912.

Heren, P., *A Spoonful of Honey: St Francis de Sales & St Gertrude.* London: Privately printed, 2002.

Hooley, T., *A Seminary in the Making.* London: Longmans Green & Co, 1927.

O'Neill, L., *Heritage 1782–1982.* Privately printed by The Daughters of the Cross, 1982.

O'Neill, L., *Venerable Mère Marie-Thérèse Haze.* Privately printed by The Daughters of the Cross, 1987.

Parry, D., *Monastic Century: St Augustine's Abbey, Ramsgate 1865–1965.* Tenbury Wells: Fowler Wright, 1965.

Reynolds, E., *The Roman Catholic Church in England and Wales: A Short History.* Wheathampstead: Anthony Clarke Books, 1973.

Seglias, L., *Our Parish: The Story of St Vincent de Paul's, Clapham Common*. London: Privately printed, 1982.

Vickers, M., *By the Thames Divided: Cardinal Bourne in Southwark and Westminster.* Leominster: Gracewing, 2013.

INDEX OF CHURCHES

Church	Diocese	Page
Christ Church, Eltham	Southwark	270
Holy Cross, Catford	Southwark	176
Holy Innocents, Orpington	Southwark	252
Most Holy Trinity, Newquay, Cornwall	Plymouth	280
Our Lady of the Assumption, Tooting	Southwark	263
Our Lady of Grace, Charlton	Southwark	197
Our Lady Help of Christians & St Joseph, Folkestone	Southwark	165
Our Lady of Loreto & St Winefride, Kew	Southwark	246
Our Lady of the Rosary & St Patrick, Walthamstow	Brentwood	278
Our Most Holy Redeemer, Keyham, Plymouth	Plymouth	279
Sacred Heart & St Ia, St Ives, Cornwall	Plymouth	282
St Alban, Herring St, South Walworth	Southwark	189
St Andrew, Thornton Heath	Southwark	206
St Bartholomew, Norbury	Southwark	256
St Bede, Clapham Park	Southwark	215
St Benet, Abbey Wood	Southwark	264
St Boniface, Tooting	Southwark	229
St Elphege, Wallington	Southwark	259
St Erconwald, Walton-on-Thames	Arundel and Brighton	274

Church	Diocese	Page
St Ethelbert & St Gertrude, Ramsgate	Southwark	162
St Francis de Sales & St Gertrude, Larkhall Lane, Stockwell	Southwark	170
St Gertrude, South Bermondsey	Southwark	173
St Gertrude, South Croydon	Southwark	166
St Gregory, Garratt Lane, Earlsfield	Southwark	180
St Helen, Robsart Street, North Brixton	Southwark	207
St Hugh of Lincoln, Knaphill, Surrey	Arundel and Brighton	275
St James the Great, Peckham	Southwark	183
St John the Evangelist, Littlewick Green, Berkshire	Oxford (CE)	156
St Joseph (formerly St Egbert), New Malden	Southwark	211
St Mary Magdalen, East Hill, Wandsworth	Southwark	227
St Matthew, West Norwood	Southwark	192
St Matthias, Worcester Park	Southwark	249
St Mildred, Minster-in-Thanet	Southwark	158
St Osmund, Barnes	Southwark	255

Index of churches

Church	Diocese	Page
St Philip & St James, Herne Hill	Southwark	242
St Simon & St Jude, Streatham Hill	Southwark	224
St Swithun, Bromley Common	Southwark	267
St Thomas Apostle, Nunhead	Southwark	194
St Vincent de Paul, Altenburg Gardens, Clapham	Southwark	236
St Wilfrid, Kennington Park	Southwark	214
St William of York, Forest Hill	Southwark	201

Index of Names

Aikens, Fr Patrick 206
Ainsworth, Sr Patricia 147
Alexander, Mrs 111, 113
Allanson, Mary 230
Alexian Brothers, Twyford Abbey 82, 83
Alton, Fr William 184–5
Amigo, Archbishop Peter xiv, xvii, xviii, 44, 47, 49, 54–56, 60–62, 67–79, 81–82, 85, 135–6, 138–141, 155, 168, 175–6, 179, 182, 185–6, 194–5, 198–200, 203–5, 210, 212–4, 216–9, 225, 230, 234, 238–9, 243–5, 248–250, 255–6, 264, 266–7, 272, 274, 288 n. 25, 289 nn. 33 & 42, 293
Archconfraternity of St Stephen 188
Archpriest of Arles (Virgilius?) 29
Armstrong, Fr 177, 190
Arrowsmith, baby John 184
Augustine, St 26–30, 39, 43, 158, 162–3, 165, 182
Augustines de Notre Dame de Consolation 197
Aust-Lawrence, Fr Henry 180

Bagshawe, Canon 246
Baily, Fr Emmanuel 198
Barlow, Sir William 197

Barrett, Fr 82
Barry, Fr Richard (death of) 222
Barstow, Mr 9
Basden, Fr Christopher viii, 165, 223
Beart Foss, J. H. 235, 258, 262, 276
Beausang, Fr 251
Beck, Archbishop Andrew 223
Bede the Venerable, St 26, 46 n.5, 78, 217, 264
Benedict XVI, Pope 6, 15 n.5
Bentley, Francis 213
Bentley, Osmund 211, 213
Berchmans, St John SJ 216
Bergh, Abbot Thomas OSB xviii, 31, 35–36, 38, 87, 92, 125–6, 140, 158–9
Bertha, Queen of Kent 27
Bishop, William Henry 67, 76
Bismarck, Otto von 34, 46 n.4
Bodson, Sr Vivinia 123
Bonaparte, Emperor Napoleon 4
Bonaparte, Emperor Napoleon III 288 n.22
Bosco, St John Melchior 51
Boulder, Miss 94

Bourne, Cardinal Francis xvii, xviii, 31, 36, 38, 40–5, 47 n.16, 49–56, 59–63, 67–74, 77–9, 81–3, 84–5 nn. 3, 5, 10 & 14, 124–6, 139–141, 144–5, 147–8, 152 nn. 6, 11 &12, 158–9, 162–3, 165, 170, 173, 180, 182, 197, 208, 215–220, 227, 246, 256, 272, 294
Bovenizer, Fr Peter CRL 127, 256
Bovington, Fr Lawrence 254
Bowen, Archbishop Michael 173, 196, 207, 248, 255, 270, 291
Bradford, FJ 238
Breuer, Sr Josepha 123
Bridgettine order 182
Brighton, Fr CRL 125, 127
Brindle, Bishop Robert 239
Brown, Fr Cosmo 232
Brown, Bishop William 65–6, 169, 177, 190, 209
Bruno, Fr CRL 127
Bullesbach, Fr Rudolph 168, 229–30
Burke, Mr A. M. 274
Butler, Lawrence 227
Butler, Fr William SJ 258
Butner, Mother Iphigènie xiii, xvi, 19, 31–6, 39, 87, 91, 97–98, 102, 107, 114–6, 119–121, 125, 130, 132, 135, 138, 141, 152 n.14,
Butt, Bishop John 42, 52, 54, 61, 63, 72–3, 81, 252, 272
Butt, Fr Joseph 61

Byrne, Fr 172

Cabrini, St Francesca 205
Cadwallader, Fiona viii, 287 n.10, 293
Cafferata, Canon Henry 260
Canons Regular of St John Lateran (CRL) 88, 124, 125, 243, 271
Cardenas, Sr Carol 224
Carew, Richard 283
Carolin, Fr James 258–9
Caron, Fr Benedict 197
Cauwenberghe, Dom Charles van OSB 149
Chew, Fr 124
Chitty, Mrs 241
Clements, Fr Peter 245
Clifton, Fr Michael xiv, xviii, 63, 85 n.8, 173, 287 n.10, 293
Clifton, Canon Thomas 236, 263
Coffin, Bishop Robert 51
Coleburt, Fr Albert 258
Collins, Katherine 210
Collins, Fr Michael 267
Collins, Myra 88
Conant, Frances Anne 22 n.2
Congreve, Sir William 197
Constable, Fr Clement 205
Conzen, Mother Mary Theophile 104, 135
Cooksey, Fr Walter 267, 270
Coote, Mgr Charles 56
Copsey, Fr Fred 274–5
Courtenay, Fr Thomas 129

Index of names

Cowderoy, Archbishop Cyril 183, 187, 200, 214, 251, 270
Cowin, Dom Norbert OSB 148
Craufurd, Rev CH 18
Crawford, Fr 250
Cribb, Joseph sculptor 192
Crommelin, Fr Peter 266
Cubitt, Thomas 215
Cummins, Fr Michael SM 246–8

Danell, Bishop James 14
Darbois, Fr AA 198
Daughters of the Cross of Liège viii, x, xiii, xv, xvi, 1, 19, 31–37, 39, 46 n.6, 87, 94, 96–99, 101, 103–4, 105 n.2, 107, 113, 115, 118–118, 120–1, 128, 130, 132, 134–5, 139–144, 146–7, 149–150, 152 n.5, 158, 249–250, 272, 289 n.39, 293
Davies, Byam Martin 22 n.2
Dawes, Charles 67
Dawes Trust 67–9, 71
Day, Sr Stanislaus Mary 109, 123
Delves, Jenny viii, xv, xviii
Denis, Mgr Jean-Marie 52
Dillon, Fr Jack viii, 188
Ditges, Sr Mary Emmanuel 37
Doubleday, Fr Arthur 61, 190
Doutreloux, Mother M Victorine 149
Drage, Fr Henry 275

Dunstan, St 262
Dupré, Anton, sculptor 196

Eafe (Domneva), St 158
Edgell, Dover 121
Edward VII, King xiii
Edwards, Canon Martin viii, 229
Edwards, Rachel viii
Egelsin, last Saxon Abbot of Canterbury 161
Ellis, Catherine 17–19, 26, 144
Ellis, Charles 17, 19, 24
Ellis, Francis Elizabeth passim
Ellis, Rose 17, 121, 144
Elphege, St, Archbishop 262
Enin, Fr James Kwabena 179
Escarguel, Fr Edward 178–9
Ethelbert, King of Kent 26
Evans, seminarian 269

Fagan, Fr Joseph 179
Fahy, Conor 262
Farrell, Fr 251
Fayers, Fr George SDB 228
Fichter, Fr Terence 168–9, 177, 185, 190, 232
Finaldi, Gabriele 179
Fitzgerald, Fr Kevin 161
Fitzgerald, Johnny 110
Fitzmaurice, Fr Louis 254
Fletcher, Fr Rory 224
Fooks, Mr 64–5, 77
Forristal, Michael 12
Franck, Mère 197–199

Franssu, Jeanne de 288 n.26
Frawley, Fr Patrick 266
Freitas, Fr Philip de 223
Furey, Fr 207

Galligan, Mgr Timothy xix
Gardner the gardener 112, 115, 120, 125, 138, 152 nn.4 & 9
Gasquet, Cardinal Francis OSB 1, 293
Gertrude of Nivelle, St x, 36, 39, 41, 162, 170
Gertrude the Great, St 46, n.9
Gervais, Eugène-Jacques, architect 197–8
Gietmann, Sr Georgia 37
Gifkins, Fr MG 174–5
Gilbert Scott, Adrian 211, 213
Gill, Eric, sculptor 192
Gillett, Fr 205
Gordon, Lord George 3
Gordon, Provost Fr Philip CO 42
Gough, Tim 259
Grady, Fr George 237–242
Graham, Bishop Charles 45, 87–88, 92, 124, 126, 129–130, 132, 152 n.8, 279–80, 284–5
Grant, Bishop Thomas 13–14
Gregory the Great, Pope 26, 30, 180–1
Guild of the Blessed Sacrament 188, 204, 234

Handmaids of Mary 224
Hanlon, Fr Michael 217
Hannigan, Fr CRL 127
Hardman & Co. (Son)163, 241, 259
Harrington, Mr and Mrs 178
Hasslacher, Mr 276
Hayes, Fr James 177, 183, 203–5
Haze, Mère Marie Thérèse 33, 89, 293
Healley, Fr 114, 121
Heneghan, Fr Tom xiv, 172
Henry 110
Hermans, Sr Florentine 114, 123
Higgins, Prior Gilbert CRL 271
Hill, Norman & Beard 246
Hill, Young p.85 n.15
Hodsdon Archard, A. J. 255
Hogan, Fr John Baptist 50–1
Holden, Fr Marcus xix, 164–5, 223
Holland, Alfred 110, 123, 136
Hooley, Fr Thomas 52–53, 61–2, 78, 217–9, 221–3, 293
Howard, St Philip 196, 225
Horspool, Miss Stephanie 178
Hull, Fr Edward OSB 164
Hunt, Fr Hugh 214
Hurley, Sr Mary Bede 141

Index of names

Iphigènie of Ethiopia, St 105 n.4

Jackman, Mgr Hugh 126, 152 n.11
Jackson, Clement 201, 203, 215, 217, 224–7
Joyce, James 6
Julien, Fr Bernard OFM 167, 177

Kavanagh, Fr A. G. 210
Kavanaugh, Fr James 208
Keble, John 6
Kelly, Fr Bernard 232, 249–50
Kelly & Dickie 236, 239–41
Keniry, Fr Augustine OSB 161
Kent, Sr Mary Marcellus 141
Kerr-Bate, C. S. 236
Kersten, Sister Honorine 33, 36, 38–9, 91, 107, 113, 128
Kingston, Sir Anthony 282–3
Knights of St Columba 185, 188
Knights-Whittome, David xviii, 118–121
Knill, Sir John and Lady 177

Labouchère, Henry 68
Lacon, Miss 178
Lagan, Fr Hugh 196
Lapworth, Dom Norbert OSB 148
Larkin, Fr Edward 168, 185
Laverty, John 142

Lawrenson, Fr Michael 255
Leach, Fr Michael 200
Leahy, James 29, 31, 46 n.6
Leahy, Frances 46 n.6
Leahy, Gertrude 46 n.6
Leake, Miss Catherine 255
Leake, Fr Oscar 255
Lee, James 46 n.6, 87–88, 93, 97, 145–6, 159, 279
Legion of Mary 188
Leidig, Fr George 195–6
Lelean, Ethel Maude 164
Linnett, Fr 253
Lockhart, Fr William IC 15 n.1
Lonergan, Fr James CRL 244–5
Luidhard, Bishop 27
Lutz, Fr Caspar 190, 211–3
Lynch, Bishop Pat 270
Lynch, Fr Tom 223

McAdam, Prior CRL 271
MacAskie, Sr Mary Alban 99
McCamphill, Fr SM 246, 248
McCarthy, Fr 190
MacDonald, Fr Aidan OSB 159–60
McElroy, Fr Alphonsus CRL 102, 271
McKenna, Fr John 166–168, 177, 206
McKenna-Whyte, Fr Adrian 226
McKinstry, Fr CRL 127
Mangan, Wilfred, architect 205

Manning, Cardinal
    Archbishop Henry Edward
    14, 17, 54, 84, 85 n.6
Margol, Fr Tomasz 259
Marix, Sr Mary Aloysie 37,
    109
Marshall, D Plaskett,
    architect 192
Mary Cyprian, Sr 117
Mary Domini, Sr 113
Mary Edwin, Sr 114
Mary Mildred, Sr 124
Mary Ursula, Sr 109
Mason, Fr Stanley 275
Maurer, Sr Micheline 123
Megalan, Fr Antony viii
Mercer, Fr Bob 270
Merry del Val, Cardinal
    Rafael 70–1, 85 n.9
St Mildred 158, 161
Minnett, Fr 177
Molesworth, Lady Jane 280
Moore, Canon 167
Moran, Fr SM 248
Morkerk, Sr Monica 109
Morris, Sr Carola Mary 141
Mostyn, Fr Arthur 175, 207
Msahala, Fr Deodat 259
Muirland of Walworth,
    builders 260
Mullins, Fr CRL 110, 114,
    121, 125, 127–8
Murnane, Canon William
    67–8
Murphy, Mr & Mrs 222
Mussner Vincenzo sculptors
    194

Newman, Cardinal St John
    Henry 5–7, 15 n.5, 31, 41
Newton, Fr 190, 232
Neylan, Sr Mary Aloyse 109,
    123
Nightingale, Florence 13
Norfolk, Duke of 12, 30, 75
Norris, Dom Charles OSB
    246, 286
Nugent, Fr 226
Nuttgens, Joseph 207
Nye, Anselm viii, xv

O'Beirne, Fr Stephen 195,
    274–5
Oblates of Mary Immaculate
    283
Oblates of St Charles 85 n.6
Oblates of the Assumption 57
O'Connell, Daniel 5
O'Connor, Fr 167
O'Donovan, Fr Bartholomew
    212, 290 n.25
O'Donoghue, Fr Cornelius
    196
O'Dowd, Martin 179
O'Flaherty, Helen 222
O'Grady, Fr William 276
O'Halloran, Canon 177, 252
O'Hanlon, J Hughes 210
Olaf Tryggvason, King of
    Norway 262
O'Leary, Prior CRL 271
O'Neill, Canon Joseph 142–3
Oppenheimer, L 238
O'Sullivan, Fr Eugene 212–3

Index of names

Pagalt, Miss 91
Palmer, Fr George 214–5
Palmer, Prior Swithburt OSB 38
Parry, Dom David OSB xviii, 293
Payne, John 282, 286
Peake, Fr 255
Peall, Fr 208–9
Perraud, Cardinal Archbishop Adolphe 29
Petre, Lord 12
Phillips, Derek, architect 193
Pioneers of the Sacred Heart 188
Pitts, Fr Reginald 185
Pius VII, Pope 4
Pius IX, Pope 7–8, 53
Pius X, Pope 45, 132–3, 199, 213
Pius XI, Pope 146, 148, 289 n.42
Plerny, Fr Emile du 204, 244, 288 n.22
Pragnell, Dom Dunstan OSB 148
Presentation Brothers 252, 289 n.39
Price, Sr Jeanne de la Croix 91–2, 107–9, 111, 114, 118, 120, 122–3, 133, 147, 152 n.10
Pritchard, Fr Erconwald 169, 171
Pritchard, Fr William 169
Pugin, Augustus Welby Northmore 12, 26, 28, 36
Pugin, Edward 30

Pugin, Peter Paul 36, 162–3
Pusey, Edward 6

Quinlan, Fr 222

Rawlings, Mr 88
Raymond, Geoffrey 270–1, 282–3
Reckitt, Frank architect 274
Reed Lewis, William 69–71
Reville, Fr 177
Riley, Fr 102, 118, 124, 129
Rinkenback, Mrs Moya 248
Robinson, Mgr Croke 239
Romaine, William 63–6, 173
Russell, Lord John 9
Ryan, Fr Laurence 245
Ryan, Fr Peter 194–5

St Aubyn, Edward 279
St John, Fr Ambrose 31, 41
St John, Anthony 22nd Baron Bletso 47 n.11
St John, Canon Edward xiii, xiv, xvi-xix, 31, 40–5, 47 n.11, Chapter 4 passim, 97, 101, 138–9, 141, 145, 147–8, 155, 162, 165–6, 173, 177, 181, 190, 202, 204–5, 207, 219, 232, 237, 243, 253, 267, 272, 274, 276
St John, Frederick 41
St John, Mary-Ann 41
St Levan, John 1st Lord 279
St Sulpice Seminary, Paris 14, 50–1, 55, 56, 61, 84 n.2
Salesian Fathers 51, 58, 228

Salmon, Fr Ronald 223
Sanders & Michelmore architects 263
Sandling, Fr CRL 125
Sandry, J. R. 285
Sankey, Fr CRL 125
Scannell, Dr 274
Scoles, Canon Alexander 246–8, 270–1, 279–3
Scoles, Fr Ignatius SJ 247, 281
Scoles, Joseph John 247, 281
Scott, Sr Gertrude Mary 108–9, 123
Shaftesbury, Earl of 12
Sheehan, Fr 177
Shenouda, Fr Romany 224
Shepperd, Fr 177
Shrewsbury, E. J. 156
Silver, R., & Sons 156
Sisters of Charity of St Vincent de Paul 242
Sisters of the Faithful Virgin 13
Sisters of Mercy 13, 158–9, 252, 289 n.39
Sisters of the Poor Servants of the Mother of God 159
Sisters of la Retraite 222, 224
Sisters of the Sacred Heart of Jesus 205
Smail, Mr & Mrs Henry 215
Smith, Fr CRL 244
Smith, Prior CRL 127–8, 271
Smith, Fr Bernard 241
Smith, Archbishop Peter 164, 173

Smith, Fr Thomas 186–7, 287 n.17
Smoker, Fr 251
Society of Saint Vincent de Paul 188, 234, 249
Society of Secular Priests 54–5, 60
Southwark Rescue Society 73, 78, 83–4, 180, 252–3
Sparling, Fr 250
Sparrow, James Sylvester 158
Spaul family 241
Spiritans (Holy Ghost Fathers) 201
Stalley, Anthony architect 258
Stiffkey, Rector of 288 n.24
Stokes, Leonard architect 165
Stone, W. 192
Stonor, Richard viii
Storey, Sr Antonia 94, 120
Stubbs, Bishop William 157
Stuflesser, Ferdinand 226

Tappley, Mr 103
Tasker, Francis William 170, 173, 176, 180, 183, 191–2, 194, 207–8, 230, 242–3, 287 n.16
Tatum, Fr G. B. 177
Taunton, Fr Ethelred 68–71
Taunton, Fr William 232, 257
Taylor, Andrew artist 226
Terodde, Sr Julia 123
Theodoric (St Ives) 282
Thomas Fr SM 246
Thompson, Fr 270

Index of names

Thornley, John 85 n.15
Tomlanovich, Ivan artist 229
Torrance, Fr John 168
Treadgold, Miss 147
Turner, Fr Charles 168, 232

Uginet, Sr Gelase 199
Unterthiner, Sr Caritas 123
Ushaw, St Cuthbert's College 5, 85 n.9

Vaughan, Cardinal Archbishop Herbert 29–31, 55–6, 85 n.9, 97, 166
Vickers, Fr Mark xvii, 84 nn.3&5, 294
Victoria, Queen 24, 152 n.7

Wade, Canon Bernard CRL 88, 92, 95, 121
Walmsley, Fr Cyril 258
Wallis, Fr 177
Ware, St Edmund's College 5, 42, 50, 52, 54
Warwick, Fr 260
Walters, Frederick Arthur 166–7, 214–5
Weeks, Elizabeth 179
Wellington, 1st Duke of 5
Wesley, Charles 283
Wesley, John 283
Wheeler, Sr Mary Cecilia 141
White, Abbot CRL 127, 271
White, Fr CRL 244
White, Mgr Leo 223
White & Co, F. G. 278

Whiteside, Archbishop Thomas 79
Whiting, Mr 178
Wilberforce, William 5
Wilderspin, Fr 177
Wilhelm, Fr Joseph 166
William 110
Williams, Agnes 179
Williams, Fr George 230, 232
Williams & Winkley 205
Williamson, Fr Benedict architect 181–2, 189, 191, 229–230, 235, 236–7, 249, 252–3, 256, 258–260, 264, 267, 276–7, 280, 287 nn.14 & 20
Windsor, Dolly 88
Winkley, Austin 259, 262
Wiseman, Archbishop Nicholas 8–11, 13–4, 15 n.6, 16 n.10, 85 n.6
Wonersh, St John's Seminary 49, 52–4, 60–2, 179, 215–7
Wren, Sir Christopher xiv

Xavier, St Francis 225
Xavieran Brothers 216

Young, Fr William OMI 283
YCW (Young Christian Workers) 81, 85 n.16

Zimmerman, Sr Mary Camilla 123

www.ingramcontent.com/pod-product-compliance
Lightning Source LLC
Chambersburg PA
CBHW032017230426
43671CB00005B/122